A QUILT
OF WORDS

*Women's Diaries, Letters
& Original Accounts of Life
in the Southwest, 1860-1960*

SHARON NIEDERMAN

Johnson Books: Boulder

Cover design by Molly Davis

ISBN 1-55566-037-1
LCCCN 88-81621

Printed in the United States of America by
Johnson Publishing Company
1880 South 57th Court
Boulder, Colorado 80301

CONTENTS

In that story I gathered up the historical and psychological threads of the life my ancestors lived, and in the writing of it I felt joy and strength and my own continuity. I had that wonderful feeling writers get sometimes, not very often, of being with a great many people, ancient spirits, all very happy to see me consulting and acknowledging them, and eager to let me know, through the joy of their presence, that, indeed, I am not alone.

Alice Walker
"Saving the Life That Is Your Own"

*As with any generation
the oral tradition depends upon each person
listening and remembering a portion
and it is together—
all of us remembering what we have heard together—
that creates the whole story
the long story of the people.
I remember only a small part.
But this is what I remember.*

Leslie Marmon Silko
Storyteller

INTRODUCTION

In her autobiography, "Journey Towards Understanding," Mary Cabot Wheelwright wrote that on coming west, ". . . I was determined that one of my missions was to convince cowboys that it was possible for a person to be a sport and also drink tea."

Her statement is a key to women's personal accounts of life in the Southwest during the late nineteenth and early twentieth centuries. Women's experiences of this era are revealed in their diaries, letters, oral histories, autobiographies, memoirs, and accounts recorded by their daughters. These intimate revelations, charming and crude, offer a version of western history that is quite different from men's tales of exploration and conquest. The unpredictable circumstances and rugged necessities of life on the frontier fractured the Victorian glass cage of "true womanhood." Some women, like Boston Brahmin Mary Cabot Wheelwright, escaped through the crack in the ornate structure that encased them and found a degree of freedom from eastern propriety through the journey west. In the West, where rules were either questionable or non-existent, women like Wheelwright could live much more as they pleased and still be "ladies," all the while enjoying the notion of themselves as "sports who also drank tea."

Then, as now, the Southwest attracts people with certain yearnings for freedom and adventure, people who like to define themselves as individuals. Those who don't fit in so well back east come west to reinvent themselves. Manifest Destiny and the opening of the great trails brought soldiers and traders with their wives, women like the eighteen-year-old Flora Spiegelberg, wife of Willi, youngest son of the German-Jewish trader family. With her European education, collection of Romantic paintings, and taste for Mendelssohn, Flora brought her refinement to a rough-and-ready Santa Fe where Billy the Kid could be found buying a new "cowboy" outfit in the family store. Flora recorded her impressions of Santa Fe in letters and anecdotes. Teaching provided another passport west enjoyed by women such as Mary Stright, a Presbyterian missionary teacher sent from Pennsylvania to Jemez Pueblo. Mary's 1882 diary tells of the journey west and her first winter in New Mexico. Health-seekers like Minnie Elliott and Katherine Davis migrated west searching for a cure for tuberculosis for themselves and their families in the fresh air and high altitudes of mountains and deserts. The remembrances of Marietta Palmer Wetherill tell the story of a woman whose life was woven between cultures—first, as a girl initiated into a Navajo clan, then as the wife of Richard Wetherill, explorer of Mesa Verde, Chaco Canyon, and other great ruins. The letter of Grace Mott Johnson, sculptor and wife of painter Andrew Dasburg, offers a behind-the-scenes look at life in the Taos art colony during the 1920s as well as a close-up look at a woman artist's struggle to balance her commitments. The West drew natural rebels like rancher-poet-painter Eleanor Williams who found in the big skies and open space both the challenge and the peace that rooted her to western life.

While living their lives as artists, mothers, teachers, homesteaders, social-ites, explorers, and survivors, these women pioneered the region. They created and built communities, social institutions, and ways of life, and they carried stories of their people to tell after their people had been destroyed. Unlike their husbands and brothers, for the most part they did not subdue or tame the land and the native people; rather, they lived with conditions as they found them or could improve them, and their fascination led them to observe and to report on their experiences. Some lived off the land, and others knew a secure, sheltered existence—and some, like Arizona New Deal Congresswoman Isabella Greenway, experienced both rags and riches. Many came in search of spiritual and artistic nourishment. And those born in the Southwest endured the inescapable violence and cultural clashes of their times.

Women didn't write adventure novels the way Jack London, Mark Twain, and James Fenimore Cooper did. These real life accounts are the equivalent of those adventure stories. And men's journals and accounts were used as practical tools, as maps, to explore and conquer the territory. The journals of Meriwether Lewis and Zebulon Pike contain personal observation, but their intent is pragmatic, unlike women's accounts. These are the other side of drawing-room fiction written by women of the era—the novels of Jane Austen, George Eliot, Charlotte Brontë, and Edith Wharton—which focused on women's social role. The adventure and res-olution of the problem of love and marriage, so central to women—not only to their emotional life but to their financial well-being and social status—which formed the core of women's novels, was replaced in these journals and accounts by the adventure of living in a new land. The South-west, with its great emptiness, provided women with vision the opportunity to create and shape their vision. In their art, their homesteads, their schools, museums, and communities, their labor and care, and through their stories, we have a record of women's participation in the shaping of the West.

Journals and quilts, two art forms of pioneer women, share many similarities. The final shape is the sum of many small, random-seeming puzzle pieces that, with patience, fit together into a whole picture. The materials to make these artworks are cheap and readily available: pen and paper for the journal and outgrown or used scraps of fabric for the quilt. The journal is written in bits of time taken from everyday, pressing chores. Both the journal and the quilt are convenient means of self-expression that can be kept close at hand and turned to when a few moments appear. While the quilt has the practical value of keeping a body warm at night, the journal can provide person-to-person warmth when sent to a cherished sister or friend back home. Both journals and quilts were passed on as heirlooms, as loving works of the hands, to beloved children and grandchildren, transmitting a personal sense of the texture of a woman's life. While the finishing of a quilt was a way for women to gather and share community in the past, women's journals and original accounts are now becoming a way for women to be together as we discover and share those which have been lost as well as our own.

The authors usually did not hope for any audience beyond their relatives, friends, and descendents. Their literary effort went not to style but to their attempt at accurately reporting and describing what they observed—nature, fairly untrammeled, and new kinds of human interactions—and to the expression of their personal impressions and opinions. Each woman is writing about how she used her resources to cope, change, and grow. Pioneer women who came to the Southwest and left records carried with them a tradition of written expression and the value of self-expression through writing. Individual reflection may not have been a value of tribal and traditional cultures, because women from oral traditions did not keep personal written accounts, or if they did, these accounts await discovery. It is the current generation of women writers who are bringing oral traditions into their poetry, fiction, and plays.

These accounts raise the kind of questions about women's lives in the West—and women's lives in general—that we have only recently begun to ask. If the frontier and the freedom it promises is our guiding national myth, how does the opportunity to make a new start coupled with the forsaking of all that is familiar affect women? These accounts show that while each woman has her individual response to this situation, life in the West stimulated and articulated women's latent personal resources. Many of these women, either through choice or because of illness, violence, and economic strain, lived without men for significant periods in their lives or for their entire lives, or they had to assume primary responsibility for their families. Did the necessity to face the world head-on lead to greater personal freedom, perhaps pushing them to become more self-determined than they would had they been shielded by a male presence?

These accounts, particularly the accounts of adversity, such as the anonymous Yavapai woman's recollections and Beatrice Nogare's story of life in the coal mining district of southern Colorado, raise the question: *What is woman's courage?* We are drawn, I believe, to stories of pioneer women because we are today searching for examples and possibilities of courage as we explore new frontiers in times when our mothers' and grandmothers' expectations of women's experience, the inheritance that colors our beliefs and feelings about ourselves and powerfully affects our action in the world, makes less sense each day. The harsh, unfamiliar and demanding circumstances of the West provided women with situations that demanded courage, a courage as personal in its expression as a daring work of art that departs from the rules and shows us something we haven't seen before. As pioneer women were dislocated from their familiar surroundings and as native women witnessed the destruction of their ancient ways of life, we are now living through a time of great dislocation as we careen toward an unnavigated new age. In such times, when we may lack even the security of shifting sands to stand on, when beliefs are transformed many times during a lifetime, and work and relationships bear little resemblance to acculturated expectations, we are asking: How does a woman create her own authentic life?

The accounts presented here represent women from different classes, races, and religious and cultural backgrounds. Some are accompanied by a great deal of biographical information; others are only a step from anonymity. Despite these differences, the thread of forthright individuality stitches these particular accounts together into a whole pattern. The sense of authenticity in these women's lives, brought into focus by their experience in the Southwest, outlasts their lifetimes and is their gift to us.

AGNES MINER
The Story of a Colorado Pioneer

A daughter of the pioneering Colorado Silverthorne family con-
fided this memoir of her girlhood in Denver during the 1860s to
her daughter, Agnes Miner, late in life. The account represents a
particular genre of western women's history, the recorded personal
memoir, passed on by word of mouth to a trusted relative, usually
a daughter or daughter-in-law, who acts as scribe. This kind of account falls somewhere between oral and written history. No doubt
the recorder, in addition to writing down the story as she heard it,
supplied a subtext of the speaker's non-verbal communication, lend-
ing emphasis according to the speaker's tone of voice, facial expres-
sions, and gestures.

The focal point of this memoir is the open discussion of the relationship between the settlers and the Arapaho people. It is a complex
relationship of mutual fear, struggle for power, and, emerging within
the strife, an occasional wary glimpse of human recognition and
sharing that might be said to amount to a kind of love.

There is absolutely no recognition on the part of the settlers that
they are unwelcome invaders in territory that is not theirs. Instead,
the native people are perceived according to stereotypes customarily
used to de-humanize and disempower indigenous people so as to make
the taking of power, land, and labor easier on the souls of the invaders.

The Arapaho are seen as tricky, thieving, dangerous killers, although paradoxically, the two groups interacted almost daily; the
Indians were hired to work in the homes of the Anglos. The relationship of mutual dependence between whites and Native Americans
in this account is similar to descriptions of the relationship between

whites and black slaves in the old South. Considering the acceptability and prevalence of Manifest Destiny thinking, the settlers' lack of responsibility is hardly surprising. Here the conviction of the pioneers is recalled through the innocence of the remembered fears of childhood that remain unchanged for a lifetime.

In addition, what we get here is a vivid picture of the impact of larger, more "historical" events on daily domestic life in school and at home, where the women and children were. There is a sense as well of the strength of women's authority in the home, based largely on the economic power held and the fact that the men were off securing the takeover of the territory.

The Silverthornes went on to pioneer in Breckenridge, where Marshall Silverthorne founded a hotel and the family was influential in the town's development. Agnes Miner, daughter and recorder of the storyteller, her mother, Martha Finding, originally prepared this memoir for the Breckenridge Women's Club.

*E*arly in the year 1859 my father, Marshall Silverthorne, decided to come to Colorado for his health, arriving in Denver May 17, 1859. Improving rapidly in health, he returned to Pennsylvania to bring back his family. With his wife and three children he started on his return trip to Denver early in March, 1860. We came by train to St. Louis, then by boat to Omaha. We were two weeks on the boat as we did not travel at night. After a short visit in Council Bluffs we outfitted for the trip. We were six weeks on the plains. We did not travel on Sundays. Mother devoted this day to washing, baking and cooking for the following week.

Twice during the trip Indians were determined that my father should trade my mother for some of their ponies. The last time they were inclined to be rather ugly about it and father had quite a time with them.

We arrived in Denver May 18, 1860, just a year and a day after my father's first arrival. We rented a house of four rooms situated at what is now Fourteenth and Lawrence streets. This house was built of rough boards, with no paint, and with most of the windows covered with white muslin. It was called Denver House after General Denver. The house was owned by Samuel Dolman who had gone back to Kansas with his family. We paid eighty-five dollars a month rent.

Soon some friends of father's wanted to board with us. These were George Clark of Clark & Grubers, Major Fillmore, Judge Hallett and others. With so many, mother had more than she could do and hired a daughter of old Left Hand, an Indian chief of the Arapahoes.

I remember one day a number of Indians were around the house and mother wanted a small pair of moccasins for my little brother who had stepped on some prickly pears near the house, hurting his feet very badly. We could not get all the needles picked out. Mother went with the Indians into the dining room, asking me to watch that the Indians outside did not enter and steal anything. I was afraid, so as soon as mother had gone I crawled under the bed and from there I watched the open door. Very soon a squaw peeped through a crack in the door and seeing something handy there stepped in and put it under her blanket. It was my new sunbonnet made with casing and run in called slate.

After a trade of sugar and moccasins had been made and the Indians had gone, I crawled out of my hiding place and said, "Mother, one of the squaws took my sunbonnet." Taking me by the hand, she said: "Come and show me which one." I was frightened but had to go. Mother asked them who had taken it, but she shook her head. "No." So mother took hold of her elbows and raised them and the sunbonnet fell out of the folds of her blanket. Mother folded up the slats and boxed the squaws' ears. They all began to cry out. In a few minutes Whites and Indians were gathered, then our friends began to cry out: "Oh, don't, Mrs. Silverthorne; we will all be killed." However, the Indians soon quieted down and walked away. They were always stealing everything they could get their hands on, but their specialties were soap, sugar and blueing.

In the fall of 1860 I went to school in Denver in a little log, one-room school building which stood on McGaa Street, on the banks of Cherry Creek. Miss Helen Ring was my teacher. One day a man came down riding on a white horse and tied the horse to a large cottonwood tree just in front of the schoolhouse. Miss Ring said: "Children I am afraid there is going to be trouble, so I will open the window and you crawl out and run home just as fast as you can."

The man was George Steel, a notorious character. He had ridden to town to make William N. Byers, the editor of the Rocky Mountain News, retract some statements regarding the man Steel's character. This Mr. Byers refused to do. When I reached home, mother wrapped my sister, brother and myself in buffalo robes and put us in the attic so that no stray bullets could touch us, since friends of Steel had gathered close to our home, prepared to fight for him. Afterwards, Steel was shot and killed at Bradford's Corner, now known as Larimer and Sixteenth streets.

About the same time a young man named Jim Gordon, who, when under the influence of liquor was very quarrelsome, had killed a young German man. After several trials he was acquitted under the flimsy excuse of "No jurisdiction." This angered the Germans and they took it into their own hands and hung Gordon on a Saturday in July, 1860. I saw this man hung. Nine years later I saw a man named Musgrove hung under the Larimer Street bridge. He was a stock thief and general outlaw.

In the latter part of May, 1861, we started for Georgia, but stopped in Breckenridge. Here we rented a house that had been a store owned by O.A. Whittemore and C.P. Elder. There was one very large front room and a smaller room at the back which we used for a bedroom and kitchen. The floor of the kitchen we made out of old sluice boxes that had been worn until the knots stood out, caused by constant washing of water and gravel. As a rule these boxes were burned and the ashes panned for gold that would collect in the knots and crevices. The front room had a dirt floor, with shelves and a counter running along one side. Father took a team and hauled sawdust from an old sawmill above town and covered the dirt floor to the depth of six inches. Mother sewed burlap sacks together and made a carpet. Then father made pins such as are used for fastening tents down and nailed the burlap down with these. All dust sifted through, so it was easy to keep clean. In this room we made three beds, end-to-end on the floor, by placing two logs, one on top of another. The enclosure was filled with hay, then feather beds that had been brought from Pennsylvania were placed on this.

This room was a dining room during the day to accommodate those who came to Breckenridge and had no place to go. The Post Office was in the front part of this room. A pigeon-holed box about three-by-five feet held all the mail. Saturday was the general Eastern mail day and the miners all came down to get their mail. There were two other arrivals of mail during the week but Saturday's mail was the principal one. The letters were distributed by calling out the names, the men answering, "Here," and the mail being tossed to them.

After a few months, Mother was asked to bake bread, pies and cakes to sell to the miners who came down for mail. This meant forty or fifty pies alone, and a hundred-pound sack of flour was very often used in a day's baking. A quart of milk was included and this was paid for in gold dust which I weighed out. I would take in between thirty and forty dollars.

One summer I was sent to the placer mine to take father's lunch to him. I walked along slowly, picking strawberries and wild flowers on my return and had been home only a few minutes when one of the men came running up and asked mother if I was home. A large buffalo had come along and in his excitement had torn up all the sluice boxes and had followed my trail up, crossing the river just before he reached town, which was all that saved me.

Larimer Street, Denver, April 1861. The crowd is watching a tightrope walker. *Colorado Historical Society.*

Martha or Agnes. *Colorado Historical Society.*

In the spring of 1862 we bought another house and moved into it. Here I helped father build a fireplace and a cellar, bringing up the dirt from the cellar in a bucket. He then papared the walls of the house with newspapers.

In the fall of 1863 we went to Denver so that my sister and I might enter school. We bought a home on Arapaho Street just where the tramway cars now come out of the Loop. This property we sold to the Tramway company in 1892.

We attended a private school in the rectory of old St. Johns church on Fourteenth and Arapaho streets, taught by Miss Irene Sopris, who later married Mr. J.S. Brown of the Brown Brothers Mercantile Company.

Each year, early in June, we would drive to Breckenridge, taking about four days for the trip. All provisions had to be hauled from Denver. We made the town of Hamilton, in South Park, the first day, and then started over Boreas Pass, leaving Hamilton about 11 or 12 o'clock at night when there was crust on the snow so that we might walk over it.

In January, 1873 I was married to Charles A. Finding and the next year was the last we were compelled to walk over the range. We carried our little baby in our arms a distance of fifteen miles.

Going back in our story to the year 1867, we made a short trip East. We took with us an Indian chief's jacket that had a fringe of two hundred and four human scalps. This was to show the Easterners what the Indians were doing out here. No wonder they thought this was the "Wild and wooly West."

At this time the Union Pacific railroad came only as far as North Platte. Finding the stage coach reservations all engaged, we decided to buy a team of horses. One of the party had a light wagon which we rode in and we had another for provisions and baggage.

The Indians were then getting very troublesome. The authorities at North Platte refused to let us start out unless we promised to drive fast enough to catch up with a company of Infantry. There were eight teams in our party. We left the road after a while and drove down near the river where the company of soldiers was camped. Two of the wagon loads decided to stay on the road near the bluffs. While eating lunch we heard the cry: "Indians, Indians!" and then we saw the Indians swoop down and circling, ride away with our horses. We went to the rescue of these people and then all together we hurried on, arriving at what was known as Beauviss's Crossing where we camped all night. After supper two soldiers came up and asked mother if she and Miss McCune would go and see two soldiers who had deserted and who had been found badly wounded

Breckenridge. *Colorado Historical Society*.

Martha Finding. *Colorado Historical Society*.

Martha and Agnes, mother
and daughter. *Colorado
Historical Society.*

Charles and Martha Finding.
Colorado Historical Society.

in the bluffs. The searching party had found them and brought them to camp. They were dying and kept calling for their mothers. The boys died at daybreak, happy in the thought that their mothers were with them.

We were taken across the river at North Platte on a ferry and then we hurried on to catch up with the soldiers who were camped that night near the right so that the Indians could not surround them. Just before reaching Wisconsin Ranch we saw a stage coach coming from Denver. On the stage was a young man who had come out to repair some telegraph lines that the Indians had cut.

While talking to the driver and this young man we saw the coach coming on its way to Denver, and since the roads were narrow we had to hurry on. We soon heard shots and turning saw the coach coming down the hill just as fast as the horses could travel. The other coach turned around and followed. The young telegraph operator had been killed. They said it seemed as though the Indians came right out of the bluffs. Following this there was no more trouble with the Indians until after we left the soldiers at Fort Morgan. We camped that night at Steven's ranch sixty-five miles from Denver. We put our horses in the barn, thinking they would be safe there. We slept in the house. About 12 o'clock we heard a shot and saw a light in the barn. There was much excitement in camp. Our Captain had given orders that anything moving should be shot. The man on guard crawled along and told the Captain something was moving. The Captain raised on his elbows and fired. Something jumped into the air. They found it was an Indian. Upon investigation we found our horses had been stolen. We could see the Indians all along the horizon. A few minutes after this Indian was killed, we heard the coach from Denver coming. We told them our horses had been stolen and that one of the Indians had been killed and that we expected an attack at daybreak. Father wrote a telegram asking for help and gave it to the driver to send from the first telegraph station along the way. When the word reached Fort Morgan the next morning, a few soldiers hurried out. Among them was a young brother of General Philip Sheridan, who had just been graduated from West Point. We traveled along, reaching Living Spring before sundown. A sad company, we were expecting never to see the rising sun again. We had been there hardly an hour when we saw in the distance, people on horseback and in wagons. They proved to be friends coming from Denver to help us. Father broke down and cried: "I did not know I had so many friends."

We reached Denver safely and had a joyous welcome home. The telegram father sent is now in the museum in Denver and may be seen at any time.

The Sand Creek battle, the massacre of the Hungate family and the

Denver flood, together with the Indian scare in Denver, were outstanding events of 1864 to 1867 which all pioneers well remember.

Old Chief Colorow at one time threatened to kill mother and to burn Breckenridge down because she refused to cook special meals for himself and squaws.

One day a team of runaway horses ran over my father, wounding him very badly. The Indians heard he had been killed and held their burial service for father. This one old Indian chief would often say to us: "If the Indians go to make war on you I tell you, I tell you." Most of the Indians were able to speak English fairly well.

FLORA SPIEGELBERG
Reminiscenses of a Jewish Bride of the Santa Fe Trail

Flora Spiegelberg probably knew the boast was not entirely accurate, but she enjoyed referring to herself as "the first Jewish woman in New Mexico." She left her mark on the territorial capital, not only with her particular down-to-earth brand of European sophistication, but as a teacher, writer, and the founder of Santa Fe's first nonsectarian school.

With her charm and curiosity, her collection of Romantic paintings, and her talent at the piano with Chopin and Mendelssohn, the young, beautiful Flora Langerman Spiegelberg was superbly equipped for her role as Santa Fe's first lady during the 1880s. As the wife of Willi Spiegelberg, Santa Fe's mayor from 1884-86, Flora hosted visiting celebrities General Philip H. Sheridan, General Ulysses S. Grant, and on October 28, 1880, President and Mrs. Rutherford B. Hayes. Perhaps her most splendid celebration was the June 1985 gala she threw in honor of her dear friend, Jean Baptiste Lamy, who had been named archbishop the preceding February. The archbishop requested that Flora be in charge of the festivities and that Willi act as toastmaster.

While receiving her education in Germany, she met Willi when she was seventeen and he was thirty, through mutual family arrangements. Willi was the youngest of the six Spiegelberg brothers, founders of New Mexico's first Jewish mercantile company and the Second National Bank of Santa Fe. As Flora put it, "I was young, and he was handsome, and I soon became Mrs. Willi Speigelberg."

Following a honeymoon trip through Vienna, Paris, and London, in 1875, Flora and Willi followed the Santa Fe Trail by stagecoach and army ambulance. "At that time I was the eighth American woman in Santa Fe," she says. "There were about fifty American men, officials and merchants, and a Mexican population of two thousand."

In addition to his accomplishments as businessman and politician, Willi, known locally as "Don Julian el Bonito," was expert with the lariat. Among his friends he counted Kit Carson and the Navajo chief Manuelito.

Flora displayed her civic-mindedness throughout her stay in Santa Fe. The mother of two daughters and the adoptive mother of an orphaned Indian boy and girl, she hired a teacher from the Presbyterian Mission to begin a nonsectarian school for girls, Santa Fe's first. Then she raised money and built a three-room schoolhouse and children's gardens, completed in 1880. On Sundays she taught Hebrew school, numbering among her pupils Arthur Seligman, future governor of New Mexico.

Flora shared her passion for gardening with Archbishop Lamy. The two enjoyed conversing on the subject in French for hours at a time. A close family friend, the archbishop planted two willow trees with his own hands in front of the Spiegelberg home on Palace Avenue. On Passover and Rosh Hoshana, the Jewish New Year, he customarily sent gifts of wine, fruit, and flowers from his own garden, and he often joined the tiny Jewish community in its holiday prayers.

Truly a woman of her times, Flora brushed elbows one day with the most famous outlaw of her era. She met Billy the Kid while he was buying a new "cowboy outfit" at the Spiegelberg family store.

In 1888 the Spiegelbergs returned to New York, where Flora took up a new career. She became an advocate for modern sanitation in New York and crusaded for updated garbage disposal methods. She became known as "The Guardian Angel of the Street Cleaners" and "The Old Garbage Woman of New York." She became intrigued with this cause on a trip to Europe, where she conducted a study of modern sanitation systems and then brought back foreign engineering reports. In 1911 she prepared a sanitary and economic plan for the collection and disposal by incineration of New York City trash and garbage. In 1912 Thomas A. Edison made a film based on Flora's plan.

She went on to serve on the New York City Health Commission, the Street Cleaning Department, the Bill Board, the Public Water

Commission and the Daylight Saving Commission. As a writer, Flora Spiegelberg achieved a modest success. In 1915, Rand McNally & Co. published her children's novel, *Princess Goldenhair and the Wonderful Flower*, which was adopted for radio broadcast on the CBS program, "Let's Pretend" in 1937. This novel saw three editions. Her radio script, "The Enchanted Toy Store of Fairyland," was broadcast on the CBS radio network in 1932, and she also wrote a collection of short stores, "Grandma Flora's Stories for Little Folks."

The anecdotes of life in Santa Fe appearing here are excerpted from Flora's personal writings, some of which were published in the *Jewish Spectator* in 1937 under the title, "Reminiscences of a Jewish Bride of the Santa Fe Trail."

What comes through in these brief, chatty pieces is the sense of a woman who is sure of herself, her place in the world, and her values. Although a twinkle of humor beams through, this work speaks of a woman capable of looking down rather imperiously from the heights of a personal code of honor composed of traditional verities, persistence and determination, and privilege. By following her enthusiams with common sense and dedication, she accomplished a great deal in Santa Fe and New York.

This extraordinary woman, who during her lifetime crossed worlds, cultures, and ages, retaining her unabashed individuality throughout her various journeys, died in 1943 at age 86.

I was born in New York in 1857 on Twelfth Street in the home of my grandfather, Moses Lichtenheim. He had come from Hamburg in 1820 and shortly after he married a very charming Christian woman . . . a Miss Riehl, who was a direct descendant of Phillip Arcalarius, a Hessian officer who had come to America to escape being sold to England for the purpose of fighting the Colonists. He settled in New York in 1783.

My father, William Langerman, came from Bavaria. He was a pioneer of 1849, a Colonel of the California State militia and a member of the Committee of Vigilantes in 1850. When I was two months old I was taken via the Isthmus of Panama to San Francisco, the home of my father. In 1866, we moved back to New York, going by steamer across the Isthmus; by steam-cars from Panama to Aspinwall (now known as Colon); and from there to New York by steamer. The journey took twenty-one days from 'Frisco to New York.

Three years later, after my father's death, I crossed the ocean and in 1874, when I was only seventeen, a very handsome young man came to pay his respects to my mother. He had returned from America to pay a visit to his family in Germany, and he knew of us through distant family connections. Well, I was young and he was handsome and in a very short time, I became Mrs. Willi Spiegelberg. Ours was the first marriage consummated in the new Reform Temple in Nuremberg.

After a honeymoon in Europe, we started out for Santa Fe. We traveled, via St. Louis, in very primitive steam-cars. Then we continued our journey to Santa Fe for six days and six nights across the famous old Santa Fe trail. . . The stage coach stopped at the log house coach stations three times daily; an hour to change horses and provide a most primitive meal. Usually we had dried buffalo chips, with beans, red or green peppers, coffee and tea without milk or sugar, and occasional delicacies such as buffalo tongues, bear and buffalo steaks. I did not relish this food, but my hardened pioneer husband never complained. Many of the station masters were old friends of my husband. When they assisted me out of the coach, they raised their big sombreros with a hearty greeting, "Welcome, Don Julian El Bonito" meaning William the Handsome, and your pretty "Tenderfoot Bride of the Santa Fe Trail."

In 1875, we returned to America for my husband had to get back to his business in Santa Fe, New Mexico. Crossing the ocean was an experience in itself in those days, but it was as nothing in comparison to the cross-country journey we had to take. The train only extended to West Las Animas. It arrived at sunset and I was fearfully tired for there was no Pullmans or any riding comforts in those days. The hotel was a small, two story ramshackle frame building surrounded by shacks that looked like large packing cases for the town was still in its infancy being but one year old. As we stepped up to register, some two hundred cowboys who had just returned from a round-up and were naturally armed to the teeth, rose as one man and, doffing their sombreros, bellowed their greetings and cheered me until the very rafters shook. "Hello, lady, glad to see you," they shouted, and they really meant it, for I was the first woman they had laid eyes on in months.

This knowledge did not add to my comfort nor did the fact that I had to climb a rope ladder in full view of all their staring eyes. My misery was complete when I found that the bed-chambers were merely cubby-holes partitioned off with thin, all revealing muslin. You may be sure that I slept in all my clothes that night and my eyes closed in a pool of tears; my body relaxed from complete exhaustion.

Early next morning, the two-horse overland coach stood waiting for us with both driver and conductor but we were the only passengers. The driver had stuffed the front seats with hay so that we might not be bruised too much while going up the rocky inclines. I got into the coach and while the baggage was being tied on, the horses, unaccustomed to the new "Iron Horse," became frightened and dashed madly away . . . and it was several blocks before they were stopped.

About midnight, we reached Trinidad, Colorado. I was so exhausted I begged the driver to permit me to rest on a buffalo rug for an hour, but even the insects were against the tenderfoot and would allow me no rest. It was a perilous and a thrilling ride all the way through but after five days and nights we finally arrived within twenty-five miles of Santa Fe where we were met by my husband's brothers and friends. When we reached home, we were welcomed by General Devens, military commander of New Mexico and his band which was playing Lohengrin's Wedding March.

Amid clean and happy surroundings, I soon forgot all the privations I had endured and I became a satisfied member of the community. I lived there for fifteen years; my children were born there, too. . . .

In 1882 I started a Sabbath school at my home and the class consisted of eight Jewish children. One member, Hyman Lowitzky, was in later life decorated by Colonel Roosevelt for bravery after the battle of San Juan. He was one of the earliest volunteers of the Roosevelt Rough Riders. At New Year's and on the Day of Atonement, services were conducted at eight in the home of my brother-in-law or at our own home for all the Jewish inhabitants. Our heads were always held high and we instilled respect into the ears and minds of the neighbors because we respected ourselves and our beliefs.

How the Spiegelbergs Obtained Their Name

Willi Spiegelberg, merchant and early pioneer (1860) of Santa Fe, New Mexico, was the first Jewish Probate Judge and Mayor of Santa Fe, in the early eighties. He was born in the little town of Natzungen, Germany in 1844, the son of Jacob and Betty Spiegelberg, and died in New York City in 1929. . . . Mr. Spiegelberg's father was one of those Jews whose forbears had not been permitted in some parts of Germany to take surnames, and in this little town was known simply as "Jacob" of Natzungen. For many years he was the commercial agent and trusted friend of a certain Baron von Spiegelberg, a powerful German nobelman whose beautiful castle stood on a hill near the village of Natzungen. When, in accordance with the celebrated Napoleonic Code which was promulgated at the beginning of the 19th century in Paris, the French Jews were granted the privilege of taking surnames, shortly afterward Germany followed this example. The Landvogt, or governor of each province summoned the Jews to the courthouse in every town and permitted them to choose their own surnames. . .

When the Landvogt came to Natzungen he summoned the small number of Jews to the courthouse, among the Christians who appeared was Baron Ottkar von Spiegelberg. And when the Landvogt said, "Du Jude Jacob von Natzungen wie willst Du heissen?" (You Jew Jacob of Natzungen what name will you select?), before he could reply, Baron von Spiegelberg said loudly, "Herr Landvogt, I wish to have Jacob be given my name. I have known him for 25 years; he is an honest, reliable man and a trusted friend of mine, and wish him to bear my name." Thus the name of Spiegelberg has come to stand for honor, faith and friendship.

The First Spiegelberg in Santa Fe

In 1845, Solomon Jacob Spiegelberg, the oldest of the five Spiegelberg brothers, then 18 years old, was on his way to Santa Fe in a covered ox-drawn wagon from Missouri. It then took over three months to cross the Santa Fe Trail to the city of Santa Fe. When halfway across, he met Colonel Doniphan with his small regiment on their way to the City of Chihuahua in Mexico. The Colonel halted the caravan, spoke to Mr. Spiegelberg, found him a very nice young man and invited him to join his regiment. He gave him a horse, which naturally greatly pleased the young man. He accompanied Colonel Doniphan first to Santa Fe, where they rested, then to Chihuahua. Colonel Doniphan found Mr. Spiegelberg's services very helpful, as he was well-educated and had quite some experiences, so he persuaded him to assist him and he remained a year. Then Colonel Doniphan obtained for him a federal permit and he opened a general merchandise wholesale and retail store in Santa Fe in 1846. He supplied the Colonel's troops, and also during the Mexican American War in 1848. Then in the early fifties and sixties he was joined by his younger four brothers.

General Sibley in Santa Fe, New Mexico

During the Civil War, General Henry Sibley, in commanding a brigade of Confederate soldiers in Texas, marched across the border to Santa Fe,

The Spiegelberg family. Flora seated left, Willi seated center. *Will Kriegsman.*

Willi Spiegelberg. *Courtesy Museum of New Mexico, Neg. No. 50486.*

Spiegelberg Building, East
San Francisco Street, Santa Fe,
about 1900-05. *Courtesy
Museum of New Mexico, Neg.
No. 35869.*

Plaza, Santa Fe, about 1895. *Courtesy Museum of New Mexico, Neg. No. 11299.*

and finding no Union forces to oppose him, took possession of the city. It has frequently happened that during wars the civilian population is mistreated by the soldiers, so, to avoid this, General Sibley declared martial law, strictly warning Mexican and American women (four American women there at that time) not to appear on the streets nor to frequent public places.

The only diversion the pioneer merchant Levi Spiegelberg could offer his young and pretty wife, Betty, was a buggy ride on Sunday to the nearby Indian pueblos where she delighted in watching the Indians, decorated with feathers and war paint, dance with their squaws, listening to their strange music and beating of tom-toms, admiring the pretty gold and silver jewlery and pottery the Indians made, while watching the squaws weave beautiful blankets. The first Sunday after the occupation of the town, Mr. Spiegelberg in his buggy drove past the military headquarters where General Sibley was seated with his officers.

He noticed that several stood up and stared at his pretty wife (the fourth American woman) but as it had happened so often before he gave it no further thought. The next morning, an old resident pioneer called on Mr. Spiegelberg and said, "Friend Levi, while I am not privileged to tell you where I got this information, but for fear of being kidnapped, I would advise you very seriously not to drive out again with your pretty young wife while our town is occupied by Confederate soldiers." He thanked his friend and immediately repeated it to his brothers and wife, warning her strictly not even to look out the little diningroom window for fear someone passing by might see her. Fearing that an attempt might be made to kidnap her, his four brothers slept in an adjoining room provided with guns and pistols to protect her.

The following morning she heard a woman moaning and crying under her bedroom window, and remembering her husband's warning, she ran to the store to call him, but it was full of a lot of shouting soldiers, so she rushed back. But when the loud sobbing continued, although strictly forbidden by her husband, she could stand it no longer. She tore open the window. She was terribly frightened, for there lay a young Negress, her clothes in rags, her face and hands covered with blood and mud. She cried out, "Oh, good lady, for God's sake save me, for I am starving and bleeding to death."

Mrs. Spiegelberg ran quickly through the yard to the street and, assisted by her Mexican maid, dragged the fainting Negress into the kitchen. They washed and fed her, gave her clean clothes, then sent for a doctor. When revived, she told how she had been stolen from her master's planatation in Texas by Confederate soldiers and outraged in a frightful manner until she reached Santa Fe, then ran away and fell helplessly under the window in the street. "Oh, good lady!" she sobbed, "I am so grateful to you for saving my life, and I pray God that you will let me serve you as maid. My name is Emily, and I promise to serve you faithfully."

Naturally, her pitiful story appealed deeply to Mrs. Spiegelberg, a young mother herself. She urged her husband to buy Emily's freedom, which he did. At the same time, he also bought the freedom of a man slave stolen from the same plantation as Emily. Both were sent to school and served as cook and maid in the family for thirty years. A little later, Mr. Spiegelberg adopted an orphan Indian boy, Joseph, and his sister Mary. They had been carried away by the Confederate soldiers.

"War is Hell!"

General Sherman was sent to Santa Fe in 1878. His mission was to settle trouble among the Navajo Indians on the nearby Indian reservation. He was successful and on his return to Santa Fe the old pioneer citizens gave a dinner in his honor. Also invited were all federal officials and their wives. At that time, Santa Fe had about 200 American citizens and only twelve American women, and they were present at the dinner.

In sparkling after-dinner speeches, the general was praised glowingly and sincerely for his achievements during the Civil War. In addition, several of the speakers related cowboy and Indian stories which were inexpressibly thrilling.

During the speech-making, it was my good fortune to be seated beside the general. "General Sherman," I suggested naively, "Do tell us something about your march from Atlanta to the sea."

The General arose from the banquet table with characteristic military dignity. Stiffly erect, and with a voice full of feeling, he spoke. "Good friends," he said, "Although I am a military officer, at heart I am a pacifist." He stared for a moment into space and then blurted out the thunderous declaration which has since become a famous saying, "War is hell!"

At first there was a profound silence among the guests, who gazed admiringly at the general. All at once, however, the tenseness was relieved by a prolonged, deafening applause, and all raised their glasses and drank to his health. The General was obliged then to undergo a hand-shaking ordeal for every guest present insisted upon commending him in person for his daring War Slogan.

My husband, Mayor Spiegelberg, knew the General well enough to venture to address him thus: "General, I hear that you are a gay Lothario and not only admire the ladies, but that you also like to kiss them." Unabashed, the genial guest of honor was upon his feet in an instant and placing his hand on his heart, and with a rougish twinkle in his eye, declared, "Good friends, I would not be a real man if I did not admire the ladies, and naturally like to kiss them."

We all laughed heartily and applauded and then the General committed himself further. "To prove that what my friend Willi Spiegelberg has said is true, ladies," said he, "If your husbands do not object, I shall be delighted to have you all give me a good night kiss before we part."

As might easily be imagined, the general smiled blissfully and complacently as each of the ladies, including myself, kissed him upon the cheek or forehead and the husbands had not objected.

Smiling and winking at the General, my husband jokingly remarked, "Good friend, it does appear to me that you would have preferred being the donor instead of the recipient of the ladies' kisses." Then we all laughed, applauded heartily, and our honored guest joined us, saying smilingly, "My friend is right."

The Author of "Ben Hur"

The executive office of the Governor was in the old El Palacio Real, built of adobes by the Pueblo Indians under the supervision of the Spanish Franciscan Friars in 1609, and was the official residence of all Spanish, Mexican and American Governors until 1924 when the new handsome state building was erected. The large window in the El Palacio Real is still shown to tourists where the Governor used to sit and work on his manuscript, "Ben Hur."

One day as I passed I looked in the window and the Governor beckoned me to come in. He said "Mrs. Spiegelberg, I have just wrapped up my manuscript of Ben Hur to forward to my publisher. Do you think it is worth the expressage?"

For a moment I stared at him, then quickly replied, "My dear Governor, judging by the success of your book, *The Prince of Peace*, I'd gladly pay half of the expressage if you will agree to divide the royalties with me."

He smiled, saying, "I will consider your offer." Then I wished him good luck. It has been said that the royalties from the book, the play and film amounted to nearly one million dollars. In later years I often joked with him about my offer and how wise he was not to have accepted it.

A Visit to Archbishop Lamy

Our good and tolerant friend Monseigneur Lamy always sent us and several other Jewish families gifts of fruit, wines and flowers as greetings to the Jewish New Year. So one day we called to thank our friend for his thoughtful attention. During our visit, my husband noticed how much I enjoyed our French conversation, so remarked, "I deeply regret that my wife has no opportunity to speak French." Then our good friend said, "I will give you a letter of introduction to my niece, Mother Superior of the Convent Little Sister of Lorette; she and the French nuns will gladly welcome your visits." I was delighted and thanked Monseigneur heartily.

A Noble Example of Tolerance

In 1904 I was in Jerusalem during Christmas week and visited the crypt of the Church of the Nativity . . . Later, mounted on donkeys, we rode to Golgatha. We rode to the Garden of the Gethsemane; we sat on stone benches under olive trees many hundred years old. At the gate I bought twelve rosaries, the beads made from the olive trees. I had them blessed in the Church of the Nativity and the Holy Sepulcher and later at the Vatican and St. Paul Church in Rome.

A Trappist monk in the Church of the Nativity blessed them and when I told him about them, he said, "My good lady, you must be a very devout Catholic." "No, Father," I replied, "I am a Jewess who believes in the Fatherhood of God and the Brotherhood of Man irrespective of Race, Creed or Color." Then he shook hands with me, saying, "Then you are a good and worthy citizen of the World."

I presented three Rosaries to German Archbishops, one to my good friend, Archbishop Lamy of New Mexico, and all others to my Catholic friends.

Great Friends

My husband passed away at the age of 84 in 1929. He was called by his Mexican friends, "Don Julian El Bonito," and he was very handsome. Highly respected and honored, in 1880 he was elected by a very large majority Mayor of Santa Fe, again, in 1884, as Probate Judge by a big majority when Bradford Prince, a former Chief Justice and Governor, was a candidate.

At present there is such great anti-semitism in many parts of the world, so it is highly interesting that in the early fifties the Mexican friends of the five Spiegelberg brothers (who established their business in 1846) used to say, "Los Hermanos Jacobos estan la misma gente que nuestro Redentor Jesus Cristos." ("We honor the five Spiegelberg brothers because they are of the same people as our Savior Jesus Christ.")

When my good, old friend, Archbishop Lamy, showed me the word, "Adonai" he had placed over the main arch of the Cathedral, I shook his hand heartily and said, "Most Reverend, you have not only preached the Fatherhood of God, and the Brotherhood of Man, but practiced it daily irrespective of Race, Creed or Color!" He was a charming gentleman and blessed good man. I never cease publishing his virtues.

Praying on the Prairies

In the early seventies on the Santa Fe Trail, the station master of the log cabin stagecoach station told the following story. One day the stagecoach arrived with four passengers, three Americans and one German. After eating a simple meal and smoking their pipes, they stood near the coach. The driver, always on the lookout for herds of buffalo and Indians, was carefully watching the horizon, when suddenly he saw a band of Indians slowly walking single file a short distance away. "Indians, Indians," he shouted, warning the passengers to jump quickly into the coach. Greatly excited, the station master could only find the four Americans, then looking behind the log cabin, he saw the German passenger praying softly in Hebrew, a black skull cap on his head, a prayer shawl about his neck, and a prayer book in his hand. "Come, come," he shouted loudly, "Don't you see the Indians are approaching?"

The German gentleman carefully wrapped up his prayer book and cap in his prayer shawl, then ran to the stagecoach and jumped in. Noticing the impatience and excitement of the passengers, he calmly said, "Good friends, put your trust in God and He will bring you safely to your journey's end." And the Indians did not attack the coach. The driver whipped up the horses and they dashed away.

Strange Names

During the long expeditions of the Conquistadors, Coronado went from Mexico to Colorado in search of gold and silver treasures. He was greatly

surprised to find among the peaceably inclined Indians a well-regulated
community life in their pueblos, or villages. While the Conquistador was
traversing what is now Oregon and Arizona, he met several tribes of
Indians with very large ears, so he called them "Orejones," or "Big Ears."
Another tribe that had very long noses, he called "Narizones," or "Big
Noses." We Americans have translated these Spanish names to "Arizona"
and "Oregon."

Another similar incident: the first explorers of what is the province of
Canada today, were Spaniards, as usual, in search of gold and silver, and
not finding it. As they marched away, they said, "Aqui Nada," meaning,
"There is nothing." Later on, when the French explorers came and asked
the Indians the name of their country, they replied what they had heard
the departing Spaniards say, "Aqui Nada," and thus the French changed
it to, "Canada."

A Lynching Party in Santa Fe in 1877

Shortly after the birth of my second daughter, Rose, in 1877, an elderly
American physician was brutally murdered by two young Mexicans. Naturally it frightened me terribly as I was often alone until late in the evening.
A month later, shortly after midnight, we were awakened by sounds of
horses' hooves and loud talking. When our doorbell was rung several
times, my husband ran to the hall door, but before opening, called out,
"Who is there?" Familiar voices replied. Willi opened the door quickly.
"We have something of importance to tell you." He instantly complied,
and to his great surprise, saw a number of intimate friends on horseback.
Two had heavy coiled ropes about their saddles, and one was leading an
extra horse. The leader of the Lynching Party then explained in a few
words the purpose of their midnight visit.

"We have this Vigilance Committee upon learning today that the two
Mexicans who so brutally murdered your neighboring American physician
are to escape their well-deserved punishment on a technicality. We fear it
may prove a very bad example for other young bandits. Therefore, to
protect ourselves, we have decided to surprise the jailor, take these murderers outside the city and hang them to a tree. I have a horse here ready for
you to mount, and surely expect you to join us."

"Oh my God, boys," exclaimed Don Julian, "I really cannot accompany
you tonight; how could I leave my wife and young baby alone? Why, she
would die of fright."

I listened at the window, and without a moment's hesitation, slipped into my wrapper, placed my three-week old baby in a blanket, and before my startled husband could utter another word, I stood beside him.

It was a bright moonlit night. These ten determined old pioneers stood silently holding the reins of their horses in the shadow of the new cathedral. Holding my baby tightly to my breast, while they no doubt saw the look of anguish on my face, and my voice trembling with emotion as I earnestly pleaded, "Good friends and neighbors, you all have wives and children. I beg of you, don't ask Willi to accompany you tonight because if he goes, I shall die of fright all alone. Besides this infant is dependent upon me for nourishment, and what will become of my other child?" Then I leaned on my husband's shoulder sobbing bitterly. There was a dead silence for a few minutes, then some whispering and the leader of the lynching party, a dear old friend of ours, in a firm yet kindly voice said, "Good wife and mother, your earnest request will be granted, as we all having families fully appreciate your responsibilities, and on that account, will let Willi off this time." Then these old pioneers turned their horses' heads and silently rode away again in the moonlight.

The two murderers were hung, and to my knowledge it was the first lynching party in Santa Fe.

General Sheridan Visits Santa Fe

In 1879 General Sheridan was sent to Santa Fe to settle trouble among the Navajo Indians. The old-time pioneers had a grand ball in his honor, inviting all prominent city and military officers with their wives, then fourteen American women. Like General Sherman, he too returned this courtesy by calling on the ladies also, in a government ambulance drawn by four mules and two soldiers as outriders, which caused quite a sensation, especially as the Indians were greatly impressed by the officers' uniforms. General Sheridan and the officers who accompanied him to the homes of the pioneers were regaled with wines and champagne.

The following anecdote is very amusing. General Sheridan was rather short, not good looking, nor of a commanding personality like General Sherman, and he was always accompanied by a very tall, handsome orderly who walked a few steps behind him. After chatting awhile with my guests, I said, in a joking way, "Kindly pardon the question, but why do you always select such a very tall orderly?" With a faint smile he quickly replied, "My dear Mrs. Spiegelberg, who do you think would take notice of me if I were not accompanied by my tall handsome orderly? Why, he makes me appear attractive."

During the late seventies and early eighties Santa Fe could boast of many prominent and distinguished men in military as well as civil life. General Miles and Pope, Colonel McCook, and General John A. Logan, whose daughter's husband was Major Tucker. General Logan happened to call while I was having a children's party. He told the little folks how, after many years of earnest work in Congress, he succeeded in having Congress pass his Bill making Decoration Day a legal holiday. General Grant had only recently returned from his trip around the world. He expressed the wish to see some of the historical places in his own country, so he came to Santa Fe, the second oldest city, accompanied by his wife, and Mrs. Colonel Fred Grant, the wife of his oldest son.

Santa Fe's First Non-Sectarian School

In the late seventies, the American community was still very small. The parochial school at the Convent of the sisters of Loretto for girls was conducted very efficiently, likewise the Christian Brothers Association school attended by boys.

In 1879 I organized the first non-sectarian school for girls in Santa Fe. I rented a room in an old adobe house near the Plaza. It was very primitive, having a mud floor, and to keep it sanitary for the twelve pupils, I disinfected it personally three times weekly. Instead of desks and benches, the pupils had little tables and three-legged stools.

Rev. Dr. Jones, Pastor of the Presbyterian Church, engaged a competent teacher from the Presbyterian Mission Society. But at my urgent request, before Miss Carpenter accepted the position, I made it obligatory that her pupils be taught to recite the Ten Commandments, and at the same time she should explain to them that the Ten Commandments are not a religious, but an ethical and moral code upon which the civilization rests today. Also, they would have weekly little talks from the Bible that the children could understand and would be of interest to them. She fully agreed with my earnest request, and all the parents approved it also.

Early in the spring of 1880, when the railroad was completed to Santa Fe, I collected $1000 from the old pioneer merchants and federal officials for the purpose of building a modern school house. At my request, General Hatch wrote to Washington and obtained from the federal government an acre of land on old Fort Marcy. Mr. Smith the contractor, who was very anxious to build my new home and the store for the Spiegelberg brothers, was told that he could not obtain these two contracts unless he was willing to build a one story frame school house with many windows to let in light and sunshine, and also modern desks and benches. After some hestitation, he finally agreed for the sum of $1000 to have this school building ready for the first week of September. The children were very happy in the two large school rooms. Meanwhile, I had planted trees, shrubs and a flower garden to afford the children pleasure. I gave a weekly medal for general excellence.

I also organized the first Children's Gardens. I taught them how to cultivate flowers and vegetables in 1880. I also gave the children nature study lessons; aided by a magnifying glass I showed a large collection of all kinds of insects and how the golden, yellow pollen carried on the tiny hairs of their wings while flitting from flower to flower dropped on the pistils of the various flowers changed their color. I also taught the children sewing and fancy needlework.

A YAVAPAI WOMAN
SPEAKS

The following account of an 85-year-old Yavapai woman was recorded during 1967 as part of the Doris Duke Native American Oral History Project and is deposited at the Arizona State Museum, University of Arizona, Tucson. The portion included here is a rarity, a Native American woman's retelling, in her own words, of the massacre of her people, as well as the capture of Geronimo as she has heard it. This oral history is powerful not only for the story it holds, but for the strong poetic movement of the voice animating the tale. Her life story contains the theme of continual displacement. First she is taken away from her family while still a young child and sent to the Indian school. After being socialized there, she is reluctant to return to her people. Her life becomes one of hard physical labor as she loses her teaching position and is pushed out of the way to make room for others believed more qualified by virtue of their race. Hers is the story not only of an individual or of a particular people, but of the many peoples for whom the settling of the American West meant being pushed out to the edge of extinction. The massacre she describes took place some time during the 1860s, when her father was a boy and the centuries-old hunting and gathering life of the isolated, peaceful Yavapai was destroyed by mining and army explorations into northern Arizona. Like the buffalo of the plains, this gentle, basket-weaving tribe of 2000 became fair game for frontier settlers who felt justified in exterminating any living creature in their way. With over half their number slaughtered, the remaining Yavapai were placed on the San Carlos Reservation in the 1870s, where their ancient culture, based on cyclic movements in search of food and clothing, died.

*T*here was an Indian reservation, a place called San Carlos, and there's where I was then, when I was young. I was born over there, too. Just across the lake. They call it Coolidge Dam now. They were not always there, my tribe. They had the central part of Arizona for their territory. Ah, the Spaniard has wrote a little history about them, and that's the way it was told, that they were peaceful Indians. They're not on a warpath all the time, but if they are attacked, they're terrible, so people leave them alone, and they were under the Spaniards then, but when the United States bought it then, of course, we come in with the United States people. They didn't want to have us live in this state owning the central part of Arizona, so he sent U.S. soldiers, and beginning at Date Creek, it's over that way. . . .

The western Yavapai, the northern Yavapai, the southern southernest Yavapai, there were three divisions, dialect languages, although it's the same language, well, they started with the western. They promised us they are going to issue them food, clothing, and about maybe two or three in the afternoon, they did give them out some unbleached muslin, and some flour and beans, and then they start shooting at them. And my daddy was a young boy then. He said he run around this way in the bushes, and went way around, and he hid back of the soldiers' camp, and he stayed there. Just before they stopped, he went in and began to chop wood with a soldier's axe, you know. He says he started chopping wood for them because he was scared of them, and he didn't even think that they might shoot him. He was just chopping wood, and the people were west of the soldiers' camp, so, he said, not many, he said that he saw with his own eyes that his mother was killed and his aunt, his mother's sister. They were both killed. That's when he run around. Around, way around, and children, men and women, just everywhere, he said. And then, they moved on to a next place called, they called it Skull Valley after they killed many of the western Yavapai, they almost wiped them out, just piled high, so they call it today, Skull Valley. That's what I told a man sent from Congress last year in November, I think, and asked me, you know, to talk. I said they had no mercy, they act like they're not human beings, and so they just slaughtered them, and it was piled so high, they had to call it, no shame, nothing, no . . . no feeling sorrow, they call it Skull Valley, and it's Skull Valley today, I said. And you can go through there, too. There's a road. And then they move on to Camp Verde, and the storm was mad. It just rain sleet of ice across the air, and everybody got sick, even the soldiers, and the Indians, of course, didn't have much clothing on. And they tried to get the northern Yavapai, they can't get them because too many woods, you know, cedar trees, just thick, and of course, that grows right close to the ground, and they hide under that, you know, but they heard that they were coming, and so they didn't hardly get many, but, anyhow, they got some, and they slaughtered the cattle. I don't know where they got it, and tried to feed them, and boil it, and then they put something white in it, and when they began to eat it, they all die with it, too. So they didn't eat. The wind stop then. Looked like it was mad, too, but it stopped in time for them to get dry up a little bit, and then it began to be spring.

They said, so quick, the grass come up, the sun shine, and they said they felt good. The Indians said that's what they needed, the sunshine, so they got all right, and that was in '72. Eighteen-seventy-two. Early, early spring, but they waited a while. They got a little bit stronger, and they said, we are to move them over to San Carlos. That's where Coolidge Dam is now. To meet with Geronimo, other soldiers were there, they're getting him, but they couldn't get him, he's just fighting furiously, and they couldn't get him. But anyhow, they took these Yavapais over there. They tried to get the southernest Yavapai, they couldn't find them. They found a few, but southern Yavapais said, they're not going to take us and starve us to death. We're just going to kill ourselves, so there's a ravine, come from the north, very deep, at Superior mine, and so they know that, and so they went over there with their children, and they just drop in themselves and died there, many of them just kill themselves. Some over in that mountain, they climb up there and they fall down and got killed and died, and they went over there looking for them, the soldiers, the white and the Indians, they get the Indians to going now, now, so they went, but they just got a few, that's what they told. They said they killed themselves. They said, they're not going to starve us to death, so many of them have thrown themselves in that deep creek, they said, canyon, and died. So they just weeped and weeped. They cried and cried, and then they went back to San Carlos, and they told the officers what happened.

These Indians told them, but they got quite a few though, they said. And then they turn around and, the soldiers said, we can't get Geronimo, you got to help us, so they ask these Yavapai men. They want the strong men. They said all right. So they joined them. And just in a few days, U.S. from Washington said, we want them to surrender, instead of killing them anymore. They heard that they killed most of the Indians, and they don't want to kill them anymore. Ask them to surrender. So the first battle they were going to have, it happened that they took one of our young men and taught him their language, and he was speaking fluently of Geronimo's language, and so they ask him to interpret what the white man says to them. That they must surrender. They don't want to kill

anymore of Geronimo's tribe. He said you can't run away, he said. We
have soldiers on the north of you. We have soldiers on the west, and on
the south, and right here on the east. You cannot get away, not one of
you. So this Yavapai learned the Apache language, told it. There was a
nice little hill, they say, just look like made for him. Little hill and kind
of flat and one tree on it, and he climb up there and stood up there and
told them what this high officer said, that a word from Washington, the
great father, what he has said to them. And so I guess he put in his own,
he said, yes, you are all about wiped out. I think you better surrender.
We don't want to kill you. We don't want to, but we just have to, and
we don't want to do it. If we did, we're going to have tears in our eyes
to do it. You know we are Yavapais, we don't belong to your tribe, but
we, we feel bad to do that. So he said please surrender. So quiet for almost
an hour, say just like death, and then Geronimo got up. They were way
down there. He got up and talked in his language, and then this Yavapai,
a young man, interpret, and another one interpret in English, you know.
Each tribe. And so it took, oh, almost half a day. They didn't say yes right
away, so they have to wait and wait. Geronimo didn't want to give up.
He'd rather die, he said, than to live on. How would you gonna treat me,
I don't know. The day is coming. As these Yavapais has said and killed
themselves, you might starve me to death, he said, and he cried they said.

I think he's right, Yavapai's right. All right. They went peacefully, he
said. And he cried just loud, they said. Everybody hear him, and then at
last they said all right, we'll surrender.

You get your best men together, they said. Your brave men, your warriors, but let the rest go back to where you have been living, so he was
told that way. And crying, everybody's crying, and then the wives, the
children, they went, but Geronimo and his warriors and their family parted
this way. He said, you can't get out, I tell you. We have trains waiting
for you already, so we'll take you to the train. By that time, it was way
late in the afternoon. Oh, crying, even the horses neigh. They said, they
seem to know, but of course, the horses, they can't take horses, so they
just let it go. With the other Indians take the horses and everything, so
they parted, soldiers got in, drove them to the train and loaded them and
took them. That's the last we seen, my daddy said. He was a scout then.

And so we all cried, and we can't eat, he said, and so we got weak and
told us to rest all that day, ah, half a day and a night, until the next day,
and then they sent us back to old San Carlos, where Coolidge Dam is.
That's the way it had been with us people, he said. They never try to say,
you can have your land back. We haven't got people here to work it right

now, maybe some years later, but you can go back where you used to live and have things to eat, your natural food, they never even say that to us, they said. They keep them over there at old San Carlos. The grass was gone, the food that grow natural was gone, there's no wood, and yet they never say. They give us ration, that's gone too. Scarce all the time. We almost go naked. They give goods in those days, even shoes for everybody, little children. He said that was short. They couldn't keep up. We almost all go naked, he said, but they manage to have little piece of goods, you know, for the women and children. And that's the way they got us to become white people. That's the way they taught us how to be white people, they said, but I don't know the other generation coming, I don't know that. I don't know how you will be, but we went through hard hardships. Lose all our people, our best relatives and people. I don't know what you're going to get for it. It's up to you, told the young people.

And then this word came, there's a school they built at old San Carlos. Said that compulsory law, you have to go to school whether you have just one child or not, you have to send it. It happened that I was the only child they had, because he was scouting, you see, he didn't stay home. And they cried, mother and grandmother just cried their heart out, but said she have to go. She ran away and took me and lived in the mountains, but they hunted her up like animal. And then they wait at the house, come over to her uncle's house. We come back way midnight and to eat, of course I don't know, she carry me on her back in a burden basket.

Asleep, and then she carry me back and forth in the mountain, where Coolidge Dam is, where those mountain is, that's where we sleep at night. And then we overslept one morning and the scouts were there with my daddy standing there crying, and said just as soon as I wake up and got up, and I saw my daddy and I just cried and run to him, and that's how he got me, and the white soldiers and the Indian soldiers, they surrounded us, said, the captain said you can't get away. If you want to be killed, he said, we'd kill everyone of you, he said, and so my mama's uncle live there so all right, he said, and he went and got his bows and arrows. I'm ready, he said, and he danced around. I remember I was crying, but I laughed because he dance around, he said, all right, shoot me, and I shoot you, too.

   . . . And then, in a year's time, I was sent to the school. I was still nursing they said, you know, some are like that, they run around, but they stop and go nurse, that's the way I was they said. And so, mama told one of the big girls, my relative, she said, you take care of her because she's that way and she's gonna cry and miss me and everything, she said, and I had to go to school, see, so I went to school, and I stayed, but I did pretty good, said, I never wake up at night. And then in a few days, the people, the children, that, this superintendent come from Grand Junction, Colorado, came and got, maybe, forty, fifty, I think firty-two, they said. He took 'em over there to go to school because a governor in that state, Colorado, said he'd like to have an Indian school there, too, so they had one.

They had to move, the crazy people that lived there, they had to move it somewhere else, then give that buildings, you know, for these Indian children to be going to school there. And so, the first party went. In the fall I had to go over there. Oh, that's the time they cried like everything, too. They camp around the building all night long. You hear crying, mamas crying, crying, and early in the morning, they wake us up to go to breakfast, then, we come back, they told us to go in the wagon right here, and so they make us climb the wagon, get in, and here my mama was, right over here. Just as soon as I sit down, she grabbed me, pull me out and take me out, and put her arm around me and said, no, you can't take her. You've got to kill me, she said, and you cannot take my only one, and she sit down, tried to hide me like, you know, between her legs. Sit there, and here comes black soldiers, hold her, then take me out, and I was afraid of the colored more than anything. I cried and I nearly died, seems like. Pick me up and put me, throw me in the wagon. Told the girls to hold me, but mama just push there so, she's a great big woman, oh, throw their, throws guns away, and she climb in and pick me out, pick me, and sit down and cover me up with her arms.

They do this then, but they got white, white color, white soldiers. So the black soldiers, they said, she's scared to death of the colored, I think, they said, you know. The teachers were around us, so they got the white one and they hold me, and I didn't cry they said, but mama won't let them take me, and she cried, but . . . my daddy tried to come and hold her, and she fight him. She said, you want her to go, she said, it's you that's giving her away, she said, and she don't want him to touch her, so these white men have to hold her, and then take me and put me in the wagon. They go, went, go quick, so she couldn't get onto me, and they held her until she cross a big river there. I think they called it Gunnison, ah, Gila River, I guess, that's what came there. And then in about two hours, when they let me go, and then, the other mothers did not do that, see, like the Apaches, like Geronimos, they did not do it. They just let it go because they have big families, you know, but with them, they only had me that's why, because he was scouting, never stayed home, that's why I was the only one they had. They did have a baby boy, but it just died in her, and she nearly died, she told me. And that's how I went away

to get my education. And it was in 1890, and I never come home until 1902.
. . . We were to go for five years, and some three years, but some did
come back, but, see, I didn't want to. I forgot my language. I just forget
it altogether when I come back here in 1902. And I had to learn it all
over, but it didn't take me long. They were glad, these superintendents,
because they wanted me to be a teacher here at Ft. McDowell. They'll
start with me, he said that. You'll be the teacher. We were wondering
who we'll get, and now it's you, they said. And so he said, come back,
they said come back. Oh, they won't let me come back, I said, my folks.
Well, we'll go after you and talk to them and see what they'll say, they
said. Sure, we're gonna get you, they said. So I went on. And the train
used to get there about twelve o'clock, at noon. You know, there were
many white people. They heard about it, you know, through my daddy.
He had many white friends in Prescott, and so they were waiting to see
me, how I come in, you know. I've been away so long, and this, I just stayed.

I cried all the time, I didn't want to come back. Isn't that awful? And
so I cried all the way over here, I think. I didn't want to come back, but
my teacher lived in Washington, D.C. and she's married. She said, you
ought to be ashamed, she said that. They are your people, she said. We
are not your people, you just went to school with us, she said. She said,
me, I went visited my boys and girls at old San Carlos. I spread down old
dirty rag, and I sit on it, and I drink out of an old cup and a frying pan
with stew in it, meat, and tortillas, she said, I eat, she said. You must do
the same thing because they are your people. You are proud girl. Come
down, she said. She just about to slap me, but I just cried and said no,
I'm just gonna get down and go away. I don't care where, I said, from
the train, and she said, you're not going to get down. You're going right
home to see your people. They're just dying, crying for you, she said. You
just act so awful.

Before long I taught over here, as they say. They went after me. One
of the superintendents, there were two superintendents, you know, one
went after me. Well, I did everything for them; when they put in whites,
you know, well, I take 'em out every time they send. They were T.B.,
they're not supposed to teach, you know, Indian school, and closed up in
a room. I fire them when they send T.B., and pretty soon, I was the
assistant matron to the Phoenix Indian School. Then I was laundress when
they can't get no laundress. . . . I was to be a nurse, when I was in
school, but the doctor said no, she's not strong enough. Got to have a
strong woman to be a nurse. I did help in a hospital in Prescott one time
. it was good money, you know. Nurse, being a nurse.

People have died hungry, old people, clothes and things. Me, I always run off and work, you know, at the Indian school. I'd be assistant matron or laundress or something down there, when I had my folks with me, and my men don't work, when they run around with other women, why I work, and we have something to eat, for my folks, and I have a little boy living, and one died, and all that, and I, and I'm never still, I'm always working, but they say I cannot do hard work. I was running the laundry one time, too. That was too much.

And then the girls, they know how to iron, and this and that, but it was good, and they like it. They said it was because it was an Indian running it, and so they work nicer. All work like everything, the girls and the Indian boys, too, and it was that easy for me, and that's the way I did in my lifetime. Of course, I taught here, but they sent in a white woman to take my place, and when they did, she was T.B., and I didn't like that, and I write to the Indian office, and they sent word that she must get out. They got to have a healthy person to teach the children, and be in a room with, with 'em is not right, that they'll take the disease. . . . Everybody afraid of me, I mean, white people. Of course, I have to look out for my people, too, see. Keep them healthy, and the children, all that. That's what I go to school for, to help my people, you know, and so that's what I did.

. . . They sent them to other places . . . so I quit that, and they won't give me jobs anymore, and then when all my people died, my babies died, and I was all alone, left in the world, I didn't care whether I live or not, I didn't care. I got discouraged. I wasn't a religious woman. I don't know anything about that. When we went to school, the government said, don't teach them the Bible because they wouldn't understand. There too many churches, but give them hymn books, let them sing, so I don't know nothing about the Bible, but I do know, from my Indian, about the Great Spirit. They teach just this: thou shalt not steal. That's what the mother tells the daughter, and the father the son. That covers everything, you know that. Covers everything. Don't steal somebody's wife or husband or horse or blanket or shoes or what. That's what they mean, see?

That one commandment covers all, I always say, from our Indians, but they have ten, they say, the whites, not the whites, it comes from heaven, they say, but they learn it, and they don't do those things. No. The Indian children. No. They feel afraid.

You know, sometimes white people don't like Indians very well, and we don't like white people very well. We are different tribes, that's how we are. We have our own ways to live, everything, we live our own way. We're given the way we should live. We are given that, too. That's how we are, see? It seems to be this way. You run your own way. Maybe God did that, we don't know, see because we'll never get along if we mingle our religion and yours, and our ways of life in living, and all that. You don't like the way we live. I don't like it now, the way you dress, see. That's the way it will be, we'll never get along.

You remember, Christ always have a long dress? Dress, long dress. The angels have long robes. That's innocence, see, purity, see. That's what it is. . . . When I come back, I ask. I went away when I was small, but when I came back, I used to say, Grandmother, tell me things that you used to try to tell me when I was too small then, but now I want to hear it. When I say that, she'd tell them to me again. Things like that. History, like I'm telling you . . . white people always want to hear history, so I says, they might ask me, and I might earn money that way, too, then, instead of washing their diapers, and day after day, oh, I used to cry and was it, oh, I used to wash, and my mama just almost cry when I tell her, she said, it's a wonder you have arms yet, she said, and hands yet, she said, ought to have been off, you know, disease, the way you washing those things.

. . . My daddy became a Christian, he and my little boy, three years old. I wouldn't do it, and he just worry to death. Well, you go to each one, then whichever you think is real right, you're gonna go in, I suppose, he said, but now, I would worry to death if where I'm going I'd be alive again, but the black book say where I'm going now, I wouldn't know anything, and I'm glad of that, he said . . . and then he died, twelve o'clock. He was talking to me all that morning.

. . . Because I wouldn't join no church. Just he and my little boy, three years old, join the Presbyterian church. I help with that, I interpreted, and I teach the Sunday school children, all that, but it didn't strike me, but I do believe. The Indians say the Great Spirit, I believe that. I believe it. They say, thou shalt not steal. That covers everything for the Indians, see?

But I did go in at last, when they all left me. I was all alone, and I cried. I said, whoever is doing this to me, I said, kill me, too, right now. I was in Prescott. I used to go over there when I have time, and stay around there and get up on a hill, and I'd sit there and cry because that's where I found them when I first came back from school in 1902 . . . I just running around all alone. I want to die, and I swear against the Great Spirit. I said, whoever is doing this, doing to me, I'm all alone now, now, why don't you kill me, too? No, I have to live on, and so I came back, and then, just then, I was living with a woman up there. . . . Whenever your men throw you away, she said, you come and live with me. . . .

. . . In those days, they don't have a hard time, they say, it comes out right away, soon, but nowadays, they say, always a long time. I went black, they say, and then the doctor from Phoenix, in those days, just buggy, you know, he came, before sundown, over here to McDowell in a buggy, and by that time, I was dying, turn black. But I can see, and a farmer's wife, white woman, always be with me, praying, she kneeling here and praying, I saw her. It was in a tipi, but I had mattress, and I saw doctor come in, sunup, and he come right away, to me, and he felt my pulse and everything, and then he rolled his sleeves, I saw him. Mrs. Gill told him that I was deaf, I guess, getting to be deaf and turning dark, purplish color. I was swollen like, just big, they said . . . Three times before he got it out. And overgrown hair, way over. And people, Indians, thought I had two maybe, or three. The way I look. Well, anyway, and I come to. I always have hard time with that . . . I was just walking around, walking around, and my mother grabbed me and put me down on the ground, of course, Indian way, you know, there's holes there, I put my heels there, and I sit down, and sit back of me, to push . . . And she said, and my grandmother came, and she said, she prayed, I think. She said pity us, she said, and help us. Have pity on us, and she, the only one we have, and it seems you are sending her a human being which she is going to receive, help her, she said. That's the first Indian prayer I ever heard. And then, that second time, I vowed I never have another one, and I have, have one the next thing, but this one, the first one, that was hard on me.

And my mother was like that with me, so as soon as I was born, my grandmother said, you just lay still, I'm hungry, I'm gonna go eat a little bit and I'll be back, she said, and get the baby and wash it, and dress it, and put things on, white people been bringing clothes, said, I'm gonna fix it, her, after I eat, you lay still, you hear, she said, to her daughter. She had a fire already there, and a bucket of water and all, she wanted to make coffee and this and that, and then, she looked because her dogs barked, and a little ways over there, mama was coming back from over there, and she yelled, what you doing over there? I told you to lie still. She went over there, and she buried me over there in the wash, and she cried and she said, and here I've been crying, and all these years we haven't got any baby, and here you go and bury it, she said, and she got me out and brought me, and she washed me, of course . . . and wash the hair with soap weeks, that has long leaves. I'm talking about myself, yes. She had that all ready, suds just foaming, you know. And she said, you really smiled, when I put it on your hair, she said, water, and put water there, one side of your face just smiled, she said, and oh, I was happy, she said. I know you're not gonna die, she said.

MARY ANNETTA
COLEMAN POMEROY
My Life Story

"Born November 20, 1862, at Pinto, Utah, Mrs. Pomeroy came to Mesa in 1881 with her husband, the late Elijah Pomeroy, among the earliest settlers in Mesa. Mr. Pomeroy was the first bishop of the first LDS ward organized in Mesa, and Mrs. Pomeroy was active in church affairs in the pioneer days."

So reads the obituary of Mary Annetta Pomeroy. Behind the description of the staid Mormon wife, however, are the far more turbulent thoughts and feelings of a woman who struggled to accept and obey the dictates of church and husband despite the pain they caused. Her autobiography, "My Life Story," reveals her true response, not just to the hardships of pioneer life, but to polygamy as practiced in her religion.

Pomeroy's primer style and limited vocabulary do not permit her much range with which to express her emotions. We get a record of events she perceives as significant—marriages, births, illnesses, deaths—and of daily activities—work and the bright spots of social activity that relieve the ongoing grind of work. The account surprises with an occasional flash of direct emotion and of poetry.

The quality of her life comes through in her succinct, homely recounting of the mundane detail of her life. Oddly, her images, in their simplicity, stand out. Despite its roughness, this account has a satisfying quality, perhaps because the language and the stories so appropriately express the writer's life.

I was born November 21, 1862, in Pinto, Utah. My father, Prime Thornton Coleman; my mother, Emma Beck Evans. Our family consisted of two girls and two boys all, except the baby, born in Pinto. . .

My father had another wife, Elizabeth Eagles. She was the mother of Willie, who died when he was a baby; Willard died 1897, in August, at Alpine. He was struck by lightning. Della, who died also; Sue, Doll, John, June, died June 1893, at Springerville, of typhoid, and George. When George was born (1882) his mother died and our mother took the children. George was then only twelve hours old. This was a lot of trouble for her, but she cared for the children as if they were her own.

Mother and father's other wife lived in the same house; each had a separate apartment, however. Ma often left me with Aunt Lizzie but she always took Lell with her because no one would take care of her. She had a terrible temper. She has changed now.

The school house was built of stone; it had a large fireplace and a small stage. We thought it very big. It served us for every purpose. When we visited it several years ago, after an absence of over 35 years, we couldn't believe our eyes. It looked too small. Only three families lived in Pinto at the time of our visit.

Mr. Eldridge, the schoolteacher, played his bass viol and led the choir also. On the first of May, he always took us to the creek for a May-day walk. I enjoyed these walks more than anything else in my life. We picked wild flowers, made a wreath of them, and crowned our May Queen.

My father was a good dairyman. He took the dairy three miles from Pinto for one summer, in 1870. The next year we lived on a ranch, but before the summer was over, the water begain to fail and we moved back to town for the winter. My father went into partnership with a Chilean. They seemed to be doing well, but when George died bills came in from every quarter. My father lost everything.

In 1872 we gave up the ranch and moved to Spring Valley where Evans was born. Mr. Heywood came from Washington, Utah, to teach school. He taught one summer and two winters. He began to make loving eyes at Lell. Charlotte and I often hid and listened to them. We enjoyed watching them "spark."

In 1875 Pa moved Aunt Lizzie out to Spring Valley and that same year Lell and Mr. Heywood were married.

July 1877, we moved to Upper Kanab. My father cared for the Cannan herd of cattle. In October the Pomeroys, Sirrines and Crosmons stopped at our ranch on their way to Arizona. They came from Bear Lake, Idaho. Elijah Pomeroy came ahead and stayed with us three days.

One night we had all the younger people come up to the house and spend the evening. We took up the carpet and with the aid of a fiddle and an organ had wonderful music to dance by. We danced, recited, sang and had a marvelous time. Emily, John Pomeroy's wife, had such a sweet voice that we made her sing several solos. At midnight the dining room was opened, the long table set, and we all ate. Coffee, hot biscuits, butter, cheese, pickles, ham and milk were served. Of course we had cream and sugar for our coffee. They seemed to enjoy the supper more than anything else. They had been on the road for almost six weeks and a home-cooked meal tasted good to them.

In July of that year, Lide [Elijah Pomeroy] and Lee Daniels came back to Kanab. They were going on North but we decided to go to St. George for the winter. Ma, Lell and her babies, Prime, Willard, Evans, John Platt and I. We rented a house with two rooms, a porch and a cellar. We took some mosquito net and put it around the porch so that we could have some place to sleep. We were very crowded.

All that summer the children went down the canyon and gathered choke cherries and service berries. We milked a hundred and fifty cows. We made butter and cheese and in the fall took them to Salt Lake or Silver Reef to trade for wearing apparel. I do not know how my parents endured that life. My mother was interested in higher education and a better way of living, so I can easily guess how she felt about it.

When Lide came back to Utah in July neither my mother nor I thought anything about it. He was an old friend of the family and Pa enjoyed having him work about the farm because he was so careful.

We had 150 milk cows and several corrals. Lide and I milked in the same corral and we often drove our cows together so we could talk while we milked. We went on several hay-rack rides and had a very good time all that summer.

One night in October 1878, a big thunder-shower came up. Lide and I had just finished washing the milk buckets. When I heard the thunder and saw the lightning, I became frightened. Lightning had struck a tree not far from me once, and it had always terrified me since. I told Lide I was frightened and he said, "Well, we'll just stay behind the kitchen door until it stops." Then he asked me to marry him! I do not remember what he said, but I could hardly say, "Yes."

October 12, 1879 Lide and I started to St. George to get married in the Temple. We got to St. George on the 15th and were married on the 16th. We drove straight through to Pinto and got there at 12 that night. Aunt Lizzie was visiting her parents at Pinto and went back with us. They had planned a reception for us at home but Lell had typhoid fever. In those days wine was almost as common as water. So many grapes were raised that nearly everybody had a cellar full of wine. Three others had typhoid so we were swamped with work.

July 4, 1880, a little girl came to take her abode with us. We called her Emma Charlotte. My girl friend and I were such good companions that we agreed to name our first girls for each other and our mothers, also.

October 30, 1880, all of us started for Arizona. We went to Mesa and the others went to Bush Valley. We went about half a mile together, then separated. It was hard for me because I had never been away from the family for more than a month, before. I didn't see them again until eight years had passed.

Our wagon was very comfortable. We had a double bed in the wagon and a shelf over it for our baggage. We got a hive of bees in St. George and put them under the bed. When we stopped for several days we took the bees out so that they could get some exercise. We traveled for six weeks and finally arrived at Mesa, Arizona, our destination.

John and Emily Pomeroy had one room made of saguaros and covered with dirt. In it were one six-paned window, and a door. The house had a brush shed on three sides where they cooked and ate. We moved in their granary which was half full of wheat. We had our little sheet iron stove, a bed on a platform off the floor, a chair and a stool. We lived there seven months, sleeping on the ground when it became too hot. We got a tent to cook in and slept in the wagon. Lide made adobes and William Newell built a house for us, with two rooms and a dirt roof. Lide had some cattle which he sold in Tempe. With the money he bought a bed, one large rocker, three chairs, a gate-legged table, a clock and a stove. We had rags enough for a carpet which we had woven. We put straw under it and tacked it down. The house was white-washed and curtains were put up. I was never so happy in my life. I sat in the rocker, listening to the clock tick and watching the baby play on the floor and thought I should burst with pride. We were surely blessed! On October 11, 1882, a son was born. We called him Thales Coleman. He grew into a lovely child.

Elijah Pomeroy was made Bishop of the Mesa Ward. He was Bishop for five years. In September 1883, small pox became prevalent. To protect our children, we traveled for three days to Horterres's ranch . . . We were surely thankful when the plague was over, but there was a vacancy that nothing could fill, especially when there were from two to four in one family who died.

In September 1884, we decided to enter into the order of celestial marriage and started to St. George. Lucretia Phelps was the woman my husband chose. It was a great trial to me. Nobody but one who is in it knows the many heartaches which one goes through while living that order.

January 1, 1885, Elijah Haskell was born. It was a wonderful gift . . . nothing but the dreary routine happened until November 20, 1886, when a bouncing baby girl, Irene Ursula, came to live with us . . . December 13, 1988, another girl came to make her home with us. We called her Francelle Aeolia after our sisters. In March 1889, whooping cough made the rounds. The five children had it. The baby nearly died. . . .

In 1890 the U.S. Government began serving warrants for all polygamists. Of course my husband had to go to Mexico. He was gone two years. Only those who have experienced this know what I went through. I had a lot of public work to do and took care of my family, too, so I was kept quite busy. On Christmas morning 1890 a wee little lady came to take her abode with us. We called her Minnie Linnfitt. . . .

In August 1892, my husband came home. The children were very happy, but I didn't know whether I wanted to live with him again or not. Finally under the circumstances we decided to let bygones be bygones and to live for the future. The winter passed very quietly. . . .

It is now the summer of 1934 and I am staying in Flagstaff. I am very satisfied with my life. I have nine children, eight of whom are living, nineteen grandchildren, and twelve great-grandchildren. I spend most of my time working in the Temple. In August 1933 I received an old age pension of $30 a month which gives me a chance to "do as I please."

MARY L. STRIGHT
A Missionary Teacher's First Winter in Jemez

Thanks to a genealogy prepared in 1973 by Hayden Leroy Stright, we have a great deal of factual information on Mary Lodisa Stright, the author of this 1882 journal. A Presbyterian missionary school-teacher, Mary kept this daily record from October 1882 until January 1883. It tells the story of her journey from her home in Pennsylvania, where her family had lived since the early nineteenth century, to New Mexico, where she spent the rest of her life, and gives us almost a photographic account of her first winter teaching at Jemez Pueblo.

Born May 6, 1857, at the Stright homestead in Deer Creek Township, Mercer County, Pennsylvania, Mary became a teacher, following the profession of many others in her family. She attended Edinboro State Normal School; then, through the influence of her teacher, Isabelle Rhuhama Leach, she went to New Mexico at age 25. Isabelle, referred to as "Belle" in the journal, had married a medical missionary, Dr. John Milton Shields, a former medic in the Union Army, and Mary joined her friend at Jemez. Following Belle's death from pneumonia in 1900, Mary helped care for her friend's five young children.

In 1894 Mary married the trader, John Wiley Miller, a fellow Pennsylvanian. She refers to him as "a nice and rather good looking man" the first time she sees him, and her references to him increase through the pages of the journal. Mr. Miller ran the Santa Fe stage station, and when it closed, he started the Jemez Pueblo trading post. The area had a population of about 500 during the time covered by the journal.

Mary and John Miller had one son, Hugh Stright Miller, born January 25, 1896. John Miller died in 1916 following a fall. Mary continued to live in Jemez Springs until her death in 1944 at age 87. They are both buried in the cemetery of the Jemez Community United Presbyterian Church.

It has been said, "You don't come to New Mexico—God sends you." God, or the church, sent many women to New Mexico in the nineteenth century, customarily in the occupation of missionary schoolteacher or nun. These energetic, optimistic, dedicated women, as typified by Mary Stright, devoted themselves to serving their communities, primarily in building and sustaining much-needed schools and hospitals.

Mary Stright's journal is filled with close observation of the details of her daily life. It is a woman's-eye view of food preparation, agricultural methods, architecture and interior decoration, holiday celebrations, human interactions, and social customs within the community. Between the lines we sense an observer who is practical, dutiful, curious, self-sufficient, and not without her prejudices. She is concerned for her students and particularly responsive to those she perceives as bright and willing to learn and cooperate. As a shield against loneliness, she quickly plunges into work upon arriving, and she readily develops close ties to community members. We come to know a woman who, taking strength from her traditional values, lives her life with a sense of purpose and adventure.

Mary Stright's no-nonsense attitude is reflected in her writing style. She writes in short, simple sentences without a trace of flighty metaphor, lacy elaboration, or introspective analysis. This journal seems to have been written for her folks back home and reads almost like an extended letter—a report on her daily experience in a new land.

O ct. 12, 1882. Left Greenville 3:30 o'clock. Met Mr. and Mrs. Jas. Carnahan and Hugh Carnahan and his brother. There is a lady, a Mrs. Smith from Oil City on the train. She has two little children with her and is going to Arizona. The youngest is eleven months and is a real good-natured little fellow. The other is three years old and is rather cross and troublesome. We traveled all night in Ohio. What I saw of Ohio I liked very much. The farms all looked nice. Could not get a sleeping car, but

Mr. C. made a bed for Kate and I by turning one and using a board that he had and a comforter and a blanket. Kate had a pillow with her so that with our shawls we had quite a comfortable bed. I slept the last part of the night pretty well. There was a horse thief captured at Akron. The sheriff led him handcuffed through our car at midnight. The thief was a tall one. They said he was 6 ft. 7 in. high. The night was very warm and the car was nearly full.

Oct. 13, 1882. Arrived at Cincinnati this morning at 6 o'clock just a little after the comet disappeared out of sight. We were awake from five o'clock watching. I think I shall never forget the sight; it was brilliant and beautiful. Our impressions of Cincinnati were not very favorable, but we did not see the finest part by any means. We passed through gardens of sweet potatoes, celery and cabbage. They were quite a sight. We took a bus to the other depot, happened to get a seat next to Mrs. Sam Overmeyers and her sister who were going to Illinois. We didn't find the station a very pleasant place. We thought we wanted a warm breakfast and went to a hotel but our fare was half roasted beef steak, raw potatoes sliced, strong butter, pretty fair bread and coffee. Two of the gentlemen took oysters which they said were good. The landlady was mad about something. She jerked around pretty lively. The dining room was pretty close—had an unpleasant odor pervading it. Mrs. C. asked Jim to open it which he did. The landlady came in and slammed it shut. We went through Indiana and Illinois. What I saw of Ind. did not look a great deal different from our part of Penna. except that is is a great deal more level, too level. They looked like floors, I thought, but the fields of grain were about like ours and there seemed to be as much woods with the difference that trees were small. I think our hemlock would be quite a curiosity for size. Did not see any pines or hemlock. I actually saw considerable rail fence. Went through two small tunnels. Ate dinner at Vincennes. Crossed the Wabash R. into Illinois—like Ind. only more so. Arrive at St. Louis at 6 pm. Crossed the great suspension bridge over the Miss. R. It is indeed a wonder of architecture, built so that steamers can pass under, and over our heads wagons and people passing all the time. Then we went through a tunnel. It was most too dark to see as well as I would have liked; still I could see enough to judge something of the size of the Miss. R. . . .

Oct. 14, 1882. Woke up in time to again see the comet. I will have to travel alone from this on, which won't be so pleasant. Met a lady in the ladies' parlor who was going to Pa. She had gone to Kansas City about a year ago. Her baby had died this summer of cholera infantium. It had been very healthy and strong before. She said the place was very hard on

children, that she had seen more funerals of little children since she had
been there than ever before. She said she never wanted to come back
here. . . I felt pretty lonesome and almost like crying for a little while,
but instead of indulging in tears I laid down and took a nap. . . . I felt
ever so much better. . . . These electric lights are beautiful. They shine
with a bluish dazzling light and are so brilliant that the gas lights look
like candles. They are caused some way by friction and are a flame like an
oil lamp. Mr. Carnahan says that paper won't burn in one. . . .

Sunday morning, Oct. 15, 1882. Waked this morning to find myself
in Kansas. As far as I can see it is level as a floor. Once in a while there
is a farmhouse to be seen, and some cattle; not a tree except the very few
which have been set out. I prefer country where, as the Irish man says,
"they have to stack it," a little at least. Stopped at one town between nine
and ten where we saw people going to church and could hear the bells
ringing and I thought of our folks at home getting ready to go to church
and I wished I could go too . . . I find it is quite a common thing for
women to travel alone. . . .

Monday, Oct. 16. I slept real well last night. But what a change greets
the eye this morning. Mountains, trees and valley all around and we are
in Colorado. The scenery is grand. I cannot describe it to do anything
like justice to it. In some places the mountains seem to touch the sky and
the rising sun makes all a scene of beauty. There is one scene which I will
try to describe. A plain as smooth and grass as even as a well kept lawn,
trees, some kind of pine I think, and of perfect proportions are scattered
over it with the regularity of park. There on one side of a deep ravine;
rocks on each bank are the mountains with masses of rocks looking like
walls and castles. In one place you could imagine Noah's ark on Mt. Ararat
. . . Las Vegas is quite a town. Have seen plenty of adobe or mud houses,
and a good many frame ones which are almost always painted brown. The
adobe are different from what I expected and look comfortable and about
as well as the wooden ones. . . . Somehow I dread my getting off the
cars; if I could only take the stage right away or if I could find a good
stopping place I would not mind, but I don't know anything about Bernalillo and from what I can find out it is a small place, but I'll not make
it any better by worrying. I have got along all right so far and I trust I
will the rest of the way. I spoke to the conductor and he said he would
see to my getting a stopping place. I get to Bernalillo at half past eight
pm, get off and go into the waiting room. The conductor tells me there
is a good hotel right across the way. . . . The place seems very quiet and
I am shown to a nice comfortable room. It is a good deal better than I expected.

Tuesday, Oct. 17, 1882. In Bernalillo now. On looking out of the window this morning I saw two Indians with their blankets around them and heads bare; what very black straight hair they have. I felt hungry for the breakfast which was very good, potatoes and meat were both cooked. . . This is quite a little place, as big as Sheakleyville if you count the mud huts of the Mexicans which make up the greater part of the town. All the buildings here are adobe except quite a large store owned by Perea Brothers, another long wooden building owned by them also, and the station house which is wood. There are three or four stores here and they keep a larger stock and more variety than in Sheakleyville. Went into one of them. They have ready made clothing for ladies as well as men, but the funniest of all are the Mexican huts which are put around anywhere and in any kind of shape. These are low one story mud concerns without windows, that is most of them, and a great string of red peppers hung over the door. The girl said the people more than half lived on peppers, not sweet ones, but the very billest kind. . . . One can't help being hungry here if they go out in the air. It is so bracing and invigorating. There is no school or church here but in a little town a mile above called Old Town there is a church, and convent. The sisters of the convent keep school and some of the children from here attend there. . . .

Wednesday, Oct. 18, 1882. After dinner, a Mexican young man came to the hotel and said he was going to Jemes in a buggy and if I wanted to do so could go with him. I did not know what to do, I was so tired of staying but he was a stranger. I asked the landlady if she knew this young man and if it would be all right for me to go with him. She said he was a nice young man and would take me there all right. . . It would have been better if I had waited. Went about a mile or two when we came to the Rio Grande River which we crossed on a very long bridge and then we were into the sand which was at least 6 inches deep. The first part of the way the plain was pretty well covered with clumps of cedar wood, some cactus and different kinds of weeds such as I had never seen before and would only see in such a place. The wonder to me was that anything at all could grow. After awhile it got worse. The clumps of cedar wood were farther apart till at last nothing could be seen but great drifts of sand. Once in a while we caught sight of the Jemes River which runs through here. The Mexican said the road or tracks rather never stayed in one place very long, for in a wind storm, a common thing, those drifts might be carried over into the track. His old horse is very pokey and he has to whip him to make him go at any kind of decent rate. I feel sorry for the horse but if we only get to Jemes I don't care. It begins to get dark and I ask him if we are nearly there, and he answers that we are not halfway. I begin to feel a little suspicious. It is moonlight and we ride on. At last the horse will go no farther. We are near an Indian pueblo and the Mexican thinks he must stop to feed his horse. The Indians live in huts on the top of the hills and he drives up that, wakes up an Indian. He wants to know if I don't want to stay all night. I tell him I don't if I can help it. He says it will be an hour and a half before the Indian can get corn and he can get his horse fed so I get out and go in. There is a good fire in the fireplace in one corner which feels very good for we had got quite cold. The nights are very cool here. They have two or three chairs. I sat down in one. The Mexican said he would get me a bed if I wanted to lie down. I told him it would not be worthwhile if we went on to Jemes. He laid down and slept awhile then got up and had the Indians bring something to eat. He had a can of peaches and a can of salmon and a bottle of beer. An Indian girl spread a cloth over a box and put a dish or two, some boiled eggs and some kind of bread that was like a very thick pancake. I could not eat much. It just seemed as if a mouthful would choke though I did manage to swallow a mouthful or two of peaches. It was then eleven o'clock and I knew it would be two or three hours before we could get to Jemes, so I concluded to lie down. They had no beds except some skins thrown down on the floor and a blanket over them with another to cover with. I could see two or three Indians lying in different parts of the hut. They showed me some skins and a blanket or two in one corner. I took my valise and spread my shawl over it and the blanket and lay down but you may be sure I did not sleep. If I ever wished for morning it was then. . . .

    October 19, 1882. Morning came at last and, oh how thankful I was. . . . We soon started on our road again which was the same as yesterday for five miles, when we came to a Mexican town where I saw a large flock of sheep, more than a thousand. . . . At last we get to Jemes and stop at Dr. Shields' door. They seemed very glad to see me. They had been quite anxious about me as they were afraid I would be directed on to Albuquerque where they said it would have been more trouble for me to get here. They set out some breakfast and I begin to feel as if I were a little hungry. . . . So all has ended right but I think I am some wiser than before. After breakfast I slept awhile and waked up feeling some better though when I got here I could hardly stand. I was so tired not having slept and being so worried, but everything has been turning around for me all day. Dr. Shields' house is an adobe but it is comfortable and homelike inside. It has large windows and plenty of room. There are two bedrooms, parlor, a bright kitchen, pantry, etc. The grounds are enclosed by a high mud wall. We are surrounded by hills and mountains which back of us seem to rise directly up but are a little distance from us.

Friday, October 20. Spent the day in the schoolroom. This schoolroom is a good sized, well lighted and pleasant room. It is furnished with an organ, maps, globe, blackboard. Books, slates, pens and ink are all provided by the government, for Dr. Shields is mostly under the government. There were not many (only about 12 or 16, mostly small ones) scholars and hasn't been since school commenced on account of corn husking and other fall work. A good many of the children go into the mountains for pinyonies, a small nut and the only kind of nut they have here. The children are scantily clothed, and are very dirty. They have bright black eyes and most of them look intelligent though here and there is one that looks as though his mind was a blank . . . We talk English to them in the schoolroom and they understand what you mean pretty well though they do not try to talk it much themselves. They act very much like white children. Some of them very fidgety. The older girls bring the babies with them as they have the care of them. The mail came in this evening. Dr. got a letter from the Genera Agent saying that the government wanted 4 scholars from this pueblo to send to Carlisle, Pa.

Saturday, Oct. 21. The Dr. has been out among the Indians to see about getting scholars and is very anxious that some should go as there never has been any sent from here. They are going to have a council meeting this evening and will meet in one of the schoolrooms. They will talk and smoke over the matter. The Indians came soon after supper. The Governor came into the house. Dr. introduced him and I shook hands with him. Wasn't I highly honored? The Indians elect a Governor every year and then they abide by whatever he says. He has 3 lieutenants. The Dr. says the Indians are fond of big talk and that they keep them up often quite late. He stays in with them.

Sunday Morning, Oct. 22, 1882. Dr. Shields says the council went off very nicely, that they were in favor of sending scholars, and that they said they would see today who would go and let him know this evening, but still he is in doubt for they may talk all right to face and do the opposite. The Indians have a good many prejudices, and are very much afraid of departing at all from their old customs. They are affectionate and indulgent to their children, letting them have their own way a great deal. If they did not we should not be able to get many into school for by getting their good will they come anyway. We give them a little candy after each session. There is a Catholic priest and he does much to hinder our work as the Indians are greatly under his influence.

The bell was rung at half past nine. We have church early (service being held in the schoolroom) for if we wait they all go off to their work. Sunday or Monday is all the same to them. Dr. did not expect many out today as it was a busy time and then they were much excited about the government scholars and would be busy talking that up. The services were in Spanish, singing and all. I could pronounce the words pretty well, but did not know the meaning. The Indians paid good attention and seemed to understand. Some days a good many come to church. At two o'clock we have Sabbath school. There were five or six small children, two large girls, Patri and Katalena, and one man. We read a chapter, each of us reading a verse in turn, sang some songs out of Gospels Hymns and had prayers. Mrs. S. took the small scholars in charge. I took the two girls, and Dr. the Indian . . . The Governor and Lieutenant came in the evening to report. Their report was rather discouraging. They made a good many excuses. Such as: one mother would cry, etc., but back of it all was a "did not want to."

Monday, Oct. 23, 1882. Dr. S. started very early this morning for Santa Fe to see the Indian Agent and to get some supplies. He can get things cheaper there than here where you have to pay two prices for almost everything except meat, beef and venison which is only 6 and 6 cents a pound. He had been wanting to go for some time but could not leave. Santa Fe is 60 miles from here so that he will be gone three or four days. He intended to get there this evening. I took almost all the charge of the school. Belle was in some of the time as I have to get her to tell the names pretty often, but I am getting some of them learned. I will give you a few, girls names: Tolela, Ogawag, boys: Pintecte, Pamper, etc.

Tuesday, Oct. 24. Two of the larger girls, Wallipe and Persingula, were at school today and I had them stay . . . We found two aprons that fitted these girls and had them sew awhile. . . .

Wednesday, Oct. 25, 1882. There were but few scholars at school today. The Indians are very busy getting their corn in and almost all large enough are at work and the smaller ones go along for the sake of a ride in their wagon (like white children there) which they only use when they are getting in their crops. They all live here, but their lands extend up and down the aciques for more than six miles. We hear their wagons drawn by oxen going along almost all the time until very late at night and again as early in the morning. They raise a great deal of corn and considerable wheat; also pumpkins, squashes, watermelons and muskmelons. They raise very good grapes. Belle has made a good deal of grape jelly and peaches too . . . There are generally plenty of apricots but were none this year. They are very early, ripening in June. Their apples are small sweet affairs and do not amount to much. Like the Mexicans they raise and eat lots of red pepper or chile. Great strings are to be seen hanging outside of every door. All their farming is done by irrigation as there is so little rain. There is a little stream above here called _____ from which there is a deep ditch dug called the acique. They all get their water for using from it. I hardly know how they manage it about irrigation yet. This morning the pump gave up so we had to go to the acique for water. It tastes very well, better than their well water. . . .

Thursday, Oct. 26, 1882. Two or three of the larger girls at school today and they had the babies with them. They often do that . . . Dr. S. got back this afternoon. Government is going to send out some supply for the school. There will be some patent seats for the school room.

Friday, Oct. 27. My trunk came this morning and wasn't I glad. . .

Sunday, Oct. 29, 1882. There were only two Indians at church today, a little girl and a large boy. Mr. Miller was there and I saw him for the first time. He is a nice and rather good looking man. Dr. Shields did not preach as his sermon was prepared in Spanish and there were not enough there . . . The work is discouraging sometimes. The Catholic bell did a good deal of ringing and we could hear them ordering the people to come to their church. Don't know whether they had any better success or not . . .

Monday, Oct. 30, 1882. We had twenty four in school today not counting the babies. Children are rather scantily clad here. The little girls will have only a little slip on though often wear a shawl or blanket, in fact they have come into the schoolroom . . . and the small boys only a shirt. Sometimes they wear shoes of their own make, though if they can get them I guess they wear bought shoes. It is no uncommon sight to see children in the pueblo stark naked. The larger boys and men wear pants or drawers and shirts, but the shirts are all out . . . The older girls and women often wear buckskin wrapped around their legs fold and fold from their ankles to their knees presenting the appearance in shape of a small stovepipe.

November 1, 1882. Tomorrow is the Catholic feast of the dead. The Indians will lay on the graves tonight offering of corn and other things for the dead. The priest will take them away of course for his own use.

Nov. 3, 1882. Received a letter from Mr. Wolf but none from home. Mr. Wolf seems to think I want some encouragement. He wants me to write for the Local. Wrote my first begging letter this evening. We want to get up a Christmas tree. . . . We do not want much help, only some toys and things for the youngsters.

Saturday, Nov. 4, 1882. Dr. S. went to the Springs this morning. He is to preach there tomorrow. An American who is married to a Mexican woman brought a wild turkey here. He had been out on a hunt with another fellow and they had killed 14. He is pretty poor and the doctor had given a good deal of medicine to his wife who is sickly; for nothing he brings them game sometimes. Wild turkeys are plenty in the mountains. There are also wild cattle there as well as bears and often mountain lions, and deer too are found. Think it would be a good place to hunt.

Monday, Nov. 6, 1882. Had only 9 scholars today. Dr. had 13. . . Tried studying Spanish little this evening. Don't know how I will get along with it yet. It doesn't seem so very hard.

Nov. 9, 1882. The Indians who started to Santa Fe Monday for freight came this evening. They brought goods home which Dr. had bought when he was there and the government supplies for the Indians which were clothing, blankets, shoes, stockings, muslin, calico, and seats for the school-room. Dr. bought a barrel of state apples, real good ones. It seemed like home to get a taste of them.

Nov. 10, 1882. Dr. Shields got some oysters among his things and invited Mr. Miller and Judge Beaumont down this evening to eat some. Judge came but Mr. Miller did not. This was the anniversary of their wedding, but neither Mr. nor Mrs. S. thought of it till the evening at supper. The judge was here when they were married. It seems strange that such a man as he should be out here. He is a well educated man, a lawyer, and has been wealthy once. He is very gentlemanly in appearance and an interesting talker. He is a Southerner by birth, his father having lived in Natchez, Miss. and once a slaveholder. He and Mr. Miller have several mining claims in this country some of which they think are gold. Last night it rained quite hard. The first there has been since I came. Could see it raining in the mts. in the evening.

Saturday, Nov. 11, 1882. Today has been quite cold. It snowed a good deal in the mts. and they looked quite white but there was just a little here and it was gone about as soon as it came. The Indians are all excitement over the feast and tomorrow will be a big day for Indians from Santa Clara and other pueblos, some Navajoes and Mexicans are gathering in. They danced last night, shooting and hollering, and making a general racket and are doing the same tonight. Tomorrow is the feast of San Diego, Catholic. The Indians all celebrate and it seems a part of their religion. Long ago they were forced to do it and now it is a part of their nature almost. This Catholic religion is a great deal more disgusting in this country than at the East.

Sunday, Nov. 12, 1882. The Indians were dancing, singing, and making all kinds of noise. They made a berth or St. house by putting up some poles and covering it with blankets. In this was an image to which they bowed down to. We did not try to have services. Dr. said it would be of no use for no one would come. Mr. Miller came down and spent the evening with us. This has not been much like a Sunday at home where all is quiet and we always go to church if not too stormy. It was quiet in the house. Mr. Miller was telling about the Navajoes. Says they have a great fear of the dead and will not touch a dead body if they can help it. If a person dies in the hut they will take the things out and pull the hut down on them though sometimes they carry them out and cover them with stones. They never use a hut or any of the wood in it after a person dies in it. . . .

Saturday, Nov. 18. It has snowed about all day, in that respect it seemed a little like winter in Pa. Perpihatiti was here most of the day. She is a pretty smart girl and can speak a good deal of English if she wants to, but she hasn't much chance, her folks rather keep her back. She and Catalena have been to the boarding school at Albuquerque. Perpihatiti ate dinner with and wiped the dishes for me. She did real well.

Tuesday, Nov. 21, 1882. Today I had 30 scholars and Dr. had 20. Our largest attendance yet. I was kept pretty busy to get around. Some great big boys were there. Their idea is to get some clothes, not to learn. Not any of them are very far along and they do look so sheepish when I call them up to read. There have been two in school who can read pretty well

Northwest corner of main plaza, Jemez Pueblo, about 1915. *Courtesy Museum of New Mexico, Neg. No. 42047.*

in the fourth reader. I got three letters tonight, one from home. They made me think I was not quite forgotten.

Wednesday, Nov. 22, 1882. This evening after school Belle and I went out into the pueblo. We went into the house of Catalena's folks. She is one of our scholars and quite a smart girl. She had not been coming very well for a while back. Her mother said it was because she had a cold. The interior of their hut was in the common Indian style. There were the same skins and other things on the wall. At one side was their mill or stones for grinding corn. From there we went to the Cacique. He is a ruler in religious doings and has a good deal to say about affairs, a sort of high priest among them. They do not allow him to work and give him all the support he needs without, but he will bring wood here to sell. The inside of his house is really neat. The floor was partly covered with carpet. Along the walls on two sides was a kind of a shelf or bench on which were laid their calchones or mattresses and blankets and covered over with calico. At night these are spread on the floor for sleeping on. The wall had a good many pictures and in a little niche was a lamp. . . .

Saturday, Nov. 25, 1882. This afternoon Belle and I went out into the pueblo. We went down to the river where the women go for water. Met quite a number with their water pots on their heads. Saw some of their vineyards. They had the vines covered with little mounds of earth. Coming back we stopped at Augustin Pecos's house. Found him engaged in making saddles for their burros. . . . Stopped in another place where there was a young baby only three days old. They had it fastened or wrapped to a board so that it could only move its head. There was a kind of framework over its head to keep the blankets from being too heavy when covering it. They keep the babies in this position most of the time till they are two or three months old and the back of their heads becomes sometimes quite flat.

Sunday, Nov. 26, 1882. A Mexican and his wife and baby from the Springs were here to church today. . . . They rode horseback all on one horse. That would seem like old times in the East. Have heard Pa tell about doing that when he was little. They stayed for dinner. After church some Mexicans stopped in on their way from the Catholic church. They were some who are quite friendly with Dr. One of the women was quite pretty. This one was quite well off having married an old man who died soon leaving her a good deal of property. She did not show her wealth in style. She had on a very bright green silk made plain waist or basque, I forget which, and skirt with two rows of red silk ribbon around it. . . .

Thursday, Nov. 30, 1882. Today is Thanksgiving day, my first away from my relations. We had no school. In the forenoon I did my ironing. Dr. and Mr. Miller went out to the mts. this afternoon. We (Belle and I) thought we would not cook until they came back so we took a piece at noon. Dr. wanted to get a turkey, but did not have a chance, but they had just got some fresh beef and Belle stuffed and roasted a piece and then we had sweet potatoes and pumpkin pie making quite a good Thanksgiving dinner or supper I thought. Dr. got back at half past three and we had dinner at a little after four. I went to the top of the mesa back of the house for the first time. Had quite a view from there. The river was in good view and looked like a thread of silver in the sand. I picked up a few specimens of stones. . . .

Friday, Dec. 1, 1882. The first day of another month found 30 scholars to begin with; if they only keep on I think we will have a pretty good report. For Nov. we averaged 37 out of over 70 enrolled. I had 20 of our average. Some of the scholars did not start till the last of the mo. and others did not attend at all regular though there were a few who did real well. Among them were Patraa who did not miss a day, and Persingula, George Teyo and Warasa. Two girls from the Springs came down today for the mail. Both were horseback. One of them, Mary Kelly, a girl of 14 or 15, and daughter of a boarding housekeeper there, had never ridden but little before. The other was a pretty good rider. Her folks are from R.I., but are living in Bernalillo now and she is staying at the Springs for awhile. They got back a little after we had dinner. Belle got another for them and they started back at 3 o'clock making 26 miles of a ride in one day on horseback. Am very much afraid it was pretty dark before they got home. Should not like to have been out myself for they say it is not hard to lose the way.

Saturday, Dec. 2, 1882. Major Beaumont called here today. He is a brother of the Judge and looks a good deal like him. He and Dr. had been up to the little river to make some measurements. Government is talking of building an aqueduct for bringing water down the other side of the pueblo for irrigation and Dr. Thomas sent word to Dr. wanting him to make some estimate of the cost.

Sunday, Dec. 3, 1882. There were 23 persons at church today. Mr. Miller was here a little while this evening. Belle and I went out into the pueblo this afternoon to see Balan, one of our small scholars who has been quite sick. Found him getting better. Stopped in one or two of the other houses. At one the woman was making and baking tortillas. These look like a thick large pancake. I tasted one and it did not taste bad. In fact I believe I could like them pretty well when they are warm. . . .

Tuesday, Dec. 5, 1882. Went to the offices for mail this evening. Some of the Indians were dancing on the first st. There were three men and three women. They had sticks and ornamented with feathers and rattles in their hands. Their dance was rather graceful. They were in a line, each fellow with his girl following him and kept up a kind of sing song noise. Three or four old men beat drums and sung, at least it was meant for that. The dancers, that is the men, had on their ornaments, belts and skins around them. I watched them a little while. The mail had not got in yet so I did not wait. They had quit dancing when I came back. While they were out dancing the children were out watching and women on top of the house. Dr. went up after a little for the mail. I got three letters and two packages. The packages were from Sheakleyville and contained Christmas gifts for the children. The things were real nice, better than I expected. There were tin cups, apron ribbons, collars, and cards.

Dec. 6, 1882. Today occurred the Transit of Venus which will not happen again for 121 years. Had seen in the papers that it would be visible to the naked eye through a smoked glass, so we tried it. Could see Venus at 9 o'clock looking like a small black spot about as large as a 5 cent piece apparently, on the lower right hand side of the sun's disc. The day has been a beautiful one for this time of year, warm and clear.

Saturday, Dec. 9, 1882. Today we had a succession of callers. First in the morning came Wallipe with milk and then some young man with milk too. While we were at dinner Augustine Pecos's wife and little girl came in and stayed an hour or two. Belle gave them a piece. Before she had gone an Indian came whose errand was to get Dr. to write a letter for him to a brother of his who is in California. He stayed till three o'clock. This brother has been gone for six years. They heard from him once or twice. He left a wife here, but she has been dead for some time. He sent $40, two blankets, and a horse to her once. The Indians seem anxious to have him back again. San Domingo, Catelena's father, with his baby was here an hour or more, and last but not least, after supper, Asuca, (his name is Jesus, but I put it down as it is pronounced) and his family consisting of wife and two boys, Pampa and Pinteca, came over. They live right next door to us. The man brought his drum and Pinteca, who was all rigged out for it, was going to dance some to show us what he could do in that line, but when he got in he changed his mind and wouldn't dance. He is only five or six years old, but I guess the Indians begin to dance from the cradle.

Tuesday, Dec. 12, 1882. This is a great feast day for the Catholics. It is the feast of Guadalupe and celebrated at the Canon. Mexicans from all around and lots of Indians went there today and I suppose with whiskey and dancing had a jolly time. It is all religion too. We only had 17 scholars and we treated them pretty well. Dr. gave them all 8 sticks of candy apiece and then gave me the same saying he wanted to treat all alike.

Friday, Dec. 15, 1882. Quite an accident happened this morning. Daniel, the boy the priest has staying with him, was riding one horse and heading another to water. He had the ropes by which they are led fastened around his body and a water keg on his back. Someway he was thrown off and dragged along on the ground, his head cut and bruised but not seriously. Dr. was sent for to see a young man at the Canon who has the delirium tremens. He was married a short time ago to a girl only 13 years old. It is against the law for girls to marry under 15, but her age was given older and then the priest will marry them if they pay extra. The young man had to pay $15.

Tuesday, Dec. 19, 1882. Was very much surprised this morning to see the ground covered with snow. That or something else brought the scholars in for we had sixty, the largest attendance of any day yet since I came. . . .

Friday, Dec. 22, 1882. Our school averaged 45 this month. I had 26 of our average. Dr. says that is the best they have ever had. We got the things that Belle and I sent for to Ehricks and we were well suited with them. Belle had sent for a silk handkerchief for Mr. Miller. It is real nice for the cost which was 60¢. I sent for a necktie for him, but it must have been lost for the package was broken open. I sent a handkerchief to each of the boys. I got a letter from Carrie Prie. It should have been here two weeks ago.

Sat., Dec. 23, 1882. Finished making little bags for candy for our Christmas tree. We made 63 altogether. Belle's baby is a real good little thing and is quite pretty now I think. It is four months old. This evening we tried arranging some of the things and dividing them out for the scholars. It was quite a job; there were so many different little things and so many to give them to.

Sunday, Dec. 24, 1882. Had preaching this morning. There were 26 present. Did not have Sunday school. The Indians have been busy baking bread, etc. for their feast. Called to see a poor blind woman. She seemed very much pleased, and had to feel Linus (whom we had with us) about all over. The Indians call him Sho-bo-er-wor-ho meaning morning star. . . The woman gave Linus a loaf of their bread. . . .

Dec. 25, 1882. This has been a Christmas in New Mexico for me and a pretty busy one too. A good many of the Mexicans stopped in today, some to see Dr. and some to ask for Christmas gifts. . . . Dr. got the trees in and put up before dinner. There were three, not large, though one reached to the ceiling, but good shape. I marked some things this forenoon and we finished making them, hung them on the tree, filled the bags with candy, and worked as hard as we could, but it was nearly four before we got everything in shape. A good many of the children hung around the door, looking in at the keyhole or were on the fence trying to see through the windows. Our tree looked splendid, almost as well as any I ever saw at home, of course not quite. The children behaved nicely and seemed very much pleased with their gifts. The house was just as full as could be and the old Indians took a great deal of interest in it. I did not expect to get anything at all, but did. Got a nice shopping basket; such a one as I often thought I would like. . . . We opened the door at five o'clock, were all through by a little after six. Sung two pieces, the scholars helped and sang pretty well and then had a prayer after it was over we had our supper. We had a roast chicken. Mr. Miller stayed for supper and spent the evening with us. Altogether I have enjoyed Christmas pretty well. I went out into the pueblo when we finished fixing the tree to see them dance. They had been dancing some all day. . . .

Wednesday, Dec. 27, 1882. I went out by myself this afternoon to see the dancing. They were dancing at this end of the plaza and I did not like to go through the crowd so I went down the first st., up across an alley and came into the plaza at the other end. There were two sets dancing. One would come on the first, would go off and come on again as the others got down to the other end. The men were naked to the waist and painted. Yesterday they had on their shirts. They wore a short blanket fastened around their waist with a belt and a squirrel skin dangling behind, bells, shells, yarn and fringe of buckskin around their legs and waist and red moccasins on their feet with a band of fir around their ankles. Each carried a big rattle in one hand and in the other a bunch of fir sprigs. The women were neater dressers. Their waists and sleeves were clean and their blankets on and belted, white moccasins and leg wrapping, bracelets of shells and necklaces. Each had a painted frame about 16 inches high and ornamented with feathers fastened upright on her head and carried a bunch of fir in their hands. I saw several of our school girls in the dance with their ribbons on which we had given them. Some had blankets on and others did not. This made me feel bad but I suppose it could not be helped. All wore their hair hanging down. The women were most graceful in the dance moving in step to the singing of the old men and beating of the drums. The men kept up a kind of jumping step to the same. Mr. Miller was out. . . .

Monday, Jan. 1, 1883. the beginning of another year and I wonder what it will have for me! I hardly expected a year ago to be where I am now, in Jemes, N.M. This has been about the same as other days in its events. Did my washing this forenoon. This evening we finished the chestnuts which I got from home and some apples which Mr. Kelly from the Springs left here this morning for a present for Belle with a Chinese Pagoda of Silver cardboard.

Saturday, Jan. 6, 1883. This is the Reyes Dias, (Kings Day) a Catholic feast and there are a good many Mexicans in the pueblo. I suppose it celebrates the coming of the Wise men from the East to adore the Savior. The Indians danced the deer dance this afternoon. They or some of them were dressed to represent deer. Some had Buffalo horns and frames on their heads, others, small pruned limbs of trees and all trimmed with feathers. There were only three women. At sunset they went stringing up on the mesa to there and after threw off their feathers and took off their costumes.

Sunday, Jan. 7, 1883. Mr. Perea came back just a little before dark. Dr. Shields had made arrangement for him to do so and to baptize the baby. We moved the organ into the parlor. Mr. Miller was present and that was all besides ourselves. I played the organ. We sang "All Hail the Power" etc., and Rock of Ages. Did not have a long service but it was a solemn one and like our meetings at home though so few were present. They named the baby Paul James. After that we had supper. Dr. and Mr. Perea had a good deal to talk about in their work among the Mexicans. Some things discouraging and some encouraging.

Saturday, Jan. 21, 1883. This has been a cold, windy day. The thermometer was down to zero last night, early in the evening it snowed quite a little, but once the wind has been drifting it all day and what a piercing wind it was. Quite like a Penn winter day. . . A party of Indians have been away hunting eagles and just returned a day or two ago. They got 21 and their skins were hung up outside of the second story of one of the houses. On the terrace were several of my scholars, so I climbed up the ladder to see those skins. They must have been large birds. . . Mr. Miller said it had not been so cold for nine years. In walking over the snow, it creaked with the frost as I went home.

Thursday, Jan. 26, 1883. The Indians had a dance today to celebrate the return and success of the eagle hunters. That is the friends of those who belong to that clan. There are three clans among them: the Eagle, Crow, and Bow and Arrow clan. I let out school at quarter past two as the children were so excited and anxious to get out and then they com-

menced to beat the drums and I knew it would be of no use to keep them
any longer. I did some ironing and then went out to see them. They were
decked out completely with feathers, the men especially who had bows
and arrows and rattles in their hands. The women had an ear of corn. It
seemed to be a kind of serenade as they did their dancing before the doors
of the hunters. Then the men came out of the houses and sprinkled meal
before them. Was out a little while yesterday and went in one house which
had no door . . . by climbing in the window. I was a little awkward and
they laughed, but seemed pleased to have me anyhow.

MARIETTA PALMER WETHERILL

Chatelaine of the Chaco

In her seventy-seventh and last year, Marietta Palmer Wetherill, wife of southwest explorer Richard Wetherill, claimed no one could have enjoyed a more wonderful life than she. The controversial murder of the man who discovered the Cliff Dweller ruins at Mesa Verde and first excavated the Anasazi civilization at Chaco Canyon left Marietta a widow at age thirty-three with five children to raise. Yet she maintained a lifelong love of travel, adventure, and independence. Marietta Wetherill actively participated in her husband's great archaeological expeditions, ran the Bonito trading post at Chaco Canyon for a dozen years, and following Richard's death, supported her family with her ranching operations. She treasured the rare opportunity history, circumstance, and character provided her, that of living harmoniously amidst the conjunction of two cultures—the one she was born to and the Navajo she adopted.

Born October 5, 1876, in Serena, Illinois, to a Quaker family, Marietta inherited her parents' musical inclinations. Her mother, Elizabeth Ann, who had studied music in Italy and once played for Queen Victoria at tea in London, was a student at the New England Conservatory of Music in Boston when she and Sidney LaVern Palmer met. He was on tour with John Philip Sousa's band, playing E flat cornet. Marietta's parents were painters as well as musicians. Of them she said: "They were always interested in books and in learning and travel and beautiful things."

The eldest of three children, Marietta was gifted with a lovely soprano voice and played many instruments, favoring the guitar and harp. Her father settled the family on a wheat farm in Burdette, Kansas, while he worked as a postal clerk for seventeen years. During this period, the family also worked as traveling musicians, playing "concert tours" across the country, sometimes in combination with a patent medicine drummer. Marietta played B flat cornet. During their travels in the Southwest, the Palmers would play at Indian ceremonials such as the Matachines in Jemez, joining right in.

Describing herself as a youngster, Marietta says: "I was so crazy about the outdoors . . . and I wanted to know about the Indians. That was the thing that I always said I was going to do, I was going to study the Indians all my life and I came very near doing it." Marietta was initiated into the Chee clan of the Navajo tribe in a two-day ceremony and, as a ten-year-old with braids, met Geronimo while he was on his last raid.

I hadn't done my lessons the day before so father said, "Well, you will have to stay in camp today." Well, I gathered a lot of those buffalo pumpkins and put sticks for legs and stuck the little ones on for horse heads and then I had to make a corral for them and I was working at that when this group of Indians rode up, I should say there was ten. One man said to me in Spanish, "Where's the water?" I thought they were Navajos, so I answered in Navajo that the water was in the spring right there below the road. And he said, "You're an Apache." And I said, "No, I'm a white girl." But anyway he insisted all the time that I had been stolen from the Apaches and he said, "I think I'll take you with me." Well, he said, "We'll take her with us," and they said, "No, we're in a hurry to get away, we can't take a child, we'd be in more trouble." And he said, "Get a piece of meat for my Apache girl off the horse." . . . And he said, "We'll come back and get you and give you a pony." I said, "I have a pony." And he says, "A bow and arrow." I said, "I have two." And he said, "Well you'll have a lot of fun with my children up in the mountains." And they rode off.

Years later, when Marietta was exhibiting Anasazi finds at the 1902 World's Fair in St. Louis, she again encountered Geronimo, under very different circumstances.

And he said, "Who are you?" And I said, "I'm your friend, I saved
you once." And he said, "I have no friends." And I said, "But I
was your friend. Do you remember the last raid you went on when
you were captured and taken to Fort Sill?" "Yes." "Well," I said,
"Do you remember the little girl that you gave the quarter of beef
to when you had the eight big mules packed with food that you
had killed those men down at the springs?" "Yes." "Well, I'm that
little girl." . . . "Have you been treated good?" He said, "Would
I be treated good, taking me from my own land that I'd always
had and my people had for generations before me and puttin' me
down among the alligators and snakes where it was always raining
and muddy and where I got sickness that I never can get over?
I've had food, yes. Here I sit, the chief of all the Apaches and sell
these little ten cent trinkets so I can eat. Is that kindness? Kindness?
Help me to get back to my own land, that's kindness."

Well one day I told him, "I've got good news for you. You're
going back to Arizona. You're going back to your old home." He
said, "I'm to die in my own ground in my own country? Mine,
mine." And I said, "Well, you ain't gonna die. You're goin' back
there to live and get well and be fine again and make a nice camp
someplace and enjoy life." He shook his head no, he couldn't do
that. Well, I put my hand out to shake hands and he stood up
and he put his hands all over my face like this and felt of me and
I said, "Well, goodbye Ski-ak'is, my friend." And he said, "Goodbye, but I still think you're an Apache."

In late summer 1895, Marietta's father, an amateur photographer
with a strong interest in anthropology, brought the family in the
music wagon to visit the Wetherill ranch in Mancos, Colorado.
Palmer had heard of Richard's discovery of the Mesa Verde cliff
dwellings and was eager to see the ruins. Marietta, then eighteen,
was not very impressed with the 37-year-old Richard when they first
met. He had just returned from the Hopi snake dance at Walpi and
his hair and beard were badly tangled; he was caked with red dust.
"He did not look like much to me," she said.

That fall, Richard guided the Palmer family on the first archaeological expedition into Chaco Canyon, the greatest ruin on the continent.
They remained in Chaco for a month, did some digging and found
many burials with pottery. Marietta often rode out with Richard
during these days.

Richard, an amateur with no formal education, spent many years torn between his passion for exploring and his responsibilities, as eldest son in a Quaker family, toward the family ranch. His attempts to gain support from the Smithsonian Institution or the Peabody Museum at Harvard met with failure. Eventually, he received some financial support from Fred and Talbot Hyde, heirs to the Babbitt (BaBo) soap fortune to assemble collections for the American Museum of Natural History in New York. The character of Tom Outland in Willa Cather's novel, *The Professor's House*, is based on Richard Wetherill and recounts much of his discouraging experience trying to bring the world's attention to the ancient civilizations he had discovered.

Marietta and Richard married in Sacramento in December 1896 and took a wedding trip to San Francisco and Mexico. That winter, Marietta insisted on accompanying her new husband on the expedition into Grand Gulch, Utah. She was probably the first woman to make such a trip. The party of thirteen men, one woman and 68 pack animals ascended the trail, of which Marietta said, "It was so crooked that even a rattlesnake would have a hard time getting down without breaking its back." Nine of the horses fell off the steep cliffs and died. Richard's intention was to document the discovery of the Basketmakers. They worked from dawn to darkness in the intense winter cold. Marietta stayed in camp keeping notes on the artifacts brought in. She also took measurements and made biscuits for supper. During one particularly snowy night, Richard became concerned, as Frank McNitt recounts in his book, *Richard Wetherill: Anasazi.*

"Those mummies," Richard said. "They'll get wet."

This night, as almost always, they had been sleeping under the protective ledge of a cave. Dimly, through her sleep, Marietta could hear footsteps, coming and going, and then there was Richard's voice, sounding pleased.

"Where would you like them—at the head of the bed or at the foot?"

Marietta started up, sleep gone and wide-eyed. There was Richard beside their bedroll, crouching, both arms circled about in supporting embrace, two of the Withered Ancients he had carried in out of the snow. Several others he had propped up close by. The mummies stared back at her sightlessly and gape-jawed,

the long wild hair of one streaming across a wizened tobacco colored face. Out of a dry throat Marietta finally answered:
"At the foot, Mr. Wetherill. At the foot of the bed."

Later in 1897 Marietta and Richard went to live in their own home—a wall tent under a high cliff in back of Pueblo Bonito in Chaco Canyon. Known locally as Anasazi, the name of the ancient people whose life he had brought to light, his wife always addressed him as "Mr. Wetherill," while he sometimes called her his pet name, "Asthanne," Navajo for "Little Woman." After years of enjoying life on the road with her family, Marietta fit comfortably into this rustic way of life. Despite constant financial pressure and uncertain support of the Hyde Exploring Expedition, Marietta thrived on a life that found her hosting interested visitors from faraway places, providing the comforts of home in the outback, working in the Bonito trading post, and attending Navajo ceremonials while, when called on, helping with births and illnesses.

Richard's murder in 1910 bore out the Navajo prohibition against living in Chaco Canyon. He was shot on June 22, a few days following Marietta's return from Albuquerque after giving birth to their daughter, Ruth. Although the Wetherills had not lacked material comfort, the settling of Richard's estate left Marietta with a bank balance of $74.23. Within a few months, she gave up trying to save the ranch. She retreated with her children to the mountains above Cuba, where, with the help of friends, she managed a small ranch. As her children grew, she moved about to various small southwestern towns. For a time, she ran a small ranch and trading post at Sanders, Arizona. Whenever she could, she continued to travel, to New York City to visit the Wetherill collections at the Museum of Natural History and to Mexico with friends.

Eventually, when her children had gone off on their own, Marietta settled on the outskirts of Albuquerque. In 1954, at age 77, she died of heart failure. At her request, her ashes were buried beside her husband's grave in back of Pueblo Bonito.

*W*hen we were in Cripple Creek on one of our tours we stopped there for a number of days. There were so many, many people there, the miners you know. There were so many men there and after we gave our entertainment they insisted on our staying and giving many of them and

then we played at night for dances. And I remember the first night that
we gave the entertainment there that I was dressed up in a little dotted
Swiss dress with the little ruffled skirts and underskirts that stood all about
and red stockings and red slippers and red . . . I was a dark-complected
girl, and I had black hair and I had a red ribbon in my hair and I walked
out on the stage and Father and Mother and the two other children, they
played this "Irish Washerwoman" on the strong instruments and the miners
threw thirty one-dollar bills on the stage!

My father played the B flat and I played the B flat and my little brother
the alto, Mother the tuba, and my little sister the triangle. Can you imagine
it? Oh, how absolutely funny! And to think . . . I could just cry when I
think of all those pictures we took. When Father passed away and all of
us had left the farm, my sister was going to move away and she sold them
to a man for glass for his greenhouse. She was twenty years younger than
I and never had seen an Indian and it didn't mean a thing to her. To me
that's the most awful thing that ever happened, I think, that and my diary
and I kept for so many, many years burning. Those two things, I just can't
let myself think of it. I can't, I just can't, because I'll cry sure.

The Rattlesnake Episode

. . . Well, I ran down this trail like kids run, you know and I saw this
big snake coiled right in the trail. He was a monster! Well, I didn't know
what to do. I just yelled for daddy at the top of my lungs but he was too
far to hear me and I thought, well, I'll have to stay with him because he'll
bite one of the cows or one of our horses sure. . . . So I stayed there
and he kept watching and wondering why I was standing in the same
place. Well, this snake got tired of my company and he decided to travel
down the trail. . . . I guess Pop said it was a half an hour that I stayed
with him and he got really annoyed, too, he was mad. He'd just rattle and
act mean and I was so deathly afraid of him. But finally Father drove
down there and he said, "What in the world are you doing?" "Oh," I said,
"Daddy, look at that." He said, "Goodness!" And he got out of the buggy
and came over there and he said, "Now I haven't a thing to kill it with."
I said, "How about the buggy whip? Whip him to death." And he said,
"Well, that's an idea." And so he went and got the buggy whip, he always
had a good one . . . you know they made awfully good cigarettes, those
buggy whips, the old ones when they wore out.

Well, he just whipped that snake and even though it coiled he just stayed
right there and just whipped it and whipped it right on the head until it

became unconscious. He said, "You know, that would be a beautiful skin and that's yours." He said, "You were a brave little girl to stay here and defend our stock."

It was six-feet-two inches long. It's a big rattler! They all said it was the biggest one they'd ever killed in Kansas. We still have the skin. He had a shop at the back of the house, a big one where he had all this plunder. And he got a long board and put it between two tables and then he went out to the buckboard to get this snake and he says, "My goodness, he seems to be coming alive! He's quite lively. He's thrashing around in here." Mother says, "I knew it. He's gonna bite you." Well, he reached in with some pliers and got him round the neck and he brought him in and put him down. He put him down on that board and straightened him out and he put an awl, stuck it right through his head and hit it with a hammer so that it went down into the wood good.

And now he said, "I'm gonna show you the inside of a snake." And then he cut him open, his body, his belly, he cut it open from right under his chin, past his heart and we could see his heart beating and he showed me the heart beating. And just then when we were all just right over him looking at him that snake gave a flop and broke that awl in two and fell on the floor and crawled in under a bench. Well my mother, she left. I got on the table. And Father didn't seem a bit afraid of him. And he went over and got him with these blacksmith tongs and pinned him down again and this time he put two awls through his head. He says, "I guess he won't break that." Then finally he stuck his knife into the heart so that I could see what that would do when you get shot. He said, "Now you see, when anybody gets knifed and they stick you in the heart or anybody shoots you in the heart, see how the blood gets all out around on everything and that kills you and your heart stops beating." He said, "Watch that now and see how long that takes and so you can see how some people die quick and some people die slow." Wasn't I blessed with a father with brains?

Meeting the Wetherills and Visiting the Ruins

We never, never went over the same routes. It might not vary more than a hundred miles east, west or some way, but we always went over a different part of the country. You see, we weren't going fast. I think it's speed that ruins fun. It makes automobile accidents, it makes people sick. I've come to the conclusion that it's this speed that everybody has that's killing them, spoiling their life, because we never had any speed. Three miles an hour was about the way we traveled and some days we didn't travel because we didn't get up early enough. But we had a lot of fun . . .

. . . We gave an entertainment at Cortez and went into the town of Mancos. And of course as usual our outfit created quite a good deal of interest. By that time we'd heard about the Wetherills. . . . Of course the Alamo Ranch was such a lovely place when we reached it and we were so delighted with it. I remember that Father stopped the team and he says, "Now that is really a ranch. That looks like a ranch." . . . I think my father first fell in love with Mr. Wetherill. I don't think that I was especially impressed at all. I think there was several other cowboys around there that looked much more intriguing to me and were a little younger. . . . There was quite a number of people around and there was tourists going out all the time to the Mesa Verde. They outfitted there. . . .

Mr. Wetherill was so interested in the Indians and he was always talking with these Indians and he could speak a good deal of Ute. So the Indians kept telling him, they says, "Up on that mountain there's big cities," they said, "big towns, big cities. . . ." Well, he didn't pay any attention to it. It seemed so ridiculous. But they lost a bunch of cattle, eight or ten, and the Utes didn't allow anyone to go up on Mesa Verde. They had made it very unpleasant for other people that had tried to go up there. Well, they had this Ute working for 'em around the barns and the gardens and he said to Richard, "We go find 'em." Acowitz, that was the Indian's name. Acowitz took 'em right to a very well-marked trail and sure enough, they started up the trail and followed these tracks clear up on top of the mesa and clear across the mesa for several miles. And then finally they got over where the ruins were and old Acowitz said to Richard, he patted him on the shoulder and he says, "Come see big city." So he and Richard rode over to the edge of the cliff and right across the canyon there was Cliff Palace. Well, Mr. Wetherill was speechless. He had never seen anything like that. He never had dreamed of anything. It was unknown.

I never knew it, that he was twice my age. He was such a young, vigorous, quick, energetic, ambitious man that you never thought about his age. He didn't have any. He was one of those people that never got old. He was the same age when he died that he was when I married him. For anything that I can say I never knew that he was older than I. Many times I felt much older than he because he was real boyish, you know. . . . He looked a hole right into ya when he looked at ya, very penetrating eyes. He didn't have time to put any fat on. He was too busy. He worked night and day. Sleeping was something that he never did unless he had to. Even the years I was married to him I always called him Mr. Wetherill. And still do. I don't know why but I just always did.

Well, anyway, he'd stay all night and have breakfast with us and we'd get up extra early so he could get a start and . . . And one time I went with Father up to the ranch to have the mules shod and Jim Ethridge—he was one of those tall, slim, kinda pasty-colored fellas with boiled gooseberry eyes and very blond hair but he worked in the hay and it was always dusty; he looked kinda gray-like. And he said, "Well," he says, "You're the first gal I ever saw Dick Wetherill ride down Mancos Canyon every day to see," and I said, "he doesn't come down there to see me." "What's he go for then. Ha, ha, ha." He made me so mad I coulda clawed his eyes out. Well, they all got to teasing me about it . . . and we took the trip to Mesa Verde and saw the ruins. Mr. Wetherill took us.

Well, by this time Father had been talking about Chaco Canyon. Mr. Wetherill had never been there, Father had never been there, and they wanted to see it so bad. So Richard said, "Well, I haven't got anything to do this winter much." He said, "How'd it be like for us to combine forces and take that trip down to Chaco? I know I could guide you down there." So the arrangements were made and we couldn't get ready quick enough. . . .

There was a trail and we just followed that trail right along and first we saw Chetro Ketl, oh, we saw all these others, Hungo Pavie and Una Vida and Wijiji, oh, those are large ruins. And then off to our left as we turned into Chaco we saw that wonderful Fahada, that great mountain that rises right up from the flat land; it was quite a wonderful sight and then you looked out this way and there was miles and miles you could see, perfectly level country going off out that way . . . we knew it was one of the greatest things that we had ever seen outside of the Mesa Verde and so very different. These ruins are built right flat on the ground right in the valley of the Chaco and both Chetro Ketl and Pueblo Bonito are built up near the cliff. . . .

We never saw Mr. Wetherill for hours and hours after we got there. He just threw the harness off the mules, turned 'em loose, and left and he was up on top of the cliff and looking down. He'd found the waterhole up there that people starve for water there and never find and he had been all over and he had sort of taken an outline of everything and he was so delighted that he was speechless.

The Marriage Proposal

. . . Well, we finally got to the San Juan and when we got there it was high and we got there late in the afternoon and we had run out of everything to eat excepting chocolate, just the bitter chocolate, and dried peaches. We still had that and nobody seemed to care for them, they hadn't gotten hungry enough yet. But, anyway, we camped on the banks of the river and Mr. Wetherill said, "We won't try a crossing until the morning. There may be Indians here by that time and we'll find out how the crossing is but," he says, "it looks very bad tonight. You, Mr. Palmer, couldn't possibly do it with your heavy load."

Well, we made camp and nobody came around and we dug a well there on the edge of the river and got fairly clear water to drink and spent the night there. And the next morning, quite earlier, he said, "Well, I'll try it." And I was on my horse, I was gonna ride across, and I said, "Why don't you take the pony and ride across first and see how it is." And he says, "Well, that's a pretty good idea but I guess I'll just drive in. It's gone down a great deal." And I said, "I think I'll ride with you. I think I'd be afraid to ride my pony across all that water. It seems very wide to me." "Well, alright," he said. And so I got in the wagon with him and we started in and, well, just right now we were in deep water. It was much deeper than he had expected it to be. And you could feel it, the wagon startin' to be lifted this way, you know, and he said, "You know those waves over there are pretty high. I can't go straight across. I've got to go up the river and you know it isn't very far down this river to the canyon. We don't want to go down into that because then we'd be lost." And I didn't say anything. I was scared. And we kept going on. We couldn't turn around because we were in deep water and the mules started to swim. And he said, "It might be possible that I'll have to cut three mules loose and, when I do, I want you to step right out on the running gears and take hold of that mule's tail and you hang onto it because your life depends on it. He'll take you to shore. Will you do it?" And I says, "Sure I will."

And so then the wagon lifted again and he turned up the stream a little more and just kept agoing and we finally got over to the bank and there it was really very swift against that bank and the mules couldn't jump up and he ran out on the tongue of the wagon, he grabbèd his rope, roped one of those mules, and snubbed it against some driftwood there and gave those mules a breathing spell for minute and they made it up the bank.

So we got out and he hollered back, I know my folks couldn't hear us. He said, "Don't try it," and he walked down to the bank and he told them emphatically not to try and then he came back to the wagon. I was still sitting in it—we were used to being either too dry or too wet anyway—and he said, "Were you frightened?" I says, "Why sure, I was scared to death." And he says, "Well, where do you put your fear?" I said, "I guess I swallowed it. I didn't say anything." "No," he says, "you didn't say a word." He says, "Will you marry me?"

Right then and there. And I said, "I don't know. I'll have to think about it." And he said, "Well," he said, "I think that it was meant that we should live our lives together and I'll do everything in the world to make you happy." And I said, "Well, I will, I'll marry you."

. . . There was no way to get out of there, there was no way to go on, but there was a trail where the Indians had come along in the soft sand, but there was no place to get the wagon. And he stayed there quite a long while and finally he said, "You know I'm gonna have to leave you here," because he couldn't ride both those mules. And he said, "I never did anything in my life that I hated to do as much as I hate to leave you here but, I have to do that because your parents have got to have help." And he said, "Will you promise me one thing, that where I leave you you'll never leave it till I come back for you?" and I said, "Why sure I'll stay where you put me." He says, "If the Indians come along and steal the mule, just let 'em have it. If they burn the wagon down, just let 'em do it. Don't you move from here." And he kissed me goodbye and then he took brush and brushed out our tracks all the way down the hill so you'd never know. You know, that was a long eight hours I waited there.

Marriage and the Grand Gulch Expedition

Well, I was married December 12, 1896 at Sacramento, California and Mr. Wetherill met us there. He'd scouted around and found a nice Justice of the Peace since we weren't affiliated with any church and he asked Mother and Father if that would be satisfactory and I of course didn't know much about it, I'd never been married before, and so I agreed to anything. Mother and I went down to the Emporium and we bought me a very nice suit. It was dark, very dark red, almost a maroon wool and trimmed with black braid and black frogs where it buttoned with large black buttons down the front. And then I wore the little bracelet, my granddaughter has it now, a little bracelet that Mr. Wetherill had given me. It was the first and the very loveliest silver bracelet that I had ever seen and he bought it for me when we were out among the Navajos.

We went all through San Francisco and then we went to Mexico City for our wedding trip. We got back the first of January and then we immediately got busy and outfitted for this trip to Grand Gulch, Utah because Mr. Wetherill had been there and had discovered the Basketmakers, another tribe of people that had lived not only in the Mesa Verde country

The Palmer family about 1895. Left to right: Elizabeth Ann, Edna, Sidney LaVern, Sidney LaVern, Jr., Marietta. *McNitt Collection, #6559, New Mexico State Records Center & Archives.*

Richard Wetherill digging. *Courtesy Museum of New Mexico, Neg. No. 8052.*

The Wetherill home. *Maxwell Museum of Anthropology, University of New Mexico.*

The Wetherill trading post at Pueblo Bonito. *Maxwell Museum of Anthropology, University of New Mexico.*

but all over this country, early, early people and were great basket weavers and he named them the Basketmakers. And of course, scientists sort of doubted that there was more than one tribe. When we went there we were out of the world. It was unexplored country and inhabited by Navajos and Paiutes and not too friendly.

So he and his mother both hesitated about my going and I said, "Well, haven't I camped out all my life? I never lived in a house very much and it won't hurt me. I'm not afraid of cold." Then Mother Wetherill said, "Well now if she feels that way about it I think she should go, Richard. I'll make her some bloomers out of heavy jeans that will come clear down to the ankles and she'll be alright." So it was arranged that I was to go.

The boys from Harvard had brought things they just thought they had to take along. They took ten times more plunder than they needed. Think of packing oats that distance for our animals, especially the pack animals had to have their dinner too, you know, breakfast, dinner and supper same as the men. We took sixty-eight pack animals and then we had to take along with us extra horses. We ate them all. Those boys had big appetites.

Well, when we got to the canyon leading into Grand Gulch there our troubles began. It would break a snake's neck to go down that canyon. We had to work on that trail for several days to get it so that we could get those packhorses down through there. We had a cook and he was one of the crankiest men I ever knew. And I didn't blame him much because I'll tell ya cooking in two feet of snow isn't a pleasant thing for a gang like we were, starving to death. But we finally got supper and Mr. Wetherill made it a rule that everybody had to clean their plate and stack your dishes up. And of course, those boys had never done anythng like that and it was very difficult for them. They forgot it three times a day but they got it done finally. We got up early and we mostly traveled late, which, of course, irritated the cook. Everybody had to work. I had to work. I had to help keep those horses going.

Here was the main cliff and here was this rock laying here and Mr. Wetherill walked and looked in there behind that. He says, "You're not in a hurry to go home, are you?" And he dug around there for a few minutes and he called me and he says, "I found something." And I went there and he was down on his knees with his brush. After he'd find any evidence of human habitation, why then the shovel was taboo. Well, he brushed there for quite awhile and I helped him. And we uncovered this beautiful basket shaped like an oval. Well, under the basket was another basket laying over a human . . . we could see that there was a mummy and over the face of that mummy was another basket. And on that mummy there was first a turkey feather blanket with big spots of bluebird feathers on it and then under that was another feather blanket with yellow bird feathers on it, wild canaries. I couldn't believe she was dead. And her face was painted red and her body was painted yellow and her hair was combed nicely down and she had on some little shells . . . And we got back late for supper and the cook was madder than hades.

The difficulty of getting such fragile and valuable things out of there worried me all the time. . . . But there was this place. And Mr. Wetherill said, "This looks like one of their turkey pens. I think we'll excavate this." And they just dug a little ways down and they found they were coming to a body and when you got to where you're going to find something, you can see the rim of a piece of pottery or maybe a person's knee stickin' up, and so he got the brushes out. They use whisk brooms and a finer brush and then all the digging is done with a small trowel, a small garden trowel in those days. And they found this marvelous mummy in there. They called it Joe Buck and it was covered first in a plain feather blanket.

When we'd go out we got so hungry that when we'd get back to camp at night we were like bears. We just couldn't wait hardly until the meal was ready and we'd gather around the fire the cook had and he got mad and swore around quite a bit. . . . We'd gather round and tell how saddlesore we were and how many stickers we'd got in us and how uncomfortable we were and how we didn't sleep at night and I know the minute we touched the bed we were all sound asleep and never woke up till morning but we had to complain, you know, and those boys were tenderfeet.

We slept in that deep snow. We'd just take the shovels and shovel it off and Mr. Wetherill cut some brush and put it down and made our bed. And just put the tarp down and put the sleeping bags down and piled in dead tired and hungry.

. . . When I visited the American Museum of Natural History a few years ago at the entrance of the Wetherill exhibit there's a big square table and this arch sitting right here in the center completely covered with turquoise. Then around this same room were the skeletons of thirteen women. And every one of them had been hit on the head with a stone hammer because the hole was there in the skull. His wives that they killed when he died, to go to heaven with him. . . .

I married the right man. There's no doubt about it because I'll tell you, in the first place I admired him for his knowledge; I admired him for being such a perfect gentleman; and I learned to love him more than . . . I never could love any man as much.

Life at Pueblo Bonito

You know those people that are putting up the money for those expeditions one never knows how long they're going to be interested in it and how much money they've got and what they want to spend for it. Those things were expensive work, let me tell you, very expensive, because every bit we ate had to be brought in for us and the Indians as well excepting the meat. And then there was the salaries and all the various things that had to be taken care of and Mr. Wetherill didn't know how much money the boys wanted to put up for it. We excavated there for the Hydes five years and then we excavated on our own a number of times while we were living there. But life there was not at all lonely or anything.

. . . Well, once I prepared this nice roast and I got it on real early in the morning because it was a big one, and instructed the Indian girls that worked for me to keep up a good fire and we roasted potatoes and onions around with it and basted it frequently and I served it up for dinner that evening, roasted it all day and it was as tender as young chicken. And Mr. Wetherill was busy in the store and so when I seated everyone at the table why I said to Mr. Putney, I said, "Mr. Putney, I guess you'll have to take Mr. Wetherill's place and carve the meat today because he's not going to be here for a few minutes he tells me." Alright, he was glad to and a very nice man, we all liked him so much. And he sat down in Mr. Wetherill's chair and he carved great slabs of this lovely, juicy meat and served it out to everybody and we all ate heartily of it of course and they were all hearty eaters. I didn't have to prepare any delicacies for my guests because by the time they got to Pueblo Bonito and did all the things they did around there, climbing the cliffs and going to all the ruins and seeing all the interesting things there were to see around there, they were ready to eat anything and it was a joy to feed them and there was one summer that I kept track of the number of people that was at my dining room table and there wasn't a meal in four months but what I had 24 people and sometimes more. Of course it wasn't any job. I loved to cook and I loved to plan the meals and I had plenty of help. But even so it kept me busy with my children and then always a few extra children that I kept there to play with mine, I didn't want to raise them alone, that isn't right.

Well, after this meal why Mr. Putney . . . he was a heavy man and quite a hearty eater, he sat back in his chair and he said, "My, Mrs. Wetherill," he said, "You know they don't serve anything better than that down there at the Alvarado." He says, "Fred Harvey can't beat that." And of course that was the real swanky place to go and eat in the early days.

If you ate at Fred Harvey's why you had done something and I felt that was a great compliment and thanked him.

The evaporation is what kept everything cool. We never had any trouble about meat. Well, of course Mr. Putney, after, we went back down into Mr. Wetherill's office—Mr. Wetherill had a magnificent office. It was all beautiful Indian rugs and various things and his hunting . . . the things he had killed, deer heads and mountain sheep and lion skins and bear skins and all the things a hunter gathers in his years of hunting and . . . some very, very wonderful blankets, old bayetas. I still have them and I'm taking good care of them and have all these years. But Mr. Wetherill still was working with this Indian, something they were buying or selling or accounts or something, and Mr. Putney said to him, "Dick, that was a wonderful dinner! You sure have a wife that knows how to cook." And he said, "Well, she gets lots of experience around here." And so after awhile I wandered down into the office and I said, "Mr. Putney, wouldn't you like to see the beef, the carcass of that beef that lovely roast came off of?"

Well, anyway, we went out there and I said, "Well, there it hangs right there." And I'd had the Navajo leave the hoofs on it. "Now," I said, "that roast came right offa there and you know I always like to tease and you made the remark that you knew that you would know horse meat because it tasted sweeter than beef and so I just wanted to tease you and show you that you wouldn't know horse meat." He turned and he says, "You rascal you."

The Murder of Richard Wetherill

I hadn't been home from the hospital (after Ruth was born) but just two or three days and while I was gone Miss Quick, the children's teacher, had had to be all that long time with the Stachers; and she was just full of talk and among other things that I remember at the dinner table that night she said, "Superintendent Stacher still declares, Mr. Wetherill, that he's going to build a school here and he has promised the Indians that Washington will build a big dam here so they can have water for all the sheep and horses and he'll fence the canyon at the lower end and the upper end and they can use it for their personal pasture." It would have been a wonderful thing for those ruins, wouldn't it?

She said the only thing would have to be done with Mr. Wetherill would have to go away, move away and live someplace else because he objected so bitterly to having a school there around the pueblos. And, of course, if he didn't have any business why he'd have to go away because if the Indians didn't come there and trade with him he wouldn't have any way of making a living and if they wouldn't take care of his stock on shares the way they did why he'd soon have to go. So he advised them that they'd better just dissolve partnership with him in any business dealings that they had and then not trade at the store, she said, and in that way why they'd run him out of the country and then they could have the school right there at Pueblo Bonito which was the most foolish idea because it wasn't the place at all. There was no room there for a school. And of course, later the government built the school at Ti-a-ah where Mr. Wetherill suggested in the first place. And made a national monument which Mr. Wetherill had tried all during his years there to get them to do but it takes them so long to do anything and it was after his death that it was made a national momument. . . They were to give him land. . . Professor Hewett manipulated that and bought it for the University for taxes. You see, I didn't know anything about those things so they just finagled me out of it. It's never made me feel bad for one minute. I just feel bad for them is all that they could stoop so low as to finagle a woman with seven children out of her home, which they did.

Well, Dez-glee-nez-pah, my girl that was always with me, she kept saying to me, "The Navajos are awfully mad. Let us go away. Let us go up to my house and take the children. Something awful is going to happen. Stacher had made the Indians awfully mad and we'd better go away." "Well," I said, "I won't go away. I'm gonna stay right here." . . . Well, you see, Stacher's lies and promises and all that. He had told them that they wouldn't have to pay what they owed Mr. Wetherill, that they could keep all the sheep and horses and cattle that they had on shares . . . I had put the baby to bed and I looked out of the back window through the gap that we always had to look down the canyon and I saw, oh, I should say five or six Indians all painted black with their hair all down over their faces, and I called Dez-glee-nez-pah to the window and I said, "What in the world are they doing that for?" And she says, "I told you they were mad. They're on the warpath, that's what you'd call it." And I says, "Well, what are they doin' that for?" And she says, "Maybe they're gonna kill somebody. They haven't told me but Stacher said that's what they should do . . ."

And I went into the kitchen to see if supper was getting on the table and I told 'em there'd be a few extrys and I said, "We have plenty though. I'd put in a big roast and I know we've got plenty of everything. We won't change anything." And then I came back to see if my baby had gone to sleep because I had been just jigglin' her on the bed to make her go to sleep. I'd fed her.

And I looked out the window and down there at the arroyo and I saw the awfullest dust. It just looked like the cattle were running in every direction, and you could see horsemen running around there and I thought what in the world is happening and I kept looking and looking and finally I saw a man coming up toward the house as hard as his horse could run. And I thought, well, he's sure crazy, what's the matter, the horse is running away with him or something . . . I'd hear them right from the start I could hear them shooting and I thought maybe he got shot. Then I saw that it was Will Finn and I thought, well, why don't he do something, he always carries a gun and he's supposed to be such a good shot. Here these Indians was right on him and they had clubs and they were hittin' him with clubs and he never stopped, he just kept spurrin' his horse . . . And he hollered to me, "Where are your children? Get your children in the house." Well, I'd run back into the house and got the sheriff's Colt revolver and I ran out to where the children played all the time and they weren't anywhere I could see, not a one of 'em, not a chick or a child anywhere.

I had the sheriff's six-shooter and I shot twice at Joe Hasteen Yazzi. I thought if you're shootin' at me I'll shoot at you and I did my best to kill him but I didn't hit him apparently because he was a long distance off, see. . .

"Well," Finn said, "the Indians attacked us." "Where's Mr. Wetherill?" I said. "Well," he says, "he's down there . . . I hate to tell you but, Mr. Wetherill's dead." I couldn't believe him.

And I said, "I'm going down there." And he says, "No, you can't go down there." "I'm not going to leave my husband down there for the coyotes to eat. You don't need to think I'm gonna do that." Well, they brought him back and put him on the back porch and we put sheets around so that the sun couldn't shine in, you know. Then the Indians they made a circle around Mr. Wetherill's body and sang and danced and I asked the Indians what it was for and they said they asked the Great Spirit to forgive them for the terrible crime they had done. They didn't know what an awful thing they had done. They thought they would scare somebody or do something like that but they didn't intend to kill Mr. Wetherill but Chiss-chillin-begay when he was in jail in Aztec he told me, he says, "Forgive me, please forgive me. I didn't want to kill the best friend I ever had. I was mad and," he said, "one time when I was a little boy about six years old I went with my father when some horses of ours ran away and they went over to the San Juan and the river was pretty high and father said, 'You're gonna have to stay here and hide in a bush til I get back.'"

"I stood there and I hung onto my father's hand and I began to cry and said, 'I'm afraid.' And we saw a cowboy come down over the hill on the other side of the river and my father got on his horse and that cowboy shot him and killed him and I thought of that and that's why I killed Mr. Wetherill because he was a white man. "Oh," he says, "forgive me, forgive me." I said, "How can I forgive you? How can I forgive you?"

Mr. Wetherill always told the Navajos and he'd always told me, he said, "You know, anybody's liable to die any time." He'd always say it in a laughing way. He said, "I want to be buried right up there by that big rock."

I never feared them. I was a Navajo, you know. . . . The Indians didn't ever kill my husband. But Stacher cleared his petticoats with his lies and he just died last year. He's had a long time to suffer over that murder. I hoped he'd live to be two hundred years old so he'd have longer time to think about it when he was trying to sleep at night but he didn't live near long enough as far as I was concerned.

I Was a Gypsy the Rest of My Life

. . . I felt so helpless . . . They had orders not to come to my house, not to come anywhere in Chaco Canyon, not to speak to me if they saw me anywhere, not to have anything to do with me in any way, shape, manner or form. Well, you know, we'd been friends. I'd saved their lives and saved their babies; I'd taken care of 'em; we'd given them medicine; we'd fed 'em when they was poor and helped 'em in every way we could; and after the tragedy was over and they got to realizing what they had done, they told me time and time again and they still tell me, that they killed the best friend they ever had. They say, "Our country has never been the same. They changed our lives in every way." But they used to come anyway at night and tap on the window and ask me if I needed anything or needed any meat or what was they gonna do about the sheep. . . . And they said, "You're not afraid of us, are you?" And I said, "No, I'm not afraid of you." And I said, "But how do you know that I'm not afraid of you?" They said, "Because every time we just tap the window once and you're wide awake and sitting up and if you were afraid you'd cover your head." And so I would go down to the arroyo and see what they wanted and they said, "You've gotten very poor, you don't eat."

"No," I said, "I can't eat." And they said, "And your eyes, you cry too much." But I guess those things have to be. It was in my life anyway.

Do you know it's only been in the last five years that I could even have Mr. Wetherill's picture around?

And I didn't know anything about Mr. Wetherill's financial condition. He had never said anything to me about it. Everything seemed to be as normal as it had always been. I'd sent for what I needed and everything was taken care of. But when we went to investigate there wasn't any money and I remember so well that Al [Wetherill] gave me a twenty dollar gold piece. That was the only person that ever gave me a dollar. I never needed it before and I wouldn't take it afterwards. I was too proud, see. I presume I could have gotten money but I had other ways. I sold things. I sold rugs. There was just quantities of them, there, you know, and I sold rugs.

For years and years they persecuted me . . . So every little thing I had to go and prove it in court, you see, that it was mine and that court just tortured me to death because when I went I had to take the children, there was no one to leave them with. I stayed all that fall and all winter till the next spring at Pueblo Bonito, and I was just slowly losing my mind. I was so confused mentally, I couldn't sleep and a very peculiar thing happened . . . I woke up in the night. I was very nervous and I'd been to sleep quite a while, and I woke up and I sat right up in bed and he stood there right in that doorway with his hands up as he always did and he shook his head and he looked so sad and he said, "Oh," he says, "I'm so sorry to leave you like this. I'm so sorry to leave you with all these children and when you know how things are, you'll know why I'm feeling so sorry and I won't see you anymore." But I knew afterwards why he talked that way because Fred Hyde had insisted on him insuring his life for twenty thousand. But business had gotten so very bad, you know, and everything had gone against him, and so he had no insurance, so I think that's what was worrying him. When I wrote to the company about it, why he had borrowed on it, see.

On account of my not appearing in court the sheriff came out there and arrested me on a bench warrant and so I went but at that time I had moved away from Chaco and was living at Luciano Lake near Cuba and the snow there was deep. And I said to him, I said, "This is a terrible time of year for me to make this trip. I don't see what the necessity of it is." And he said, "Well, the court wasn't satisfied with the way I was paying the debts of the company or something." And I said, "How can I pay the debts when Chambers and these other white people have stolen everything that there was?"

. . . "Well," the judge said, "Mrs. Wetherill, they're treating you kinda rough, aren't they?" "Yes, I'm getting used to rough treatment," I said, "I've had several years of it and I'm getting awfully tired of it." I was getting to that place where I could have done a little shooting and it's funny I didn't do it. It's a wonder I didn't go and shoot Shelton and Stacher both . . . If I hadn't of had those two babies I would have done it, see, but I thought, I'm their mother and I must take care of them. The others could get along, somebody would take care of 'em, but those two little babies, I couldn't do it, because I knew I'd hang for it.

. . . I'm gonna tell you that I have seen some of the most marvelous sights there. I have stood in that porch when we'd have those terrific lightning storms and the thunder would just crash and it just sounded like it was tearing the earth in two and see it strike those big pine trees and make kindling wood of 'em . . . I had forgotten how beautiful trees were. I had forgotten how lovely it was to have the winter right there at the door and that beautiful spring with those deer coming down there and they'd stand there . . . and go on ahead and drink and walk away.

E.J. ELLIOTT
Fighting Death in the Desert

In the flowery language befitting a Victorian tale of rescue from the jaws of death, E.J. Elliott tells in this 1927 memoir how her mother, Minnie, won her battle against tuberculosis. Given six months to live, Minnie Elliott and her two small children arrived in Scottsdale, Arizona, when the settlement was populated mainly by gila monsters and rattlesnakes. Having received a death sentence from her eastern doctors, Minnie proceeded to discover freedom and inspiration in the desert as she invented her own cure. Throwing off her corset and the bondage and anxieties the garment represented for Victorian women, she proceeded to create her own whole grain diet, to simplify her life, and to surprise everyone by getting well.

The impositions of necessity in the rugged desert setting, certainly perceived as "hardships" back east, proved a restorative blessing. Taking responsibility for herself and her family, her well-being was enhanced by a life in nature on the open desert.

Minnie is another example of a woman who, because of her separation from her husband, when forced by circumstance to make decisions and act on her own, rejects conventional expectations and thrives.

*M*y mother's experience is the thrilling story of a sickly young woman given "six months to live" by the finest of eastern specialists, resolving to go west to wage the battle of her life against tuberculosis for the sake of her husband and three children. For herself she would have preferred her "six months" and death among her family and friends in the east, rather than face the wearisome trip across vast wilderness to the then unknown Territory of Arizona, supposedly full of hostile Indians and armed desperadoes.

My father could not accompany us as he was a young minister, earning a meager salary and forced to remain by his post, for a time, to finance the trip. He wrote to the only person they knew in the west that we were coming and that he would appreciate any information or courtesy shown us. We arrived in a small valley town, Tempe, composed of adobe huts and shacks; my mother so weak from the tiresome journey she could scarcely drag herself off the train, my younger brother coughing continually, and I a tiny, frail baby in arms, but soon the few kind neighbors took pity and did everything in their power to aid us. The first few weeks were too sad to relate: I soon took dangerously ill with typhoid fever, and my mother, too weak to nurse me constantly, was relieved by a kind missionary and my oldest brother, who watched over my little cot with unwearied devotion. I shall never cease to love that dear old man, who found time in his weary round of duties, to hover over a little child and help win her back to life.

As our family health did not seem to improve, the kind friends advised us to go farther out into the desert, and a generous-hearted, retired army officer, Chaplain Scott, offered to aid us in putting up a tent-shack near his ranch. There the battle for life was started. My poor mother was afraid of the Indians, whose reservation was near, and timorous of the snakes, gila monsters, skunks, tarantulas, and kindred insects that infested those regions and visited us frequently. She was dismayed in finding herself ten miles from the nearest stores, markets, druggist and doctor. Little did she then dream that the absence of them plus the healing air and the very struggle for existence were the basic principles of her recovery.

Her unwavering courage and faith, in spite of all odds and her keen resourcefulness soon changed the sickening dread to bouyant cheer, banishing loneliness and transforming that barren shack into a cozy, attractive home. She wrote the cheeriest letters to Father, never telling him of the panics of fear she suffered over the frequent visits of the Indian squaws, the dread of sudden sand-storms, changing day to night, or the presence of creeping, crawling "critters" that caused cold chills to shake her frail, pain-spent body. Little brother began to improve almost immediately and he proved to be an encouraging topic of letter interest, but Father pleaded in vain for exact data on herself.

She would tell how the little lads would fare forth, sling-shots in hand, to bring back tender, juicy quail, rabbit, etc. for mother (thus helping to keep hunger from the door), but of her progress she was silent: it was a long, hard fight. It was exceedingly difficult to get food, so she began to look about for the best the region afforded. She discovered that by toasting and putting ordinary wheat through a coffee mill, a delicious and nutritive mush could be made to fill our empty stomachs. The desert sage honey was an available sweet, and milk could be purchased from the nearby ranch. There were also a few orchards and vineyards in those days, so that during the summer season we had plenty of ripe fruit, the necessary completion of our menu. "What a meagre diet for a tubercular patient," some sympathizing friends were wont to say, but that simple diet, with a few variations on special holiday or festive occasions, constituted the most sensible nature cure with which Providence could have blessed us. In fact, the absence of denatured, predigested, concocted canned foods was blessing in disguise. The theory of stuffing TB patients with numerous steaks and raw eggs is frequently a blind alley to their digestive downfall and hastened death. This she learned later, in experience with well-to-do patients. Our extreme poverty was not against us, so take hope all you, who, with empty pockets, are waging the same grim battle!

At first Mother coughed so hard she could scarcely walk, but she gradually increased her breathing and bed exercises, finally dragging herself out into the desert to indulge instinctively in the daily, healing sunbath. Being one of the early disciples of Physical Culture, she determined to put it to the test, although she seemed a hopeless case. She gradually increased her early morning walks, until in few months she found herself reaching the canal, about a mile distant. There on the bridge she would rest and watch the glorious sunrises and drink in the rich, dry, healing desert breezes, wafted over boundless spaces of pure ozone. Soon the charm of those endless vistas broken here and there by fantastic buttes and mountains, tinted crimson and gold at daybreak, filled her soul with peace, and she learned to love her "Desert of Hope." The longing for the home times and familiar faces seemed to give way to a sense of rest and secure abiding.

Thus, with a whole-souled determination by God's grace to put all fear and discouragement out of her heart, she resolved on "VICTORY" in her battle for life. This very resolve marked the turning point toward recovery. Her cough gradually subsided, her persistent temperature faded away, and as she increased her exercises her weight began to increase. In less than three years she gained 50 pounds. She abandoned the hour-glass, tight-corseted styles then in vogue, and dressed in simple, loose-fitting garments;

she moved about with ever quicker step and the returning bloom of youth replaced the pallor of death.

Our little village, Scottsdale, was fast becoming a health resort, all the patients living as we did, in tents or shacks, or on the few ranches. They were a delightful class of people and included professors, lawyers, ministers, writers, etc. Mother was the leading spirit among them, for she always went about doing good; many a poor dejected "lunger," as we playfully called them, took courage, observing her phenomenal recovery, then in progress. Many of them came "too late," but also many stayed it out and recovered, but never to return to the east.

Mother's genius for comforting and consoling people took her mind off our own troubles, and filled her life with blessed experiences and many a heart with new courage and hope. She staged little performances, put on programs, started a little Sunday School, taught the young Indians who aspired to better things, and made fast and life-long friendships among the little exiled colony of healthseekers, who, like herself, had been sent "out west to die."

Father, realizing that our little family could never live in the east again, joined us; and later took Mother east, where for a summer she amazed all her former friends and her relatives with her marvelous recovery and her interesting accounts of life in the west. The physicians who had given her "six months" examined her, and amazedly pronounced her lungs "sound." They declared they never would have known that she had been so hopelessly ill. Many others, hearing of her recovery, came west later and my father established, in gratitude for Mother's recovery, one of the first sanatoriums near the capitol of the state, Phoenix.

Many were the hardships and even dangers experienced in that new land, but we look back on those "pioneer" days as our best, for not only did we find the priceless boon of health, but also we were enabled to weave our lives into the fabric of the last American frontier. The fellowship with dauntless souls bent on seeking out the natural and physical treasures and beauties, the "pioneer souls that blaze their paths where highways never ran," and the young souls that faced the same life and death struggle in the desert, was our greatest reward and most noble inheritance.

Our "Desert of Waiting" was changed by the alchemy of high courage and dauntless faith in God into a haven of life and health.

ISABELLA GREENWAY
A Charmed Girlhood

Isabella Greenway, Arizona's colorful New Deal Congresswoman, typifies the well-bred, well-connected eastern women who found in the West a wide-open arena for their talents, and through the confidence of their personalities, seized the opportunities presented by their special time and place to make enormous contributions that flowed naturally out of who they were. While the fragment of autobiography Isabella wrote in 1948 pertains to her early memories in St. Paul, on the family farm in Kentucky ("where we are sometimes born and always buried"), and her upperclass, rather storybook Manhattan girlhood, it is included here to show the roots of a woman who became one of the Southwest's most powerful and influential females, as well as for its lighthearted wit and historical interest.

The woman known as "Arizona's Sweetheart," who homesteaded, became a prominent rancher, a mining, hotel and real estate magnate and ran Gilpin Airlines was born Isabella Selmes in 1886 in Kentucky. Following her father's death when she was nine, she and her mother went east. Her lifelong friendship with Eleanor Roosevelt began in their private school days. Isabella was a bridesmaid at the wedding of Eleanor and Franklin and in 1932 made the seconding speech for FDR's presidential nomination.

The story behind Isabella Greenway's rise to national prominence is an intriguing mixture of personal triumph and tragedy. In 1905, at age nineteen, she married Robert H. Munro Ferguson, a former Rough Rider and friend of Teddy Roosevelt. Her father, also an intimate of Teddy Roosevelt's, had, before her birth, gone into partnership with him in a North Dakota cattle ranch, an operation which failed miserably. In 1908, her husband contracted TB, precipitating their move to Silver City, New Mexico, where they lived in tents and then homesteaded on a ranch in the Burro Mountains.

The fourteen years preceding his death in 1922 must have been difficult for Isabella as she nursed an invalid husband and raised two children in relative isolation and tough financial straits which echoed the experience of the reduced financial circumstances of her genteel southern girlhood.

During these years in Silver City she began her political life on the School Board and in 1918 as Chairman of the Women's Land Army of New Mexico, in which women performed the work of men who had gone to war.

Following her husband's death, in 1923 Isabella married his best friend, another former Rough Rider and a distinguished WW I hero, General John Greenway. John and Isabella had been in love for eleven years, and had even informed Ferguson of this, but had never been alone except for one half-hour in a hansom cab in Central Park on the eve of Greenway's departure for Europe and WW I.

John Greenway, a leader of the Arizona mining industry, died of a blood clot only two years after the marriage, leaving Isabella his fortune and considerable business holdings.

Moving to Tuscon, she established the "Arizona Hut," a craft workshop which employed disabled veterans. She furnished her hotel, the Arizona Inn, with its products. In addition, she purchased the Quarter Circle Double X Ranch in Williams, Arizona, where she hosted the Roosevelts.

Becoming active in Democratic politics was a natural step as Greenway's widow and a prominent business and social leader in her own right. In a special election in 1933, she defeated two male rivals for the Congressional seat. Republicans did not even bother to nominate an opponent. She was re-elected for a second term by a huge margin, but declined a third term. She served on three House committees: Indian Affairs, Irrigation and Reclamation, and Public Lands. In addition, she brought a $14 million public works project employing 3000 to her state.

Isabella's statement declining a third term reads with the characteristic charming forthrightness that endeared her to her constituency. Speculations were that she was retiring from Congress to (1) get married (2) to run for Governor (3) to work out some special philosophy of life after fifty. She made her announcement on her fiftieth birthday.

> I would be an unhappy woman indeed, not to have the compliment of conjecture thrown about even my fifty years. At home my friends take these rumors about marriage in stride, attaching significance to political rumor only. . . . The advent of the fiftieth year is surprisingly thrilling! I'll tell you how it feels. You come face to face with the fact that you're crazy to live. You begin to budget your resources with an eagerness akin to greed, and all the while you discover how generous, beyond any deserts, are the compensations of our good providence.
>
> The refreshing part of the milestone is the revelation that goes with it, convincing us the intense pleasures come from the simpler things, that should be available to all, and the lucky people are those who have kept the fundamentals clear-cut—counting the quality of energy spent rather than the tangible result.

Isabella did eventually marry a third time. The "New York Society Girl Who Became an Arizona Cattle Queen" died December 18, 1953, at age 67.

*H*aving never discovered a beginning or an ending to anything, we'll plunge in where memory first registered.

I think the first incident that made a lasting vivid impression on me was reaching for a piece of floating gum in a very large fountain in Irving Park, St. Paul, Minnesota. I remember falling in headlong, floundering and being pulled out by a policeman and taken home by my colored mammy and punished aplenty. All day in bed on bread and milk. Modern psychologists doubtless would explain this as the beginning of an aversion to baths and a terror of bodies of water. Back in that year of probably 1888 when I was two and a half years old, the incident proved that if you accompanied poor judgment with faulty performance you paid an inflated price and that the harsh obligation of parents was to prove this logic locally in the home as a preparation for life's highways.

Be that as it may, the next memory log kindled confused emotions of so fundamental a kind they have flared ever since and their light has clarified little.

Our house was one of a row of very small brick houses edging the Park. My Father and Mother had lost the lavish side of money that Father had inherited but they continued to sustain as many of its evidences as possible. They were dining out this particular day. Father, in evening clothes, came downstairs ahead of Mother and stepped in to the kitchen from which was coming that special and wonderful fragrance of newly-baked bread just one out of the oven. The cook was telling a tramp, who had come in the back kitchen door, that she would not give him the loaf of bread he asked. Father, always generous and human, and probably thirty years old, protested and gave the man several loaves. I was moved with approval. At this point the man went out the back door, took careful aim from the dark and hurled the loaves back at Father who was placating the cook.

Then it all happened—out the door, over the rail, I saw Father jump into the dark and a scuffling mass. They struggled round to the front sidewalk. In the light of a street lamp I could see my Father being attacked by three or four men. He called to my Mother to bring him his pistol. My Uncle, Franklin Cutcheon, then a frail young lawyer also in evening clothes, plunged into the melee while Mother, truly beautiful, (I know yours and everyone else's Mother is beautiful) held the pistol and refused to give it to Father, who, bruised and battered and his clothes torn, was definitely getting the worst of it. When the neighbors joined in, the marauders vanished.

The impulse (rarely resisted) to plunge into the dark of unmeasured conflict has been mine since that night. Father taught me my principle prayer: "Dear God, please *make me good and brave and true.*"

Perhaps this is the place to explain how my Mother and Father came to be living in this particular little house in St. Paul.

My Father, Tilden Russell Selmes, was the son of an Englishman from Rye, England, whose family were yeomen. Just what that implies I have never had time to find out but have been proud in hoping it meant soil and the security of feet on the ground. Grandfather became a banker in this country and his second marriage was to my Grandmother from Bennington, Vermont. He was, I've been told, a member of Lincoln's staff and helped finance the Civil War. The story goes that he went to England to ask aid and was refused on the grounds that all *gentlemen* lived in the South. He never returned to England. His death came as a result of injuries when his horse was shot under him while he was observing a battle in the Civil War.

Grandmother looked like Queen Victoria and brought her two girls up in Europe and Concord, Massachusetts, among the famous circle of notables that included Emerson, Thoreau, Miss Alcott, Hawthorne and other distinguished men and women of letters and books.

Father, I gather, found buoyant release in the good fellowship of cheerful young men and a merry progress through Andover and Yale, underwritten by detached independence through inherited means.

Grandmother nagged and irritated him excessively and upon a Sunday, when Father was at home from college and was carving the roast, she aggravated him to such a point of unendurance that he threw the platter, roast beef and all, through a plate glass window. This roast beef incident has brought secret solace and justification to me upon a regrettable number of occasions. His quick temper became my heirloom and during the years I have fostered and cherished its circulatory benefits.

Father studied law in Lincoln's firm in Illinois with, I believe, no idea at the time of practising it—and then went forth to find whatever it is that adventurous young men go forth to find.

Well, he found my Mother—a glorious, vital, restless and beautiful young woman whose golden red hair came to her knees and whose flower white shoulders, arms and exquisite hands stirred even a child to a sense of exciting phenomenon and worship. Her mind submerged the lure of her beautiful body and challenged only the best. From the morass of a fantastically Victorian upbringing she struggled for reality and her years were beset with disturbance between theory and discovery—recoil and courage.

Hers was not a master's but a mistress' genius of knowing how not to bore a man (or a woman for that matter). On casual statement that I was writing a book called "Men Who Loved My Mother," a surprising number and variety of men asked that they be allowed a full chapter and invariably their wives wanted to cooperate. Her maiden name was Martha McComb Flandreau.

Father and Mother decided on a way of life. A cattle ranch at Mandau, South Dakota, with three winter months in Washington. For 1884 that was progressive.

Friendships of that era must have had a special quality of dignity, under-written as they were by relative leisure, pauses for appraisal and a cozy emphasis on gossip and humor that made it all so exciting and personally important. The raconteur held his own and wrist watches had not been invented.

Cultural gems sparkled while Nazis and Communists lay smoldering in the nebulous darkness of pre-birth. So, at least, it seems to me as I think of all I heard about those days and friendships with Mr. and Mrs. Henry

Adams, Senator and Mrs. Cabot Lodge, Mr. and Mrs. James T. Blaine and sundry other personages.

One day Mother and Father drove into Mandau for supplies for the ranch. Mother, who was waiting for Father in a small restaurant, became conscious of a commotion across the room. A number of cowboys were surrounding a young man, who was obviously a stranger and enthusiastically telling the story of his day's hunting. With clenched first he reached his emphatic climax: "And if there had not *BEAN* mist on my *GLASSES*, I'd been gotten another." His language and the way he told it fascinated the cowboys who kept calling others to hear the story again and again amid whoops and yells.

When Father returned he went over and spoke to the young Easterner, who said his name was Theodore Roosevelt. In his pocket were letters of introduction to Father and Mother.

He and Father became partners in the cattle ranch business and Mr. Roosevelt stayed much of the time with them. I was a year old and my colored mammy always remembered he needed several pillows on account of his asthma. He was grateful and Mammy would say to him: "You're going to be President one of these days," and his reply was, "Well, when I'm President, I want you and this child of yours (referring to me) to visit me in the White House." It was thus I received my first invitation to pay a visit. Seventeen years later President Theodore Roosevelt remembered and Mammy (not Mother) received a written invitation reminding her of their talks and asking us to pay a visit to the White House.

Night after night, over Mother's protests, Father and Mr. Roosevelt would plan what was to be the Rough Riders' Regiment—and hoped for a war that would make the Regiment a reality.

They were not very practical ranchers, or maybe a series of bad winters ruined their business. Father lost everything he had and was left with debts which he finally paid in full just before his death.

Mr. Roosevelt was more fortunate. He lost all he could but a trust saved his sharing Father's plight. His and Father's friendship remained constant and unfailing all their lives.

When the ranch was gone, Father took up the practice of law in St. Paul, which brings us to the little brick house where my memory began.

We moved to a bigger house, which Grandfather Flandreau gave us on Virginia Avenue. The skating rink opposite gave me enviable advantages and charley horse tortures at night and no end of good friends' backyards to play in, bobbing parties, taffy pulls and a sort of undercurrent called "school"—(private some years, public another).

If any phases of my mental processes could be dignified as remarkable those that have enabled me to pass through every educational institution that befell my childhood and youth without a ripple of consciousness as to what they were all about are those. My immunity to knowledge has remained miraculous over the years. Devoid of intellectual curiosity I have had to develop a shameless (but ingenious) system of self-preservation among those whom respect I covet—a technique of listening and asking rather impressive questions fools a few but never for long.

History to me is fascinating hearsay that I'm sure I'd enjoy if I had a prolonged illness. Good literature is too exciting for my health. A beautiful sentence can dislocate the continuity of my best planned day and leave me on an oasis without a compass.

It was important, I think, to insert the above paragraph lest some unsuspecting person waste time through to the discovery point of my abysmal ignorance.

Our old family farm in Kentucky, where we are sometimes born and always buried, became our resort for summer.

Minnesota zeroes in the winter and the Ohio River dog days in the summer was the somewhat topsy turvey system that enabled us to live on as little as possible and at the same time be with my beloved Great Aunt, Julia Dinsmore, who really was the head of our family. She was a poet. Theodore Roosevelt said she was (with the exception of Lord Gray) the best educated person he had ever known.

She owned the farm and had foregone all (including marriage) in order to bring up her dead sister's daughters. Literally she lived off these 400 knobby acres and we often with her.

Livestock, tobacco, corn, vegetables and fruit—fabulously old colored people who had left us to try freedom and returned preferring home.

No plumbing, electricity or telephone and the damp cool cellar our ice box.

A surrey, a spring wagon and buggies in various stages of dilapidation— the one painted was always loaned for funerals. Hogsheads full of carpet rags destined to become our floor covering. Twisted shreds of newspapers for lamplighters to save matches. This was our farm.

We farmed by the Almanac, and in Aunty's finest Spencerian penmanship her Day Book recorded all matters, births, deaths, cash paid for horse shoes, the traveling preacher's visit, who called last for a gallon of vinegar and which hollow the neighbors' hogs broke through to ravage our corn.

So often I've rushed barefoot on the roof to save the drying apples—it's difficult to keep my shoes on when I hear a sprinkle.

With my friends, the tenant's children, I've succored and warmed tobacco and even met the strange test of fortitude imposed among ourselves of biting a big beaded green worm in half.

Thirty-six years later my ability to report this agricultural feat brought me many votes of confidence in the farming district of Buckeye, Arizona where there are many Kentuckians. I have sometimes wondered if Political Science covers this procedure of how to get votes.

Our summer crises came regularly and could be depended upon. Always one, and sometimes two, trips to the County Court House in Burlington to attend to our business. The spring wagon had to be washed, my blue checkered gingham had to have extra starch, we ate fried chicken at our "dear Hilda's" house—where the big pink shells on the hearth impressed me greatly and the must smell was an irretrievable part of the structure.

Then there was Threshing Day when the neighbors helped and we served everything we could find to eat and the women waited on the men and we had blackberry cordial and cherry bounce.

The advent of the boat bearing the stuffed whale down the Ohio River was probably the most exciting of all. The whale's mouth was propped open and had a crimson carpet and a sofa and chairs and a place where people could kneel to be married in its mouth. Many took advantage of the unusual distinction of being married in the whale's mouth. Sometimes when the wind was right I thought I could smell that whale two miles inland.

A calliope heralded its arrival and played in the evening while it was there—which made me feel gay and in touch—although I wasn't quite sure what I was in touch with.

Somehow I was never allowed to go to the County Fair. Maybe it was because the other girls, after bleaching themselves for weeks with sunbonnet, fascinators, and homemade mitts, usually met a young man, who, after keeping company with they married at the age of 14 or 15 and began having babies. I always wondered why my friends wouldn't rather have played a little longer. We had such good times.

The 296th piano made by Mr. Steinway is in our parlor and when my aunt's little, bent figure leaned over to play "Moonlight and Roses" and her fading voice, uplifted by her soaring soul sang "Meet Me by Moonlight Alone at the end of the Grove" I sensed that there was something somewhere that maybe I, too, might find some day. It seemed to be something you could live on, and that while you couldn't see it or touch it, you could feel it. I wondered what it was.

Then came my Father's illness and death. He developed cancer and he and Mother went to Johns Hopkins Hospital where Theodore Roosevelt went to be with him. He wrote a letter to Bob Ferguson whom I later married.

Father's last months were in Kentucky where the house was filled with various members of the family, standing by and wishing they could help. Until almost his last day he was lifted on a horse in his pajamas and Mother led it about.

I think my interpretation was not that Father had left me but that he had left me a responsibility—my Mother. In that responsibility I came to consciousness rapidly—I was *nine years old.*

Mother had $50 a month on which to support us both. Mammy and I were sent to live with Grandfather Flandreau in his house in St. Paul. The home was ample and amply filled with remarkable individuals, beginning with my lovely to behold Step-grandmother who prided herself upon not having seen her kitchen for over a year and who translated Swedish books for amusement and had Caffe Chattels where only German was spoken.

She had three sons—my half Uncle, John Riddle, who I best remember in a stiff chair in the big library learning Russian. He was preparing to be appointed Ambassador to Russia. His immaculate sophistication, his waxed mustaches and his aloofness from all current participation was that of a bird of passage in a seasonal flight finding himself pausing among birds of another feather.

His brother, my Uncle Charles Flandreau, had written some amusing books and conceded brilliant essays while at Rivalry. His room was isolated and he could never be disturbed. He impressed me with the fact that civilized people should not meet before 3 p.m. under any circumstances. So I always took my school friends home to lunch in another room if he was breakfasting in the dining room. He was always expected to be caustic and ruthless in comment and rarely failed his expectant listeners.

The third Uncle, Judge Flandreau, and I (I was his only grandchild) lived normal lives—ate and walked together and consorted with his cronies in the Minnesota Historical Society. Mammy bought my clothes, arranged my parties, etc., and Mother was there for short times only.

In spite of the fact that I was only 12 when Mother, Mammy and I went to live with my Aunt and Uncle (Mr. and Mrs. Franking Cutcheon) in New York, the childhood friends of that period in St. Paul are cherished and held dear.

At the generous suggestion of her sister we lived at 128 East 75th Street with my Aunt and Uncle. He had become one of New York's promising lawyers.

Isabella Greenway.
Buehman Collection,
Arizona Historical Society.

FDR, Eleanor Roosevelt, Isabella Greenway, and Senator T. Walsh of Arizona at
the Greenway ranch in 1932. *Arizona Historical Society.*

Isabella Greenway at the 1932 Democratic Convention in Chicago. She never wore rouge or lipstick. *Arizona Historical Society*.

New York spelled first Miss Chapin's, then transfer to Miss Spence's school—*no graduation*—(I mentioned previously my inability to take educational institutions seriously and in this case I felt Latin to be definitely no subject for a young lady to anguish over)—and finally a debut in New York.

But it was these years, from 12 to 18, the endowed me with friends to adore the rest of my life—though few of them went to the schools I did nor were they particularly each other's friends and over the years I lost them from time to time, contactwise but never devotion-wise.

Eleanor Roosevelt was one of the first. Her Godmother, Mrs. Henry Parrish, was my Mother's closest friend and I can see her as if yesterday, when I first saw her in Grandmother's house—I suppose we were 15 or 16.

A lot of us were feeling our way toward maturity in a varying set of circumstances and many with major home problems which precluded a carefree approach but nevertheless, no matter how serious-minded we were, we realized that to appear to be having fun was a part you played.

It is with chagrin that I must accept the verdict of some of my dearest friends who say that through life I have proceeded without plan and that I become effective only when intolerable pressure from self-created chaos necessitates action for self-preservation. The explanation of that was arrived at by another friend who said: "Isabella's undoing is that every PROBLEM that presents itself is translated by her into a multitude of OPPOR-TUNITIES. She has something."

Uncle became MY Uncle inevitably and very soon. Later in life he told me he loved me more than anyone except his wife and in spite of the fact that I had caused him more trouble than probably all the rest of the people in his life.

We always walked to school together, first to Miss Chapin's and later to Miss Spence's. Mine was a special importance in having Uncle take me to school when Fathers rarely brought their girls. Through Central Park I stumbled, hanging on to his arm, month after month and year after year while he tried to explain the fundamentals of Latin and my day's homework. It could not be done. I was discovering life and not exploring dead languages and convinced myself that Latin was not a subject for young girls to anguish over and that ultimately head mistresses would come to this realization. Alas, they did not in time for me to graduate. But I was happy in my white muslin dress on the occasion although I received no little roll of paper tied up in ribbon and was just proud to death of my friends who did graduate. Ironically enough, I later became quite in demand as a commencement speaker and found I made a hit with the young by explaining that I believed their first, and probably most difficult, problem on stepping into life was to wean themselves from their parents with patience, indulgence and tenderness. They seemed delighted that this could be aired openly and I hope some parents have in consequence ridden into freedom through the kind and adult guidance of their children.

Uncle paid my school bills and bought my clothes and I was sheltered from all knowledge of their cost or the burden of meeting them, which seems to have been the conceded system of keeping a girl sweet and untarnished by materialism.

When it was finally decided that I must use a check book, I entered into the spirit enthusiastically and used it so conscientiously that Uncle was finally called to the bank to be told that they could not meet the situation when I met my overdrafts with more checks and gracious patronage.

Speaking of finances, I find it difficult to believe but many of us girls growing up, who were on allowances, developed a banking system with Mrs. Winthrop Chandler's butler who advanced us enough, not infrequently, to meet our tips on visits, including his own, and often when we ran out of taxi money we would drop in to the Chandler residence on lower Fifth Avenue to be refinanced by Reece.

In that era, in the particular Victorian circle with which I was familiar, no girl went on the streets of New York at any time until she was married except in the company of another girl, maid or governess.

Mammy should be explained. She was with my mother before I was born. She was big, dark, intelligent, high tempered and hideously temperamental. But we belonged to her as completely as she belonged to us and it was she who was always with me. She was afraid of nothing and no one. Once in Paris when we were sketching in the Tuileries, a large crowd of over 50 people gathered around the spectacle of herself and myself. A very impertinent remark was made to me by a young Frenchman who was taking advantage of the crowd to do a ballet in a circle around his gloves and cane which he had laid on the sidewalk.

Mammy drew herself up, entered the ballet arena and in loud and clear tones announced to him: "Je pense que vous ete un fou," at which point a large part of the crowd stayed with us until we reached our hotel on foot.

While Mammy did not take up Latin she learned all the French that I did by sitting through every private lesson and studying incessantly at home, with the happy result that when I finally made my debut, she enjoyed talking fluent French to the multitude of others, who were French and waiting also to take their young ladies home.

Mammy took my mail very seriously, especially my love letters. She opened them before I did, read them and marked them and always explained that when there were 36 pages she knew I would not read them anyway and she did not think it fair to the young men. When I had callers of whom she did not wholly approve (she had her favorites) she would appear in a large white apron and cap and announce firmly that it was time to dress for dinner.

Mrs. Joseph Alsop, daughter of Mrs. Douglas Robinson, niece of Theodore Roosevelt, was fun out of this world but serious and able in spite of an upbringing very like mine in its concentration on the social side as a principal objective. We used to drive together to balls and she used to take Jack London's book with her and read aloud to me because she said she felt we were forgetting the serious side of the human problem. She later became a member of the State Legislature. Her two sons are Joseph and Steward Alsop.

Eleanor Roosevelt I met through her godmother, Mrs. Henry Parrish, with whom she came to live some time after her mother's death. I adored Eleanor from the moment we met, slender, graceful, gorgeous golden hair to her knees, eyes that crinkled with friendship and a certain humor peculiarly her own that all through life has never failed.

KATHERINE DAVIS
Memoir of a Health-Seeker

During the early 1900s, health-seekers traveled from camp to camp in covered wagons the way people do today in recreation vehicles. Katherine Davis, a frail woman with a sick husband, four children and very little money, lived this nomadic life for several years. In her memoir of this extended journey, she tells of her family's stay on the Navajo reservation, of her life in Moriarity, where she assisted her husband with his job of Justice of the Peace, and of her adventures in Albuquerque during a bad flood year. Her open-minded appreciation of the landscape, the native people and their crafts and traditions and the people she met of different nationalities is remarkable, even by the standards of our times. She obviously relished the chance for adventure and downplayed the hardships involved.

This is a simple and readable account written by a woman who "liked to write" but who was not a writer in the sense that she did not expand on her basic responses to her experience. Katherine Davis was one of New Mexico's original tourists. Her unschooled style is the equivalent of naive painting or folk art.

Aside from specifics noted in the journal, we know little of Mrs. Davis. The journal is dated 1900; the big flood she witnessed in Albuquerque occurred in 1902. We know the Davis family had been living in "one of the middle states" before receiving medical advice to come west for Mr. Davis's tuberculosis. They sold everything but their home, which they rented out to finance their trip. Mrs. Davis is a writer one step removed from anonymous—we have at least her name and family background. Her attitude toward her writing, for example, in her omission of documentation, is that of a modest woman, one who, because of her working class status and lack of formal education lacks confidence that anyone would take a serious interest in her account. This attitude is frequently encountered in women today, as when we attempt to record oral histories and are met with women's doubts that they "have anything to say."

Mrs. Davis's daughter, Ermina, who was about five years old when the family began its travels, sent the memoir to the Museum of New Mexico in 1951, the year following Mrs. Davis's death, hoping to fulfill her promise to her mother to help publish the tale.

The real charm of this piece is that it gives us the "ordinary" woman's perspective on the western journey, which, while undertaken by so many, held great discomfort, some danger, and much worry. Mrs. Davis's resourcefulness, open-mindedness and her ability to find delight and beauty in the people and settings she encountered are characteristics that, while contributing to the settling of the West, transcend her time and place.

*T*ime casts a haze over most of our experiences in life, yet there are some incidents that are so deeply imprinted upon the mind that a lifetime cannot erase them. Such are some of our experiences during a few years of travel in a covered wagon out in the west. The parts of the west we were covering were in most instances seldom traveled by white men. We were for some time in the Indian Reservation. We camped at intervals; at some places we remained as long as two months.

Before we began our trip overland, we had lived over a year in the Navajo Reservation. The Navajos are a peaceful tribe naturally and easy to get along with; they are very interesting. Their famous blankets are known far and wide—there are no other like them. They have been copied, but anyone who has lived among the Navajos and has seen the Indians weave them knows a real Navajo blanket the moment they see one. I purchased several fine specimens. There are two grades of these blankets, but more about them later.

This trip was not planned as a pleasure trip, but in the interest of my husband's health. His doctor back home had ordered him to go to New Mexico and try the climate for a while, and then he might try a higher altitude if he felt he needed it. His health began to fail again after we had been there a year or more, and his doctor advised an overland trip to the Rockies.

On the Desert

We purchased a team of mules and a wagon and fixed it up for the trip. We soon came to a desert that took us a week to cross. Our first day brought us to an Indian village where we camped for the night. The Indians were very friendly and some of them came to where we were camped and talked with us. Some of the squaws were weaving a blanket a little way from us. There was a large spring near the village, and they named the place the Indian Springs. Soon after leaving there we came to a sort of table land, and from then on we had nothing but hot sand and dry short grass and sagebrush for almost a week. Not a tree in sight and water only at twenty to thirty miles apart. We had to haul water for ourselves and for the teams; there were six in our party.

The nights were chilly and the days were very hot, and nowhere could we find the friendly shelter from the blazing sun. We usually traveled in the early mornings and evenings, and let the teams rest during the heat of the day. We would get out and stretch ourselves in the shade of the wagon for a little while and eat something and climb back into the wagon. We seldom saw a living creature, and for days it was like that.

At the U.S. Indian Trading Post

Then one day we saw two men on horses coming down the path behind us. There was no road but a sort of bare place that had been used by traders during the summer and by the scattering tribes of Indians that occasionally came along that way. We traveled by direction to reach the point we were headed for the bottom, and peaks along the way were our guides. The two men were going the same way we were. The only houses we saw on the desert were the school for the Indians of the reservation and the U.S. Indian Trading Post. The trading post and school were thirty miles apart. Each was out on the desert in the blazing sun. We only stopped at the school long enough to buy something to eat, but we spent the night at the trading post. They only had their own rooms, but a very roomy, comfortable dugout they let us have for the night. It was furnished with beds or rather cots. We were glad to get any place that was better than sleeping on the ground or crowded up in the wagon. We were taking along everything the team could pull. We had a sewing machine in the wagon, for where there are children there is always sewing to be done, but Mrs. Manny at the trading post had no machine and had to drive to the Indian School to do her sewing, so we let her have our machine and took one of the beautiful Navajo rugs in pay. The rug could not be called a blanket as it was just as much as I could find strength to lift it from the floor of the salesroom. At that, it was not as heavy as the sewing machine. The keepers of the trading post were very glad to have us stop with them. They had only recently been married and came to take the position at the trading post. They came from California and its fruits and flowers to this lonely desert where only seldom any but Indians came. The Indians brought their wares and vegetables, and most of all, their lovely blankets. The U.S. Government found buyers for them (some way). We bade goodbye to our hosts and took up the trail again, but the time we spent was refreshing and we had already put the longer part of the desert behind us. From then on the San Juan (San Wan) River [journey] was less tiresome.

A Stay in a Paradise

At the near side of the river, there were Navajo Indians camped. They were weaving blankets, pulling and twisting the wool of which the heavy blankets are made. The Navajos raise sheep, and of the wool they take from them they pick and clean and then dye some of the white and part of it they leave white. The dye is obtained from rocks and berries. They pull and twist the wool into coarse but smooth threads, but the finer grade of their blankets are made of commercial yarns such as Germantown. It is said that the women of the tribe are the weavers, but I have seen the calluses on the hands of the men where they were made by pressing down firmly the threads as they were woven into the blankets. In fact I bought the blanket from a man whose hands had callused in its making. I bought all of my blankets from men, except one I bought at the trading post. All of them are works of Art. The Navajos are also artists in other lives, as I can attest to, for instance, jewelry. I have seen beautiful rings, charms and many other forms of adornments. They often adorn their jewelry with stones which they seem to know where to find.

A Mormon Village

To return to where we left our party at the camp by the San Juan River, we were happily surprised to see a beautiful land of trees, houses and gardens, a small town whose inhabitants were thrifty Mormons. They permitted us to camp a while just out of town, long enough to rest up from our long and tiresome trip across the hot sandy desert. Our trip had only started, really, and much of the worst was yet to come. I don't mean there was not a great deal of enjoyment and much of great interest all along the way from the first, however, one remembers the most exciting incidents, those more deeply imprinted upon our minds. It is of these I am writing. At the same time I wish to say to all who are interested in travel they should, by all means wander off the beaten path, as we did. Most tourists follow well-known routes and thereby miss much of the natural beauty of the country. We had unlimited time to spare, in fact, that was the reason for the overland and covered wagon mode of reaching the Rockies. It gave my husband the opportunity to get the utmost benefit of the gradual change of climate.

Now, we have resumed our journey up toward Colorado. There was a great difference in the trip as we rode along by the river, very different from the week of the sameness of the desert, sand, sand, sand, hot burning sand. Not one tree, not a bird. Of course there were holes of water at distances of twenty or thirty miles, and there were the cool evenings around the camp fire, after supper, for though the days were clear and burning hot, the nights were cold enough to require blankets. The pleasant time was before sunrise and after the sun went down. Those periods we used to relax and enjoy the respite from the heat of the days.

Strings of Red Peppers and White Adobe Walls

But now the extreme heat was behind us. It was now June, and everywhere there were signs that summer would be upon us soon, and now we were traveling in a part of the country that was new to us yet very interesting, meeting and becoming acquainted with a race of people we had had no opportunity to know, the Mexicans. Let me say in all sincerity I have never known finer people, nor a more hospitable and kindly people. We were as strangers in a foreign land, in fact we were strangers among a race of people we had only learned of from books. Now we were meeting them face to face. It was all so strange. The buildings were mostly adobe, clean inside and out. Often against the white walls on the outside of the dwellings we would see long strings of red pepper, the chili pepper. Usually there would be many of these long strings of peppers hanging out to dry, long bright red strings against a white wall. There was no monotony here, and the unusual and beautiful red sandstone formations, ever changing form and color as we moved along.

On Top of Truchas Mountain

We went up to the top of a mountain, eleven thousand feet above sea level, and think of it! There was an Old Mexican town with its ever present church. It was a quaint little town, and there was a logging camp up there on top of the mountain, a sawmill and houses for the workers. We took one of the houses, and there were vegetables in the garden, but most of them were gone, however, there were peas still blooming. They were not the garden variety, but sweet peas, and lovely.

The children enjoyed this change of surroundings, and the opportunity to climb upon the stacks of lumber at the mill, or climb the young trees, or many other things children do who have been so long cramped in a wagon. It was a dangerous drive up the mountain with only a small margin of ground between us and thousands of feet down below, but before our trip was over, we became used to climbing around mountains. We passed a wall, or rather we passed through it, for there was a road put through that part of the country and it had to cross this wall.

The Strange Stone Wall and Hieroglyphics

The wall was built—or had the appearance of having been built, the rocks were of immense size, and trees had grown in openings in the wall, and there were markings resembling hieroglyphics, and also pictures. These markings were high up on the wall. This strange rock formation ran for a long distance in each direction. The break in the wall was wide enough for a railroad to pass through. The rest of the surrounding country was as I remember not rocky. We stopped there to inspect the strange wall. One thing was certain, it had been there a long, long time, and I would like very much to hear the story of those hieroglyphics, they were so high up on those immense stones, how did those stones get up there? That is an unsolved story. One of the lovely places we stopped to rest was on the top of a mountain—a mesa, as they call them out that way, a table land of tall straight pines. As we reached the top of the mesa we passed a few houses with white painted fronts, and after we had prepared to get our dinners, a man came to us with goat cheese. It was very good, and was the first and last goat cheese I have ever seen. After finishing our dinners, we moved on. We stopped at Durango and made camp for a day or two, out of the city, but near. It was now July, and Colorado was lovely. It was Springtime in the Rockies. At that time of the year Colorado is delightful, the roads in the valley were lined with wild roses, and the rivers were cold, and it was good drinking water.

In Quick Sand

We wandered around and stopped a while at different places. Once while crossing a river we started to sink down in quick sand while the mules had stopped to drink. Fortunately, my husband noticed the mule trying to start the wagon. He got out of the wagon and carried us all to the shore of the river, then hurried to get the mules and wagon out. The mules surged and finally got out, with the shouts and urgings of a whip. Poor animals, the water was shallow, and if one moves fast it is possible to cross alright. As it happened, we were near the edge of the water after crossing to the far side. We would have been alright if the team had not stopped to drink, but if we had not been near the side of the river, no one would have ever known what had become of us. There were not people living near enough to hear our cries.

We spent a week at Santa Fe, N.M. Nothing important happened until a circus rolled into town, but we visited several places, including the ancient church. However, I am diverging from my story of the west as we saw it.

Lost in the Rain

After a few weeks in Colorado, we found a good place to camp, except the water was down below us about a quarter of a mile. We stayed there over a month. There had been a sawmill camp there, but they had moved about everything to another site. We were fortunate enough to find a cabin all clean and with bunks and old chairs, a table, an old stove and shelves, and with our bedding, dishes and cooking vessels we managed fine. Here an incident happened that I think I shall always remember as one of the most frightening I ever experienced. Some men [were] living near and my husband had been cutting some timber for a railroad that was to come through there. They were over on the side of a mountain some distance from our cabin. There was a valley in between, not a wide one however. My husband didn't come home at noon along with the other men and the two oldest children had been carrying his dinner to him, but this day they were to be working farther around the mountain and the children were afraid to go for there had been a mountain Lion heard in the neighborhood.

Lost on a Mountain

So I went taking the youngest with me to show me the place they had been going to before. I thought we could find them by the sound of their axes chopping, but if they had been chopping we couldn't have heard them, for a sudden thunder storm had come up since we had left the cabin. It was the season of the year when it rained at noon. Everyday we listened for the sound of the axes, but the thunder and rain drowned any sound we might have heard. We wandered around in the storm til we were nearly exhausted. There we saw a large bull coming toward us. We could not run nor climb a tree, what would we do? The rain was coming down in torrents and the thunder and lightning all together were almost driving us frantic, then, the bull! He stopped just a little way from us, stared at us, then turned in another direction and about that time we heard a noise that we thought was a panther's scream. We were lost, and not knowing which way to go, we started toward the valley we had crossed. We couldn't see it, but it was down and if we got to it we would be safer if there were a panther or a mountain lion following us. The sounds came nearer and almost ready to drop from fright and exhaustion, we stumbled along as the sound came nearer.

A Mountain Lion Pays us a Visit

We could hear it plainer—it was my husband calling us. He was hunting for us. He had waited, and decided to go home, then when he found we were out on the mountain he came to look for us.

Our stay there was interesting in many ways. The cabin was on the side of a mountain facing the one we were lost on, and out of sight of any of the few remaining families of the camp and very wild. We were pretty close to stark nature. We had two glassless windows. The ground squirrels came in at both the windows and the door. They got into everything they could, even drank out of the bucket of water when they found it uncovered. They were beautiful little creatures and were not afraid of our dog, Navajo. Navajo followed us from the Navajo camp beside the San Juan River. We didn't notice him until we were too far to send him back. He had swum the river after us and stuck with us til we got to Albuquerque late in the fall.

The little ground squirrels were not the only visitors we had from the animal world. Perhaps these animals were hungry. One night while we were deep in sleep the night air was pierced with a scream from a mountain lion! Navajo was barking from under the house. He must have halted the beast. . . .

At Moriarity

We camped along as we had on our trip north, sometimes for weeks before taking to the road again. We came to a small railroad town that we thought we would like to stop at for the mules to rest up and graze on the tall grass. Moriarity was a small railroad town made up of a mixed population. Colored people were not often found. There were a few at one place, a mining town where we lived for a year or more while my husband was appointed Justice of the Peace to fill out the term of a Justice who had died before his term expired. We found a two room adobe house, but we had to let the Superintendent and his family have one. Our stay there was not a very happy one.

We Now Lose Our Mules

We had a small flood that came almost to our door and kept us in until the water receded. It happened when a heavy downpour filled the bog in the prairie and washed out a part of the tracks of the rail board. It wasn't long, however, until the water had drained off. We lost our mules while we were at Moriarity. We were never sure what became of them, we had always turned them loose to eat all the grass they wanted, but here we had fastened them together to keep them from becoming separated from each other. Since they had always come to get water and feed, we were not worried about them. But one afternoon two Mexicans came looking for some burros. That day our mules didn't show up. The whole neighborhood was searched but we never saw them again. Perhaps the band of thieves who had a hideout in some mountains some miles away, known as Chillie. . . . Those desperadoes had long preyed on the cattle and horses of the people of the community, stealing cattle and then butchering them and bringing in the meat and selling it to those they stole it from. They were so well entrenched that the officers got little chance to catch up with them. Perhaps they are gone from there by this time, at any rate, we never heard from our mules again.

From there we went to Albuquerque. We arrived in Albuquerque in late autumn and in the following spring returned to the small town we had lived in before. My husband was much improved, and so we stayed on for a while until he had to have another climate.

In the Courtroom

While we lived out in the west, my husband was appointed Justice of the Peace, as he was employed at the mines during the daytime. We fixed up a room we could easily spare, and there he held court of evenings. There was no building especially for holding court, so we arranged for using our spare room. This meant I would be kept very busy, with the children all small, they required more attention. We got along alright. Some of the people were Indians, some Italians, some Japanese and other nationalities I didn't know. All had to come to court on some offense or another. Some of the cases called for fines; for small infractions that only called for reprimands. None of the cases were of a too serious nature. Of course a few were federal court cases that had to go to a higher court. My job was to make out copies to be sent to the other higher courts in the state and to make records of the cases, also to make out complaints and warrants for the sheriff. All the writing fell to me. He, as I said, was employed during the day and of course he had no time to take care of all the writing. I liked to do it, and as there was not enough cases to require a great deal of it, I got along alright.

The cases were sometimes humorous and sometimes the oppposite. No doubt the inability to understand the offended because of his nationality, for sometimes two and three different nationalities were on trial in the same case. One night we had two Indian brothers. One was named Thomas Thomas, the other was Five Cent Thomas. They had been brought in on a charge of drunkeness. You see, the Indians were wards of Uncle Sam, and anyone giving or selling intoxicating liquor committed a federal offense. The Thomases were witnesses against the one selling them liquor. There were a lot of those cases. The Sheriff was from Kentucky and so was the Justice of the Peace, and from the same part of the state. They had never met before. It was a queer crowd sometimes, with different languages and interpreters. It's likely that sometimes truth may have been on the scaffold, and errors on the throne, however, I hope not.

Children are children the world over, and nationalities make little difference where games are concerned. The children of the foreign population were learning English very fast. Our daughter had no sister to play with, but she and a little Italian girl named Mary became pals. They got along fine. The difference in nationalities seemed to make no difference whatever.

Indians Come to See us

The Navajos were trustworthy and honest too, as we learned while living on the Reservation. When we first went out to New Mexico, we lived in a place where there were many Indians. We didn't know what to think when on the first night we spent in the place, Indians came and stood in our rooms. We naturally were frightened, but we weren't used to having strangers open our doors and walk in, but they were hungry, for they went to the cans beside the homes where bread and cabbage or other waste vegetables were put and gathered food to take home. I watched them and then I learned why they stood by the doors and looked in. Now these were a class that were unable to get work and not a sample of the tribe in general. I have seen enough of the Indians to realize all they need is an opportunity. . . .

The blue skies on New Mexico are the bluest I ever saw. They are so free from clouds and the bright moonlit nights! The moon really does shine bright in New Mexico, while crossing the desert, as I told you, we traveled by the peaks of mountains, as that was the way we knew how to find the direction. Our wanderings took us through out of the way places, some of which at that time were not on the map, for there were no highways in the places we toured. I mention a few: Astee, Cedar Hill, Farmington, Tierra Amarillo (Yellow Earth), Tres Piedras (Three Rocks), El Rito, Ojo Caliente (Hot Eye), Abiquiu, Espanola, Santa Cruz, and many others. There were spots of scenic beauty beyond description. We drove along a road which gave us a panoramic of Manzano Mountains and if an artist could have painted it as we saw it, no one would have believed he had painted it as it looked to him. Those lovely colors we saw looked like large daubs of bright paint spread out in artistic design.

A Beautiful Picture in a River

At one place we stopped, there was a river nearby, and beyond the river lay a mountain of beautiful colors, and beyond and above it a background of purest cobalt, all mirrored in the still waters of the river, the most beautiful painting! It was painted by Nature. Just imagine a full moon just coming over the mountain. I had gone down to the river to get some water. I wished for some paints and canvas.

There were many such beautiful sights. If only I had packed some crayons or something to make stetches! But there were too many other more important things to think about. . . .

By the Rio Grande

After we lost our mules, our covered wagon trip ended. We had to go
by train from then on. From Moriarity we went to Albuquerque. It lies
beside the Rio Grande River. It was then a pleasant little city with mild
climate. The children and I had to spend the winter there, for my husband
had to go back to the mine where he had been employed before. He
thought it best to leave us in Albuquerque until Spring. That was the first
time we had lived near the Rio Grande. It is a river that like many others
in the west changes its course. I was in a store on the opposite side of
town from the river's present course. Two men were talking about the
river, the storekeeper said, when I first came here that street out there was
the river bed.

The river at that time was the subject of much discussion, as it was
rising and threatening to flood the city. The fear of everyone in the city
proper was that the dikes would give way. As the river came nearer to
our door, we began packing and moving to a safer place, even in the
highlands, where we had moved we still worried about the dikes breaking.
I was afraid to go to sleep, for the children and I were alone, but if the
dikes were to begin to give way, the whistles would start blowing all over
the city. We stayed on until spring when my husband came down to take
us back with him. In Albuquerque, flowers and fruit trees were blooming. . . .

I doubt if these experiences could happen again to anyone. We camped
two weeks at Santa Fe, a winter in Albuquerque, and intervals at many
other points both east and west of the Great Divide, two years in the
Navajo Indian Reservation. Taken together, all things considered, the trip
was not a waste of time, for there were many pleasant hours to balance
the strange and often dangerous experiences. Then there was the ever-pre-
sent anxiety over my husband's health, which often became such that he
was unable to continue until he took a few weeks' rest. As I look back
over those anxious years of travel in strange and out of the way places,
off the beaten path with a sick husband and four children and a small
income from our home in the east that barely kept us in the necessities of
life—and often that was delayed in reaching us—and what with lying
under a tent made of a tarpulin, the rain seeping in and under us as we
tried to sleep, and at other times the yelping of coyotes around our camp
at night, it is almost a miracle that we came through as well as we did.

FRANCES BEEBE
I Never Was a Person To Get Lonely

Frances Beebe, an early settler of Roosevelt County, New Mexico, originally came to the Portales area to homestead with her family from Texas. Her oral history, recorded by Mary Jo Walker of the Golden Library, Eastern New Mexico University in 1981 when Mrs. Beebe was 91 years old, introduces a woman who possesses the traditional virtues we expect of a proud pioneer homesteader—common sense, determination, industriousness, pragmatism, and natural courage. Yet Frances Beebe's story is distinguished from other tales of hardship on the eastern plains by her sense of fun. She refuses to see life as a difficult, bitter struggle for survival. Rather, her perception, which informs her life story, is that life is an arena for exercising her talents and personality. She refuses to accept limitations, or even to acknowledge difficult situations have any power whatsoever to stand in her way. Neither is hers a stance of false bravado. She is simply a rare individual with a constant readiness to plunge into life, to hold back nothing, and to see no reason why life shouldn't treat her well.

As of this writing, Frances Graves Beebe is 98 years old and living in Corpus Christi, Texas. She wrote me recently: "Fly down some day and if the water is warm enough, we will put on our bathing suits and show the spectators what real women look like!!"

*M*y father was William Pickett Graves and my mother was Sam Houston Ross. And they grew up in Texas in the early days shortly after Texas became a state. They were born and reared in Colorado County, Texas. Austin colony was built on my great-grandfather's land that the Mexican government had given him as a grant. Way back before the Mexican War, they were having trouble with Texas.

Sam Houston was a great friend of my grandfather, and he named my mother. She was supposed to have been a boy, but she was a girl, and they named her Sam Houston Ross, and she always went by that name. My parents married in December 1878 near La Grange at Ross's prairie, Fayette County, Texas. I was born soon after they moved down to Wilson County in a little village they called Pleasant Valley on the tenth day of September, 1889. My father was postmaster and ran a general country store. He kept books for three places; for the gin, and when the cotton was all ginned and ready to be sold, he went with the farmers to San Antonio to sell their cotton. In those days there were very few people that had much of an education. He was seven years old when the war broke out. His father was a civil engineer and his mother had been a teacher and he had a very good education by the time he was twelve years old. He was good in math of any kind and later he got to be a civil engineer and a surveyor. That was about all they had to do in those days, things like damming up rivers and building big places to supply water. There were rivers running in every direction, the water was out of control.

I started to school when I was eight years old; my mother and father taught us at home before then. My mother would teach us spelling lessons and geography and father had math and grammar. We had to come up with our lessons. There were nine children in the family, and I was the fifth one. My parents were both musically inclined. They taught us music, and we always had just a ball at home. If we had anything going on, everybody would gather at our house because we had music and fun. We had an old-time piano and later we finally began to get stringed instruments.

Well after the others married, my mother's health began to get bad, and it seemed like I didn't have the time to spare from music, between my time at school and my other jobs. I went to work for the newspaper people and helped the others with their music education. And I helped them through school.

I went to work for the newspaper. It wasn't easy in those days to get a job of it. Nothing to do. People had offices and they sometimes gave their children jobs in them. The same way with working in the bank. The banker would have either a son or daughter that would come in and learn the banking business. And I found that newspaper work was the only thing I could find. I worked for four dollars a week. I went to work for the *Robert Lee Observer*.

I was about sixteen or seventeen. We moved to Coke County in 1904, and my father went to work in the bank there. My mother's health was real bad and by the time I would get the housework done. . . . I didn't get to go to school regularly, but I kept up my math and grammar. My father saw that I kept up with that. And when I went to work, I worked a few weeks in the bank, but the banker had a daughter that was ready to take over, so I just went right on across the street to the newspaper office. I don't know why I thought I would get a job there, but they gave me a job.

I told them what my situation was. It was 1907 and that was the year of the money panic. Very few people know anything about the money panic. We had a depression then, worse than anything that we have had since. All of the banks failed and there wasn't anything for people to do. Just everything stopped. So I just walked over to this office and asked them. I wanted to look around and see if they needed an apprentice, and they said that they did. And they took me and it wasn't any time until I felt right at home with that.

In those days you had to set all the type by hand. They had big cases with all the letters in those cases, called a stick, in a seven column newspaper. They had to have seven of those. They had galleys that we would set the type for. We would get it all set up and then we would put it on a big slab of marble with an iron frame around it and lock it in. Then we took the impressions of it and read the proof to get all of the mistakes out of it.

I worked there for about two years and the editor said, "Now you have advanced to the stage where you could go anywhere and you could draw twice the salary you are getting here," and he advised me to investigate.

We worked from 8 o'clock to six, six days a week. It was the only paper in the county. We printed all the school catalogs, and the chamber of commerce things, and the *Old Soldiers Review* and *Confederate Union*. And all of that was set by hand and made into book forms. Times like that if we had a deadline and we thought that we were not going to get finished by the deadline, sometimes we would work until 11 o'clock at night, no overtime either—just something that had to be done.

In 1910 I went to Lubbock and went to work there. I like to never got there. It was the first time I had ever been away from home. Everywhere I went, everywhere I had to stop, everyone was so friendly and nice that

I didn't worry. To make a long story short, after I bought my ticket from Lamesa to Lubbock, I had 25 cents left in my purse. . . .

And so I went to the newspaper office and I introduced myself. And the editor said that he had been looking for me on almost every train coming in. He took me around and we went back to meet the crew. He said, "Now the last girl that worked here, the boys ran her off." He said they teased her and tormented her so much that she quit. I thought, "Well, my goodness, what kind of group am I getting into?" But I went in and I don't think I ever met nicer people. . . . The editor and his wife were very nice. They would come and take me to church every Sunday morning and try to see that I met the right people. Our advertising manager decided that El Paso would be a better opening for him, and I took up his work and did my work at the same salary. They didn't raise my salary. I felt that I was discriminated against. But it was the finest thing that ever happened to me, because I learned things there after he left that I wouldn't have learned. So when I left there and went to Winters, Texas—it was closer to where my parents lived—I doubled my salary because I would take care of the machines, and I could do anything that anybody could do in the office, you know. I did everything except the editorials. I would pick up the daily papers and get my ideas from them. It was an education and I was determined to get all of it.

By 1912, my parents had moved to New Mexico and homesteaded out here. It was in Roosevelt County and it went on into Chaves County. Later they put it all in Roosevelt County. I joined this wagon train in San Angelo and I think it was twelve days from the time we left San Angelo until we got to Eagle Hill. The only person we saw, from the time we left Big Springs until we got 18 miles south of here was a sheepherder way off herding sheep.

We took three wagons, and one of those old-time Spalding Hacks that four or five people could ride in. They had the beds of the wagons fixed so that you could put two beds end to end on them. Most of this was along in September and it was getting cool by this time. Most everybody slept in under those places with wagon sheets and everything. They had the chuck boxes, you know, and the big barrels on each side to hold water for drinking purposes. They had a big, what they called "grub box" on the back of the wagon. They would put the lid down and there was a big work table with all of your provisions above. Everyone had that. They all cooked by the campfire and everybody ate together. My brother-in-law was the only man in the bunch.

There were two families and I was considered to be the third family.

But each family had three children apiece. All of those kids had saddle horses. How in the world his man kept up with all these teams and saddle horses—he certainly had the patience of Job, you might say. . . . I had two half sections across the section line from my parents' and my brother's land. My brother-in-law and sister went over about two sections away and settled down.

I was 24 years old. If you were married, why, one of you had to give up that homestead. But I didn't marry until 1916. By that time they had passed a law that a man and woman that married, they could both keep their homestead. It was either seven months or five months out of each year for three years. [to prove your claim] And at the end of these months I would always go back to Texas and work. I always had a job waiting for me. I would go and work until time for me to go back to the homestead. . . . Well, they thought I was very ambitious!. . . . Go west young woman! It was quite an experience. Some would disagree bitterly with me. Some of them just thought they were going to starve to death. But I don't know, people who knew how to manage had their chickens and cows and hogs and a beef to butcher. Some of them say that they remember going hungry, that they just lived on cornmeal and mush or something like that. But I think very few people had to live that way.

The law was that you had to put in 40 acres of cultivation for every 60 acres. But some way I got by for two or three years before I married without putting anything in much, without plowing anything. But most people had to. When I was there in August, it had a lot of rain and the grass, the gramma grass, was *that* high. And you couldn't find a place where they didn't homestead. Everybody put out shade trees and fruit trees, you know.

Some men dug an eight by ten for me. And they covered it with sheet iron and put dirt on top of that. It was about five feet deep, I guess, and then the roof came up like a regular roof to a house. The stairs went down into the dugout and the door fell over like that. I had a little two burner stove to burn oil.

I wasn't a teacher. The teachers got $30 a month and they had to live with any family they could live with, you know. Some of them had to sleep with two or three children. But they only taught four months. . . . Some of them didn't stay long enough to live their homestead out. Some did, and then sold it. We bought the ones adjoining us. Finally we wound up with a nice little body of land down there.

My husband-to-be lived down in the next township, and the people did the same way there. About the time they lived to prove up on it, all they

Frances Beebe, left, with friends, about 1909. *Frances Beebe*.

A farm near Clovis, New Mexico, about 1905. *Courtesy Museum of New Mexico, Neg. No. 5077.*

Corn and melons, Quay County, New Mexico. *Courtesy Museum of New Mexico, Neg. No. 58023.*

wanted was enough money to get out of New Mexico and go back to
Oklahoma, Texas, or wherever they came from. I think we paid $5 an
acre or $1600 total. But some of them would settle for a good team or
horses and wagon and a few dollars, enough to get them out of the state.

They didn't have any way of making a living. Some of them came in
here and built nice little shacks, you know, instead of building a dugout
and living in that, and taking the money and buying a milk cow or some
hogs or some chickens. They never thought about what they were going
to live on, and they spent what few dollars they had on the improvements,
a house to live in. They couldn't live in a dugout like the rest of us did.
And there was no way they could raise big enough crops of corn and
maize. It was 30 miles to market, and hardly worth. . . .

I had a little oil stove and I had somebody make me a little table, and
I had a comfortable bed. It was an old iron bedstead, and good springs
and a mattress. My mother and father divided that with me. I was lucky.

I never was a person to get lonely. Of course I missed some things. We
didn't have any church. But we were lucky. Most of the people that moved
in there were retired teachers or retired doctors. Some people were musicians and we were just real lucky. They were all people that wanted to
provide the best they could for their children, do the best that they could
for them.

I got here on about the 10th of September, and about a month after
that, there were so many people. The only way they had to make any
money at all to carry them over the year was to go to Roswell and work
in the apple harvest, or go to Texas and pick cotton. So many of them
would go to Roswell to get a wagon load of apples so they could bring
them back to can, and to divide with the neighbors. My parents were
going down there after a load of apples, and I went with them. The ladies
were all there working, and they were dressed up just like they were going
to church. You had to wear gloves to keep from bruising the apples. So
I thought, I will just stay here and work, and they paid well. It was a part
of my vacation. I had some friends that were camped there, so we camped
together. I worked there until the apple harvest was over. I learned to peel
apples. . . .

When I went back to Winters, Texas, the last time, I had a very good
friend, a sweetheart. And we had agreed that I was to come back and
marry at Christmas time. But I don't know. I had been gone six to eight
months. I had changed and he had changed. And that day that I had
landed into Clovis coming from Winters, well, that was the day that the
Germans had declared war. We knew sooner or later that the United States

would be involved and all the young men would be drafted. I thought it would be a very foolish thing to think about marriage under conditions like that. He agreed with me. He was a farmer down in that part of the country. It was agreed that if he saw someone that he thought more of than me, why then that was his privilege. He gave me the same privilege. All this time I couldn't stop thinking about this cowboy back in New Mexico. I liked his looks and his attitude. When I left there on the 29th of January, I was so glad when I got across the New Mexico line. I never did feel the least bit guilty.

When I came back, I had to make preparations for the year. Henry would always come every Sunday afternoon if he wasn't working, moving cattle or seeing about a water well or something. We would go to the singings around the community. At the time, he had a nice little herd of cattle. We both had the same birthday, and the same age. September 10, 1889. But he always contended that he must have been born a few minutes before I—so that he could be boss. I don't think that ever made any difference. I never felt like I was bossed around.

There was a little girl that lived down in the community, between us, about five miles from Elida. We would always take her with us wherever we went. We were driving across my 320, and we were always joking, and he just made the remark that he would sure like to have this 320. I told him, I said, "Well, the only way a person is going to get it, is any man that comes along with a marriage certificate in one hand and a preacher in the other, that is the one that is going to get it." He said, "Well, you certainly know how to drive a hard bargain." This little girl was so embarrassed, the first house we got to she got out. We asked her what was the matter. She said, "I can't afford to ride around with them," she said, "they are too fast."

Once we were going home from a singing, and he stopped very suddenly and he said. . . . "I would just like to know how I rate with you, anyway." And I looked at him and I said, "Do you honestly want to know what I think about you?" and he said, "Let me have it." I said, "Well, this is it. Do you remember the afternoon you came over and asked me to go to the party with you when I was on my way back to Texas? You knocked me off the Christmas tree then, and I have never got back on." He said, "That is all I wanted to know." And from then on we began to plan to be married. . . .

We stayed down there on our land about twelve or thirteen years before we moved up here to Portales. But all three of my children were born down there. Now when Graham was around four-and-a-half years old,

Henry came in one day and said, "Do you know what I would like to have?" I didn't have any idea—"a million dollars, I suppose." He said, "I want a little curly-headed girl." And I said, "Well, I'll do the best I can." So then we made plans for a little girl, and sure enough it was. . . .

All three of the children graduated from Portales High School. Then the Depression hit. We lived through the winter panic of 1907, and then that came along. It wasn't anything new at all. People in those days lived according to their means. "Easy credit" wasn't so easy in those days. The ones that didn't owe anything, and had a little something to go on, made it through all right. . . .

I got a very nice man. I can't remember ever getting angry at him about anything. If he ever was angry at me, I never knew it. He always had the idea nobody could do anything like I did, and there wasn't a man that could do things like he could do. He had a lot of friends. He was a person who had a lot of fun about him, but he had a serious. . . . He would never say anything about what anybody else should do. . . .

Since I was a child, life has been one adventure after another. Everything has always been wonderful to me. I can't see anything in my life that, if I could do it over, that I'd do it differently. Maybe I am simple minded and didn't realize anything better. Anyway, I'm glad I'm simple minded.

My attitude, the one I grew up with, is you're not expecting life to be a bed of roses. That's been my attitude always. . . . I know no one owes me anything, but I owe everybody a great deal that I'll never be able to pay.

BEATRICE NOGARE
Life in the Southern Colorado Coal Mining Camps

The story of Beatrice Nogare, daughter of an Italian immigrant mining family of southern Colorado, tells poignantly of the power of social and economic forces over an individual's life. The brutal realities of life in the coal mines, the ongoing violence punctuated by strikes equivalent to warfare, and the aftermath of poverty, illness, and despair were enough destiny for any woman, and completely determined the course of Beatrice's life. In a stoic, matter-of-fact way, she describes the murderous working conditions that maimed and killed the men of her family, and how she spent most of her life as a caretaker, nursing them.

In her oral history, Beatrice leaves a record of what life was like for women in the mining districts of southern Colorado during the early twentieth century; it is a personal response to the conditions that led to larger historical events of her era, such as the Ludlow Massacre of 1914.

In 1912, the time of Beatrice's account, the number of miners accidentally killed in Colorado per million tons of coal was double the national average. Miners and their families, largely an immigrant population of whom only thirty percent spoke English, had to live in company houses, buy at company stores with company-issued scrip and accept company-run schools. Towns like Walsenberg and Trinidad were virtually governed by CF&I (Colorado Fuel & Iron), controled by John D. Rockefeller, Jr., through a forty percent ownership interest. The miners lived in a feudal conditions.

In the 1913 strike to which Beatrice refers, nine thousand miners struck, rallied by Mother Jones, for the implementation of many demands already passed into law but ignored. Serious violence followed, with a build up of militia in Ludlow. The previous two decades had been filled with confrontation bordering on open warfare in the mining districts of Cripple Creek, Telluride, and Leadville and the mills of Colorado City, two decades in which miners resorted to rifles, torches and dynamite and owners retaliated with Pinkertons, paid armies, militia, and National Guardsmen. On April 20, 1914, the militia at Ludlow rioted, opening machine gun fire on the tents of miners and their families, triggering ten days of rebellion throughout Colorado and actually putting the entire nation on the brink of revolution. Miners seized Trinidad, and while the United Mine Workers considered calling out every union miner in the United States to Ludlow, the nation was shocked by the atrocities committed there, particularly the reports of mothers' and children's charred remains found in the "Black Hole of Ludlow." A crowd of five thousand gathered in Denver to denounce Rockefeller, and President Woodrow Wilson's mediators worked to find a solution as the strike dragged into the summer of 1914.

The 1927 Wobbly strike to which Beatrice refers could have been a walk-out called by the IWW in August, in which half of Colorado's twelve thousand miners protested the execution of Sacco and Vanzetti, but, more likely, she is referring to the October 1927 IWW strike which lasted through February 1928, which, for all the violence of vigilantes, police, and National Guard who shot and beat miners, resulted in only a $1.00 a day wage increase.

This account is part of the Huerfano County Ethno-History Project housed in the Pueblo Library District.

*I*t was hard in the mining camps to live. Course, they went to the mines and they didn't get very much pay. They had to come out on strike to have them raise the pay. Then we had to buy everything at the store, at the company store. And in some places, like Trinidad, right here when I came to this part of the country, I came from Italy when I was 21 months old, but I don't remember then. My daddy came in 1906 here and he went to the Maitland Mine, that was his first one. Then he went to McNough and to Camaron. And from there we went down to Trinidad. Now that's down by Bone. From there the mine, they closed it down, and my daddy got a job at Sofield. That's just about a mile from one camp to the other. Of course, there at Bone they had the train station there. Well, anyway, we went to Sofield, I think in 1912 and in 1913 there was a strike, so we had to go down into tents. They were about a mile from Sofield and we lived there. I don't remember exactly how much we lived, but my brother was born in 1913 and he was only one month old when we brought him under the tent. Let's see, that's in April, he was a month old, and my daddy didn't get another job until he was 26 months. We were out 26 months without pay, no nothing. The union gave us a little bit, $5 a month, but it wasn't enough. We finally got the same superintendent who was there in Sofield, and he was a good man, and he tried to get my daddy work again but the shift was about $1.50 and that was all right, if they had the props and rails when they went in. But who was first in the line got there and needed the rails, they took it, and the props and the one on the end of the line, he didn't have the rails and props he needed and they had to come home. No shift.

We had to buy everything at the store. The pay was only scrip money, like the stamps that they give here now, they were just a little different, you know, but they purchased stuff at the store. You couldn't go to Trinidad to buy anything. You had to buy everything at the store, with your scrips, at the company store. You probably heard of that song, "Sixteen Tons," it was just like that. If anybody would go down to Trinidad and buy something in Trinidad, then when they'd come home if the superintendent found out, next morning they would have their check typed. They would have to move away from there, no more work. That was pretty tough.

What the 1913 strike won was all this freedom. They had to pay money and not scrips and could go where they want to buy their stuff. That's what they won, and then they raised their pay up.

The safety conditions, they didn't change them right away. When they won more was the 1922 strike. Now we were here in 1922, at Gordon Mine. That's what brought up the higher wages, I think, it was $7 a day then, and they got these safety rules and then the men didn't get killed like they did before.

I got a brother that worked at the Del Carbon. I just forget how old he was. He's in California. And the whole top came down on him. And we never expected him to live. He got a big lump on the back of his spine and the doctor's don't dare to operate on him or it would kill him. They paid him for a dead man. He got a little insurance. They didn't have any insurance before 1913. No insurance. They get killed, they take them out in the night and just bury them without even the family knowing, at that time.

You know where Ludlow is? You just go west from there. There was Hastings and Delow. My dad worked in both mines. Let's see Hastings, in 1918 or 1919. I can't remember when the explosion was there that killed many people. I was so young then. I was just seven years old in 1913. I can't remember all of it. but some way or other, my dad he moved away from there. I don't know the reason, he moved away just in time. Otherwise he would have been in there, too. There was over a hundred people killed in that explosion.

In Delow we went down in 1919 to see, my dad didn't want to be a scab. You know, he didn't want to work during the strike, the strike of 1919, so my dad went to California, he had friends down there, and my dad knew how to weld, so we went to California, for $5 a day, not $5 an hour like now. Well, my mother got sick. She went down from here and she was going through a change, so the doctor, they couldn't do anything for her. The doctor says to come back here, up here, for the air, a little higher, that would make a difference. When she came back she got well.

So we went down there in 1919, and I went to school, 13 months there in San Francisco. That was then I was about 13 years old. Then we came back to . . . Durango, we went to Durango, instead of going to Trinidad. My dad worked in the mine, they called it Camp Perspeak. He was out there for a couuple years. Then that slacked, they'd lay them off. So he had to look for another job. So he came back here to Walsenburg. That I can remember better because I was older. We packed all our things. We packed everything, you know, we shipped our furniture, we got all of our things and we got here to Walsenburg and there was nobody we knew.

We were four children, I was the oldest, and my dad and my mother, and we started walking from Walsenburg. When we got off the train and we came here, because my daddy knew the road and we walked up to Gordon. I can't remember how we got to know this man that worked there, he was Italian, too. So he told my dad, I think, another man told my dad to go down to this man. I think, that's the way, so my dad went and we all wanted jobs, see. So this man, I remember, they gave up supper, and we didn't have no place to go, we didn't know where to go without much money, you know. So they put us up and the next day they went out to the mines to the superintendent and dad got work there. So my dad stayed there until I got married, in 1926. My dad moved up to Big Turner and he worked until he retired. Then he passed away. He had asthma of the mines, so he just passed away. At that time they didn't even think about black lung, the way it is now. Never heard of it. But the asthma, yes. It may be possible it is the same thing. Could be the bad air or dust in the mine that causes the black lung.

After that my brothers worked in the mine. My brother passed away in 1974, he had black lungs. He was in Pueblo, a custodian, after that, but he worked in the mines. He started at 16 years old, he graduated from school and worked in the mine instead. That's how they used to do. He worked up to 1950 and they closed the mine. They closed them up, otherwise he would have died, but they closed the mine and he got a job up at Lakeview school in Pueblo from '50 to '74. We, he was a retirer. In about a year they found him dead. See, I took care of him, you see, I had a son in Farmington, my own son he got cancer. And so I had to go up there. Because he always wanted me to go up there, and I knew I wouldn't see him very much longer.

So I went up there eight times, when he was operated for tumor, it traveled, that tumor, cancer of the rectum then. From there it moved to the lungs, both lungs, and to the brain, and there was no way of removing it. Finally it moved to the bladder and the doctors didn't want to operate any more. It was terminal and he died. He didn't know he had it. The sister-in-law didn't want me to tell him, but it was better to tell him, cause I like to know what I have and that's the way he was. He always asked, "Why am I like this?" And I couldn't say cause if I did she'd get mad and I didn't want to make any trouble. So, anyway, he died. First my brother and then my son. So I had to care for both of them and I couldn't be with them steady.

Well, my husband got cancer in '77 . . . . Well, my life was a terrible one. A hard time, boy, I tell you I have. He was a miner. He came in 1922 from Italy, and he came from Venice, on the outskirts, and they call that place Skio, where he was born and raised. And he went down to World War I and in 1922 he came over. I met him in 1925 here in Gordon. He went to Pryor and Rouse mines. I think Rouse was where he started. And then down there, well, the mine was slacking down and they laid him off, and he came up here to Gordon. He worked there til the Depression. Then he brought this home and we moved down there, cause, there was no work in Gordon, at that time. In the depression there was no work nowhere. You were lucky if you had a job, but they didn't hire. My brothers were working and my dad, all three of them worked at Gordon, but my husband worked at Morning Glory and that mine was closed down.

So we decided, course, we didn't pay no cash, we just paid as we could pay. He was out almost a year. He was on WPA and we got $32, we were four. Then another man that was working at Big Four, I told him, my husband, why don't you ask this man, he was very nice, maybe he will help you out, cause they always have to get somebody a job like that and he did ask him and he got this, so this is the way my husband quit the mining. My husband, he nearly got killed and out of that he didn't want to go to the mines no more. He tried it, but he didn't succeed. He's still alive. He's not feeling so good but he's still alive.

. . . Then we had the Wobbly strike of 1927. But it was a Wobbly strike. We didn't gain anything then. We had a lot of little strikes every so often, until our wages got up high, now they are way up high. Before the 1913 strike they made about $1.50 a day, if you could work.

All three of my brothers worked in the mine. One, the first time he started , he was working on the tipple, next to the mine, and tipple burned down one day. I was already married then in July and this happened in September. The Tipple burned down and I had six boarders. They were so scarce. And one of the boarders there was kind of off. He got injured down in the mine back east somewhere. He had a car, and he asked my brother to go hunting. My brother loved to go hunting. And so my mother sends him down, says, "Go down to your sister and see if she will give you a dollar for the shells," you know. I told him, I said, "Joe," I says, "you ask me anything else?" I said, just like I knew something was going to happen.

He went out to the Buttes to this lake, you know? It's near Pueblo. With this man. And they shot the ducks and my brother was going to go into get them. He was a good swimmer. And that's why I have always said that something happened to him because I know he was a good swimmer. I couldn't see how he could drown. It was an argument, I guess, like that. The other man said it was him that shot the ducks down and my brother knew that it was him. So he was going to try to go in to get them. You know the big BVDs they call them, underwear, well, he had these BVDs on and he had his shoes on. He didn't have the time to take those off to go in. I know that he would take his clothes off because he was a good swimmer and I told them a long time, I said, I think, something happened. It was the truth. Somebody saw them. And he throwed him in. And he throwed him in there and then he came home and said that he drowned. And my mother came down and they hadn't found him. My eyes were red and she thought I'd been quarreling with my husband and said, "Well, I can walk down tomorrow and find out," she said. Me, I was trying not to cry, you know, show her that anything happened, cause I knowed, she got sick again, course we didn't have the money to get her to the doctor. The mine wasn't working too good at the time. They had the funeral in September and he was only 17 years old. Well, down at Morning Glory, as you go off the water gully there's a little hill you have to pass in order to go over to Morning Glory. That's where this man got killed. Somebody killed him. I assumed that somebody killed him. Because he was mean to people, see. That's what happened cause we never found out anything else. His brother was in the old country. I think the county buried him.

And my mother, you know, she was a good singer, and you know, she never sang no more. It was like she lost faith in everything.

I remember something else. We were in the tents in Sofield, one day while I was in school. And my mother was washing that day and here comes the militia, two men only. She was hanging clothes. These militia men hollered at her and they was going to drive the horse on top of her. These other people hollered at her, Mrs. Manolinos, stop, you know, but they hollered in Italian, because they're going to run the horses on you, and kill you. The reason they did that was they thought she was going in to hide the guns, see.

At Louis School one time they was going to burn the school down. So the teacher sent the kids home right away, and tell the kids to hide down in the arroyo, cause there was an arroyo there. So that's what happened there and what we done many times we had to do that. It was a serious business down that way. You know, it's the young ones now that are gaining the profit of 1913, but it was the older people who did it. How much they suffered. Many lost their lives. Now they are doing good now. The strikes don't last so long now, either.

I heard it so many times from my father. I don't know what place it was but it was in some camps, the 1902 strike. But where it was I don't remember. But anyway, there was a woman then, who had some little child, and they had to build a house down under the ground, to hide themselves. There was a lot of massacres in that strike, too. They made a house underground and they went down there and all they had to eat was that goat's milk. It lasted a long time, too, that strike.

MARY CABOT WHEELWRIGHT
Journey Towards Understanding

Born October 2, 1878, the daughter of a Boston Brahmin family at whose home Ralph Waldo Emerson was a frequent guest, Mary Cabot Wheelwright enjoyed a lifelong spiritual quest and love of music and travel. These interests combined beautifully when, at age forty, traveling through Arizona and New Mexico for the first time, she made friends with the Hubbells, the Newcombs, and other southwestern traders who introduced her to Navajo ceremonials. Despite the taboo on recording these sacred rituals, Mary was drawn to document them, working as a do-it-yourself ethnologist who devised her own methods to suit circumstances she encountered along the way.

Wheelwright's meeting and ensuing friendship with Hosteen Klah, the great Navajo medicine man, had far-reaching effect. Klah's awareness that his culture's rituals must either be preserved or lost led him to break the Navajo taboo against replicating sandpaintings and ceremonials. Together, Wheelwright and Klah established in 1937 what is now the Wheelwright Museum of the American Indian in Santa Fe.

In addition to her ethnographic writings, Wheelwright left an unpublished autobiography, "Journey Towards Understanding" (1957) which is excerpted here. More than a telling of her adventures in the Southwest, "Journey" also describes later travels. Wheelwright went to India in 1940 to search for symbols related to those she had found in Navajo art. In addition, she traveled to Europe, Greece, Egypt, and China.

Her other great love was sailing, and she spent summers on the Maine coast, where, for a time she lived alone in a shipmaster's cottage on Sutton's Island. Her passport read, "The Cranberry Isles."

Walter Whitehill writes in the *Dictionary of American Biography*:

> For 40 years Wheelwright remained the dutiful Victorian daughter, devoting herself to good works, particularly a settlement-house music school in the South End of Boston. Since she was dyspeptic, gawky and opinionated, she did not attract suitors; but, after her mother's death in 1917, she conquered her shyness and set out to see the world. . . . She became so attached to the Southwest that in 1923 she bought the Los Luceros Ranch near Alcalde, N.M. . . .
>
> (Being the victim of a prudent Boston family trust, she had a handsome income for life but no control of the capital. This protection against fortune-hunting suitors made it impossible for her to endow the museum as she would have wished.)

Mary Cabot Wheelwright is among those eastern women "to the manor born" who, on coming west and discovering a certain amount of freedom from accustomed Victorian propriety, realized their personal visions on a much more influential plane than was permitted back home. Travel in the West had the exotic flavor of travel in a foreign country, and Mary relished her emergence from the confines of the drawing room.

She had little formal education, and her autobiography reads like a somewhat disorganized and choppy first draft. She may have intended to revise it, but she died in 1958, only a year after she wrote it. Nevertheless, "Journey Towards Understanding," fragmentary and unfinished as it is, is a wonderful record of the life of a significant, neglected historical figure who found her purpose in bringing her considerable resources to the challenge of preserving the heritage of native people of the West.

I shall begin by going backwards because I think that a capacity to understand primitive people must come from love, and my mother's people seem to like nature and simple people.

At about the time I began my recording of the religion of the Navajo I had been discouraged by many professional anthropologists who said the Navajo did not have any religion, that the Singers, or medicine men, had their own individual rites, and that no woman could do that sort of work. I happened to sit beside Dr. Henry Fairfield Osborn at a dinner in New York. He knew nothing about me, but the first thing he asked me was what I was working at.

"How do you know I am working at anything?" I replied.

"You must be," he said. "You are a really happy person. . . ."

There have been many doctors and some inventors in the Cabot family. Occasionally these inventors have made fortunes, but it was the search that interested them, not the expectation of riches. . . . One brother of my mother's—an intimate friend of Ralph Waldo Emerson—was so devoted to bird study that his very practical wife once said to him, "I think if you heard that the inhabitants of Boston all had the plague you would care less than if the thrushes had suffered this winter."

They got their refreshment almost always from nature. They were not particularly artistic, but seemed to need much time and space to breathe. . . My mother once wanted to see what the White Mountains were like in mid-winter and went on an expedition with the mailman by sledge.

Also, after she was married she cured her invalid husband of a bad cough by taking him camping in the Adirondacks, which at that time was not the usual cure for tuberculosis. A cousin explored the interior of Labrador alone.

I think that any fundamental success in creating something must come from a certain fire, from an intense desire to help and from love of the activity. A painter must love what he paints, a musician must love his music above technique, a writer must love his characters even if they are not apparently admirable people. My feeling is that people are moved too much by theory and so-called science and too little by warmth, enthusiasm and the intuition that makes one man different from another. Above all, one must have courage to decide on a course of action and stick to it until the job is finished. Although nothing is ever finished, one can supply part of the structure.

In middle life when my parents had died, I went West, not only to California, but to the Southwest where I seemed to get near to something I had always wanted, a simple way of living, more adventurous and more exciting than the safety of Boston. . . . While I lived in the east I had particularly enjoyed sailing, and when I found that the desert gave me a similar feeling of escape, I came to love it, too. I rode a great deal which was how I came to know the Navajo and their reservation. The slow progress, depending on the pace of the pack train, gave a wonderful feeling of independence and self-sufficiency of your own little world when you settled down in a place near water, not necessarily a beautiful place but adequate for the horses needed water and so did you. Also, the feeling of being part of the earth when you slept on it, night after night, was an enormous experience. It made it so much more possible to understand the connection—intimate and consoling—of the Indian to his earth.

We have put so much between us and the earth, with our houses and our motors. Particulary motors, which remove the action of two of our senses—we can neither hear nor smell the earth but only see it. Also, either on the sea or traveling by horse, the element of danger or uncertainty adds spice to life. "Safety first" is a poor motto.

Adventure in a New Life

Rio Arriba County, New Mexico, where I first stayed, was not particularly safe in those days. I first lived at Alcalde, near Santa Fe, in a "dude ranch. . . ."

Many people in the Southwest at that time were not particularly interested in the Indians as being either picturesque, curious or subjects for study, but fortunately Santa Fe had a large number of artists who did appreciate these qualities and the picturesqueness of it all. It was exciting to come to a region where individuals counted so much, coming as I had from a community where family customs and possessions made a great deal of difference. It was stimulating to find individuals as free as they were out there. People were accustomed to having possessions at one time and nothing at another, and were able to cope with both situations. They almost seemed to enjoy the difficult. Roads were practically non-existent then and the tracks were often washed out. I was amazed to find elderly people talking of breakdowns and sticking in the mud as though it were fun. They seemed disappointed when things went too smoothly.

I found that being from Boston was a distinct handicap, and I determined that one of my missions was to convince cowboys that it was possible for a person to be a good sport and also drink tea.

I had often been to Europe, but it was not until I came west that I had any conception of my own country. I think possibly it was just because I had come from a settled community that I could appreciate the extraordinary differences between my own country and any other place in the world, and it helped me to go further into the spirit of the west by way of Indian life. People brought up with or near the Indians accepted them without analyzing their differences, and without comparing their cultures with others of the world. . . . I had always been interested in different types of religion. . . . I remember quite well when this idea came to me—of religion as a great tide which moved men all around the world. It gave me a feeling of peace and took away much of the feeling of loneliness from my life.

D.H. Lawrence in his book, *Mornings in Mexico*, describes the Corn Dance and the Snake Dance of the Hopi, and writes of what the Indians' rituals give them—freedom from two of the curses of civilization: loneliness and boredom. Because they feel very close to the earth, their Mother, they also feel that their ritual helps the processes of nature.

In those days, pioneer anthropologists, archaeologists and others stayed at the Wetherill ranch and they were among the first white people to realize the possibilities of studies of the Indians.

I thought museums probably had made records of the chants of the Navajo, but I found that although records had been made they were of wax, and most of them had been used so often they were valueless. No proper record of what they were existed. I realized that my only qualifications for the undertaking were that I had enough money to live on, a somewhat limited amount of time for working, as I had an aged mother and commitments in the East, a great deal of interest in religions, although I had made no study of them at that time, and some musical background. My religious background was liberal as I had been brought up a Unitarian, a simple religion lacking dogma, so I had no prejudice against other forms of religion. I did have the belief that religion was very much a necessity for man.

I was also interested in improving the quality of Navajo blankets and Cozy McSparron said he would find out whether any of the old dyes were being used. I had sent him patterns of the older blankets, which he feared would not be saleable, but I offered to buy any doubtful experiments. We found they were much easier to sell in the east than the modern types. . . .

In a later camping trip to Canyon de Chelly . . . we arrived on the night of a big Navajo ceremony, the Teiji or Night Chant, which was out on the plain. While we were still a long way off, we could hear the singing and I shall never forget that strange sound. It was falsetto, more like coyotes than human beings. Over the ceremony hung a pall of smoke, so thick it was like a tent, and the fires shone up on it from below.

Of course I didn't understand it at all—bands of dancers coming in, singing the same chant and dancing in competition with each other. . . . The next day as we came down the mountains I saw something I have

Mary Cabot Wheelwright, around the age of twenty, with one of her Lhasa terriers. *Wheelwright Museum of the American Indian Photoarchive*.

Mary and friend sailing near the coast of Maine aboard the *Hesper*. *Wheelwright Museum of the American Indian Photoarchive*.

Mary Cabot Wheelwright and Clyde Boyal with Hosteen Klah rowing in Northeast Harbor, Maine, 1930. *Wheelwright Museum of the American Indian Photoarchive*.

never understood, a solitary Indian on horseback, pursued by an eagle. I suppose he had robbed the eagle's nest, but I do not know.

On Hosteen Klah

We had heard that we could stay at Nava, for Mr. and Mrs. Arthur Newcomb had . . . fixed up some rooms in what, I think, had been a chicken house. There we heard that a Yebechei (Night Chant) was to be given by their great friend, Hosteen Klah, at Kimpeto, about seventy miles away. So we started off . . . it was a desolate day, with gray skies and wind, and the country was featureless and grim and it grew more stormy as we went along. It began to snow hard, but we managed to reach the ceremony nearby where the dances were to be seen through the whirling snow, while the fires blew out sideways.

Out of this turmoil appeared Klah, calm and benign. I got a very strong impression of his power. The next day dawned serene and still, but cooking breakfast was quite an ordeal . . . soon Klah arrived and asked me if I was the one who had bought the sandpainting blanket he had exhibited in Gallup. . . . I asked him about the meaning of the Fire Dance. He asked, "Why do you want this information?" I answered that it was because I was interested in religion. Then he asked, "How deep is the sea?"

I thought this a curious coincidence as my chief interest had always been the sea. . . .

Klah decided he wanted to have some of his songs recorded. He realized that he must have help in preserving the great knowledge he had, for he knew part of five ceremonies and was the only person who knew the Hail Chant. He had given the Wind Chant and the Blessing Chant, he knew the story of the Mountain Chant, and he was the most sought-after priest of the Night Chant, or Yebechei.

He told the Newcombs that he began to learn his ceremonies when he was five years old. He learned the Hail Chant from his maternal uncle and spent twenty years studying the ceremonies with "Tall Chanter" and with "Smiling Man·" He was 37 when he gave his first Yebechei alone. He lived east of Nava near a rocky hill and was much pestered by snakes, which he would ask Arthur Newcomb to kill as he would not. Later he moved into the Cornfield region, west of Nava, where he built a tall hogan in which he could weave sandpainting blankets. He made about one or two a year, and he did this to record his sandpaintings permanently.

In some books it has been stated that Klah was a transvestite but this is not true. He never married and was a child when the Long Walk took place, at the time the Navajos were exiled. His mother went on the long Walk, but we understand he was hidden up north on the Reservation.

The system by which a man became a Medicine Man at that time was not passed from father to son, but through a maternal uncle. The aspirant was supposed to learn the ceremony from one man and the myth from another. In other words, it was an elaborate and diffused kind of education. Klah began with his grandfather and learned from him the Evil-Chasing type of ceremony in which star crosses were cut into his back, his thighs and wrists with a red-hot stone knife.

Once when Klah was traveling with the Newcombs in their car they saw a whirlwind coming toward them, a real little tornado, a rare occurrence in that region, and they were badly frightened. Klah was asleep in the back of the car, but when he awoke, he cried, "Let me out! Let me out!" and he got out and stood, facing the storm.

He was the last priest of the Hail Chant and by that time the storm was near and it was hailing hard. He stopped and put some of the hailstones in his mouth. Then he blew them toward the whirling storm and it dissolved. He was perfectly confident and unafraid.

Because Mr. and Mrs. Newcomb had a deep interest in the Indians and had the friendship of one of their most respected Medicine Men, I was able to start on my career of recording the Navajo religion. Also, Klah was ready to pass on his knowledge by making blankets to record his sandpaintings. He told me that the Great Spirit had told him to pass this knowledge on to people who could write it down. Very soon after our meeting he decided he wanted to have his songs recorded and came to my house in Alcalde . . . . It was tragic that Klah's nephew, his only disciple, died long before Klah did.

The technique of recording a story is that the Medicine Man first tells a small section. This is translated by the interpreter to the person recording, who takes it down. it could not be done on the typewriter as the sound of the machine would interrupt the flow of the narrative. I found that one should not ask too many questions during the course of the narrative, for the story is told in a kind of rhythm which should not be broken any more than necessary. We worked usually for three hours in the morning and three hours in the afternoon, or until Klah got tired.

. . . I felt I should get in touch with other people interested in the Navajos and went to see Dr. Edward Sapir, an authority on linguistics. He was deeply impressed by the Navajo and their language, which he felt was most nearly allied to Tibetan. . . .

I also discovered that Dr. Jung, the psychologist, had been to the southwest. When Mrs. Henderson sent him the first volume of the Creation Story, he sent me a message that I had done a most valuable thing in collecting the source material.

I was extremely fortunate to have come in contact with Hosteen Klah, who had already faced the fact that his great lore would need to be written down to be preserved. At first many of the Medicine Men did not approve of opening up the secret gates of their beliefs and I doubt if it could have been done except that many of the Medicine Men were growing old and most of the young Navajo could not memorize the mass of material. With the pressure of trying to learn English, trying to understand about money, and the impact of great numbers of white people coming to their ceremonies, most of the medicine men I met were ready to have me record their knowledge. I learned from Klah proper procedure on meeting a new Medicine Man. They liked very much to have presents of things useful to their ceremonies, such as abalone shells, turkey feathers, turquoise, small white shells, tobacco and crystals, which stand for truth. I always paid them for the time they gave me and usually provided transportation to and from their homes, and I always told them exactly why I wanted to record their myths.

. . . One friend, Mary Austin, saw a short ceremony of the Great Star Chant. This was given in a beautiful large Hogan which had been built for Klah's Yebechei. It was a night of bright moonlight with passing clouds, The patient had been blackened all over and spotted with white stars and, as the moonlight waxed and waned, it made a most extraordinary effect. At times you could see the patient, but when the clouds came over the moon you could see only the stars on his body.

Olive Rush, the artist, came to a ceremony of the Bead Chant and when she went back she painted her impression of the Sun God on his turquoise horse, rising from the symbols of the sandpainting. . . .

. . . Frances Newcomb would take rough notes on the sandpaintings and sometimes the Medicine Man would go over those during the intervals of the ritual and say whether or not they were correct. At first we both needed Klah's authority behind our recording, but gradually the Indians began to accept us . . . I helped quite often with the ceremony by sending for the Medicine Man, and providing food for the sandpainters. . . .

I felt in Klah great integrity and nobility, and also such a naturally studious mind that both Mrs. Newcomb and I could ask him questions about the "why?" of various ideas in his religion . . . I should like to elaborate on the concept of "why?" because I have found a tendency among professional anthropologists to make lists of articles or actions, but never to ask, "why?" or "what does it mean?" Of course, these are the most difficult things to find out, but without them no research has life in it, only facts, and facts without the exercise of intuition and imagination and sympathy are dead.

Hence arises the fact which strikes the eye everywhere in the record of ethnology and folklore, the fact that the same frigid and detached spirit which leads to success in the study of astronomy or botany leads to disaster in the study of mythology or human origins. . . . That same suppression of sympathy, that same waving away of intuition and guess-work which makes a man preternaturally clever at dealing with the stomach of a spider will make him preternaturally stupid in dealing with the heart of man.

At one time Mrs. Newcomb thought she should take a course in anthropology, but I advised her strongly not to do so. She knew enough of the Navajo language to be able to communicate with them, and was so deeply interested in the sandpainting ritual that she was often consulted and invited to help with sandpaintings.

It is fascinating to professional anthropologists to have a preconceived idea of what they are going to find, but to me every new Medicine Man I met was an exciting experience, because I never knew what door he was going to open. My only aim was to give him confidence in my integrity and try as best I could to get the knowledge he had to give me. . . . I always tried to make the language simple when writing down a myth. The use of long, sophisticated words in one of these stories is completely out of tune, and destroys the direct impression of the speech.

I believe that anyone recording a primitive religion should have a knowledge of many religions. I had always been interested in the religious practices of different peoples and had read a good deal about them. On the whole, I had found that Christianity seemed to be the most exclusive in its point of view, for both Mohammedanism and Hinduism accdept the concept that there are different paths to the same summit. . . .

. . . I began gradually to accept the Indian's trust in the plan behind nature, and to accept the Navajo and the Hindu concept of no absolute evil or absolute good in human beings. Their belief is that every power or human being is dual, one side inspired by the positive and the other by the negative.

I was anxious to record Klah's Creation myth, feeling that then I would have a basic understanding of his belief. In the spring of 1930, I went to Santa Barbara, California and stayed at San Ysidro Ranch. There, in about ten days, Klah told me the Creation Myth. He came with Arthur Newcomb and his nephew, Clyde Boyal, who was the interpreter. After that I tried to use Clyde with Klah because it was the natural thing for a nephew to help his uncle ceremonially, and Clyde was an intelligent interpreter. I asked Klah if the form of the Navajo religion stemmed from the Creation Story, but he said the ceremonies were more like a group of trees, not one single tree of Creation with branches.

Klah enjoyed Santa Barbara very much because in his Creation Story there was an episode when the Great Mother, or "Changing Woman," had gone from the Navajo country to an island off the California coast. She lived there in a crystal house where the sun, whom she married, could visit her. This tradition caused the Navajo to make annual pilgrimages to the Pacific, and in the myth it tells of the various places that were visited on the way from Navajo country.

. . . The only ritual that Fr. Haile over attended was one connected with the Hanalthnayhey Myth, a ritual against evil—what they call Hotch-onjai versus Hozhonji, which is Blessed. Later I saw Klah give that ceremony. To me it was a most moving and universal thing—simple, consisting of three days of prayer and on the third day the making of the sandpainting of the Path of Life, while the person for whom it was given held the symbol of the Great Mother, a decorated ear of corn. After they had finished the songs, everyone in the Hogan walked the Path of Life, carrying seeds and their children. I said to Klah, "I wish I could have walked that path with you." He replied, "You would have been welcome."

As I recorded myth after myth I felt so strongly that the material had universal application that during ten years, beginning about 1926, I felt impelled to collect all that I could of this extraordinary material, which had come out of our own soil.

Much later, I talked about this to a Hindu Swami, Nikelenanda, of the Vedanta Center in New York. I asked him where these people could have found such flashes of fundamental wisdom and insight. He replied that he thought it had probably come with them when they migrated from the east, and also from an intense perception of their own world, seeing the phenomena of nature in a way we have forgotten. From it they have speculated and made use of their observations.

The Hozhonji Blessing Chant is really part of all ceremonies. When a ceremony is complete it begins with the Casting out of Evil, including purification of the body—taking of an emetic and sweet baths for four days in the morning, and in the evening of the rite of the Untying of Knots on the body of the patient, while the Medicine Man sings and prays. This rite seems to me to typify the untying of knots of the person's mind. Although Fr. Haile felt that this part of the ceremony was the oldest form and that the other was possibly a reflection of Christianity, I am quite sure this is not the case, for there is no inclusion in their concept of the world of Devil or Absolute Evil. Even in the Scalp Dance, which was the reconciliation of the Spirit of the Dead with those who killed him, there is a part of the ceremony which is a Blessing.

Before I came to the period from about 1938 to 1941 in which I felt the great pressure of time in recording the Navajo ceremonies, which were fast becoming obsolete, I would like to give some idea of the country over which I was riding. The first camping I did was from the Grand Canyon when I was very much a greenhorn. I went with a friend and one guide, who had never taken women camping before, along the rim of the Canyon and down into Cataract Canyon where some of the Indians lived. It was spring and when we got into the Canyon it was glowing with cacti in flower and evening primroses. I did not realize then that I should probably never see anything so wonderful in the way of canyon flowers again.

On this trip we suffered very much from thirst, we were very much sunburned, we drank any water we could find, and when we got down to the camping place we found that most of the trading post had been washed away. There were only two men there, the supervisor of the Indians and a man who had come to take a census of the Indians.

I was taken deathly sick from the water on the first night—in fact, even the horses were sick—but after a day I was well enough to ride out. It was at this time that I had a curious experience which was useful to me later in understanding what the Cleansing Ceremony of the Navajo does for the patient. I had a rheumatic condition in my hands, but after this tremendous purging and drinking quantities of rain water when I reached the top of the Canyon, I realized a kind of exaltation of mind and body, and I have never had the rheumatic condition again. I knew then what the cleansing of the Navajo meant.

Almost every spring I would come west and came for ten days or two weeks when I could leave my mother. I first explored the Jemez Mountains, the country of the Jicarilla Apaches, and I saw one of their ceremonies, which was extremely picturesque. The Indians were camped in tents on the shores of Stone Lake, and at night when the fires were lighted and the ceremonial races were in progress it made an unforgettable picture.

The longest trip I took was to the great Bridge of Navajo Mountain, starting from Fort Defiance by way of Kayenta. Here we got Ben Wetherill as a guide and went into the really terrible country and trails on the way to the Bridge. No one who has not been can imagine the difficulties of the trail. It was necessary for the horses to climb up the slick rocks or petrified sand dunes and we went afoot for the horses to follow Ben Wetherill's horse as best they could. At times I felt I could not possibly get through. At one point the trail was so steep that I could only get up by hanging onto the tail of my horse. One of the horses was of better blood and would lose his nerve at the most difficult places, just like humans, but most of the horses and mules were used to the country and somehow got through. Finally we came to the bridge and slept under the arch in full moonlight. We signed a book for visitors, and I think were among the first hundred who reached there.

We eventually came out at Tuba City, Arizona, and rose to the Grand Canyon, having traveled 550 miles in 29 days.

The most moving adventure of the trip happened near Lee's Ferry, on the Colorado River. We had slid down a great sand slope to the river and spent a day there resting. When we went on, singing as we often did to pass the time on our slow pace, we heard a voice calling, "Help! Help!"

The guide told us to wait while he went back to the arroyo from where the voice had come. Then he called to us to come to him and we saw a little bundle lying in the full sun at the bottom of the dry arroyo. As we slid down, a faint voice said, "Be careful there, that's where I hurt myself."

It was from a little elderly man with a broken hip, quite self-possessed, who had fallen into the arroyo in the dark and had lain there from Monday to Thursday, not knowing he was near a road until he heard us singing. We draped a canvas over him for shade and fed him water slowly, and then fruit juice. He showed no fear, and as he gained strength he told us his story.

He had been walking up to Utah and had run out of water and the water holes were at least twenty miles apart in that region. He had food, but had not been able to reach it, and now offered it to us. We sent the younger guide to try to find the only water in that region. The older guide asked why he hadn't gone mad, and the old man answered, "I guess it was my religion."

He was a Christian Scientist and when I asked him why he had chosen that faith, he replied that it seemed to be something simple he could understand, and added, "I haven't made a success of my life because I don't feel it is right to fight for things."

Eventually the guide returned with a motor, and we made the old man as comfortable as we could in the car. The nearest doctor was 350 miles away, over a rough road. I offered him some brandy. He was a small man, of Welsh birth, and he looked me quietly in the eye and said, "I am all right."

As we had used up our water during this incident we had to turn back to a place half way up a terrible red rock mountain where miraculously there was a spring and a pool of water. None of us will ever forget that night. There was moon and the desert, burned almost black by the sun, was unearthly. We did not sleep much and the next day we were so tired it seemed we would never reach the next trading post thirty miles away.

When the old man recovered I sent him down to his daughter in the south, and sent her money every month to take care of him. She wrote me, "Many people think he should be shut up, for he wants the desert, but I think he has a right to his own life."

A few months later she telegraphed me that he had received my check and had gone, and soon after I got a note from him from Albuquerque, asking if I would stake him to a burro and tent. Of course I did this and he went back to the desert.

A year or so after this I rode over that same desert after a rain and the flowers were as tall as the horses' legs, as far as you could see. It was a great contrast to the way we had seen it a few years before, but even then its horror was not enough to frighten one small old man. Now there is a motor road and a bridge over the river, and the spring in the mountain supplies water for a forester's house.

Camping in the mountains was exceedingly beautiful in late May and early June. White mariposa lilies grew under the delicate green aspen trees, pale iris bordered the bracks, and flax, prickly phlox and larkspur were abundant. When the desert flowered after a rain, wild heliotrope, orange colored mallows and many others burst into bloom. I remember one marvelous combination of flowers in northern New Mexico where bright yellow lilies, about a foot high, their petals turned up like little hats, grew among acres of Blue Martensia, with blue bells and pink buds.

The extraordinary contrast between the vegetation in the mountains and the desert made camping trips fascinating. One trip we took, starting in great heat, went from Lee's Ferry up a long canyon leading to Bryce Canyon Park, then through upper country where there is snow, over very rough country with no trail, and down to Zion Park. When we got down to Zion Park I asked the ranger why he hadn't marked the trail coming down from the top. "Because I never heard of anyone coming in from that direction," he said.

From there we went across country to the north side of the Grand Canyon, and as it was June and very hot at the bottom we spent the day under the waterfall at the end of Bright Angel Canyon.

Recording Period

As I became more and more interested in getting a comprehensive picture of the religion, wherever we went Frances Newcomb and I would ask, "What Medicine Men are here? What do they do?" In a great many cases the traders would not have the faintest idea of what it was all about, but we usually took an intelligent interpreter with us who could hunt out prospects.

To give an idea of this search, we heard of a ceremony to be given just south of the Utah border, so we started for it with a good interpreter. When we got there we found that no ceremony was being given, so we turned west through an unfamiliar region with very bad roads. We stopped at a place called Sweetwater, a small Mormon trading post. Three nice men were there but no woman, and the only accommodation was one small double bed. We spent three days investigating the region. Frances Newcomb did the cooking for everybody, and we had to wash in the kitchen. The toilet was in the corral where there was a dog that did not like us. We found nothing of interest in this region and went on to another trading post. This was Round Rock. Here Frances Newcomb recorded two fine sandpaintings.

Then I went on a tour on the western edge of the Reservation, up near Navajo Mountain, but did not find very complete records. Finally we came to the conclusion that the central part of the Reservation, where the farming was better and there was more prosperity, was the more fertile field, since more people had money for the complete ceremony.

At about this time, when Klah was doing so much in giving me information on where to find certain ceremonials and the proper Medicine Man for each one, I decided I would give him great pleasure by bringing him to the Atlantic Ocean. It would give him great prestige among the Indians to have visited both the Pacific and Atlantic, so I invited Mr. and Mrs. Arthur Newcomb, Klah and his nephew, Clyde, to visit me at Northeast Harbor, Maine.

As they traveled over the country in the Newcomb's motor, Klah kept asking if there were Indians here. When he got to Northeast Harbor I introduced him to a half-breed Penobscot, the last of a tribe who once lived on Mt. Desert. Fortunately I had an ideal place where Klah and his nephew could live, the upper part of a boathouse on the beach. This enabled them to be independent, and Klah enjoyed very much wandering about in my woods of tall spruce trees. He and Clyde had their meals with us, and the members of my household were amazed at their enjoyment of our kind of food.

It was great fun to take Klah and his nephew rowing. They were frightened at first, but about a fortnight before they left they were going out on my schooner and enjoying it intensely, when the spray flew over them. Klah wore his traditional dress of cotton trousers and lovely velveteen blouse, his silver necklace and belt . . . I was afraid he might get poison ivy and warned him of this, but he said he knew of it. He also said he could feed himself in the woods. He was certain the Great God was there because it smelled so sweet.

My cousin, Mrs. Murphy, who had been to one of Klah's ceremonies in the west, invited us to a Japanese tea ceremony. It was conducted by two Japanese in a Japanese tea house which Mrs. Murphy's mother had brought from Japan. Klah was very happy to do this ceremonial eating and admired the Japanese.

Frances Newcomb suggested that before he left, Klah might show one of his sandpaintings on the terrace overlooking the sea. On the spur of the moment he collected sand, charcoal and tintex to color the sand as needed, and Klah made a little sandpainting on the Black Wind for a few of my friends. The Indian from Northeast harbor came to see it but did not understand. Later Klah went to visit him with an interpreter, trying to make a contact, but found it impossible as the eastern Indian had forgotten his lore. The sandpainting was preserved for a few days so that a student of metaphysics could see it. We protected it with a barricade of chairs, but to Klah's joy many animals walked on it—squirrels, mice and snakes. Just before Klah left a north wind came and destroyed it, which pleased him very much.

Klah give me his Hail Chant in Tucson, in the same year I recorded his Night Chant at Newcomb. The people who took part in it were mostly members of Klah's family. He told me also of the ceremony of the Feather Chant and went with me to the last day of that ceremony. It was interesting and different from any other I saw. Even at that time it was a rare type of ceremony and I am afraid that by this time it has died out. In it two of the gods came and mixed liquid food in the hogan and a large round loaf of bread was made and buried in the earth to bake during the night. The participants took the food prepared by the gods and in the dawn we all ate this bread together.

GRACE MOTT JOHNSON
Two Weeks in New Mexico

"Two Weeks in New Mexico," a 1921 letter written by sculptor Grace Mott Johnson to her friend Ray Rosenbaum in California, gives an arch, behind-the-scenes look at the Taos art colony and its queen, Mabel Dodge Lujan. Many women will resonate with the personal concerns Johnson (she insisted on being called "Johnson" by everyone, including her son) expresses. We hear the voice of a woman trying to juggle her commitments as she tries to find time for her art, to care for her son, to take care of the finances and logistics of her life, and to maintain her personal well-being amidst the upheaval of her disintegrating marriage to painter Andrew Dasburg. The tone is decidedly gossipy. Mabel Dodge Lujan is portrayed as a meddler who invited people into her home as guests ostensibly to support their art, then proceeded to manipulate their relationships destructively. While undergoing this treatment, it is to her credit that Johnson maintained a basically compassionate view of Mabel and the other players surrounding her. She relates this experience with tongue-in-cheek humor and the confidence of a woman who knows and likes herself and who is certain of being understood by the close woman friend addressed.

Artist, feminist, civil rights activist and utterly independent spirit that she was, Johnson's unconventional upbringing likely accounted for the woman she became. Born July 28, 1882, she was only two when her mother died, was raised by her father on a farm in Yonkers, New York, and was entirely home-schooled. Her father, a minister, following a run-in with his congregation, left the church and, in effect, society. Grace was brought up with the notion she could do anything a man could do and paid no attention to traditional limitations placed on the female sex. She loved physical labor, she loved animals, and she loved to draw, and when she was eighteen, she pedaled off on her bicycle to begin her life.

In New York, she studied at the Art Students League and her sculpture was included in the 1914 Armory Show. Her desire to draw animals led her to Paris in 1910 to study Percheron horses and to Egypt in 1924 to draw camels. In pursuit of her studies, she followed the circus as well, drawing and sculpting from memory. She spent time off and on in New Mexico during the course of her largely long-distance relationship with Dasburg. She believed marriage was an unnecessary convention and rebelled against the formality of the marriage ceremony. She consented to be married only at Dasburg's insistence, and she never married again.

Johnson was a pioneer in her own way. She de-segregated Jones Beach when she insisted her black friends be allowed to join her there. She customarily stayed at the Harlem YWCA while in New York. At the center of the artistic and political movements of her day, she was close to important figures of the times such as John Reed, Louise Bryant, and Walter Lippmann.

Johnson believed women's clothes were unfit to wear because they lacked sufficient pockets. Consequently, she always dressed in a tattered old brown sweater, which, we may assume, had enough pockets to suit her.

Grace Mott Johnson died on March 12, 1967.

*T*hey had been back from their historic trip to the Hopi Snake Dance for a week or more. (Mabel had taken cold, she thought, from sleeping on the ground during it, and said that had stopped her menstruation for a week.) Now, after lying around some days, she was all over this and seemed interested in doing something, but mostly, to judge from remarks dropped by her and others, in meeting Eve Young-Hunter before she and Mr. Young-Hunter went East again. They had been camping some distance from Taos and making various attempts to meet Mabel without coming to Taos where the former Mrs. Young-Hunter is still living near Mabel's place.

Mabel said once impatiently that "it did seem a nuisance that they can't come here." Which seemed to me a characteristic specimen of Mabel's tendency to foment an uncomfortable or exciting situation, and her childish obviousness in it, and her heartlessness.

Since the former (I was about to say, *the real*) Mrs. Young-Hunter is ill or hysterical because of the divorce, and her husband's marriage to Eve who was acting as Mabel's housekeeper when they met, and which one feels was, indirectly at least, another case of Mabel's separations of married people. Mary Young-Hunter is living next door to Mabel still, alone or with the daughter Gabriel in her home and studio acquired there two years ago. She is an English lady.

I heard Mabel arrange by telegram, etc., to meet the present Young-Hunters on their way to an Apache Indian Dance, the roads to which were reported impassable and so on. There was always some hitch so that Mabel said "it looked as if she were not to get there."

All her arrangements were made with her son, John Evans, and Tony without a word of the possibility of myself or Alfred being invited for the trip, so that I took it for granted that we were not going in any event and made no preparation for a camping trip.

Meanwhile Mabel turned over John's Ford to Alfred and me to use if we asked permission. The battery had been taken out to be put into a Monroe runabout that John was interested in at the moment, which had been left in Mabel's garage by two boys arrested for cattle stealing. The Ford was hard to crank and I had vowed that I would not drive any cars this time while in New Mexico, for the time required to take care of them, the attention and mental attitude involved is directly opposed to my natural condition of observing nature and my mood for work.

Nevertheless, here was an opportunity to let Alfred learn to drive the car, now that mine is sold (he could not drive in N.Y. at 10 years old anyway) and also to take some little trips with him—as to the Hot Spring for a bath, etc.

I broke my resolution not to touch a car and, paying for gas and oil, of course, took him out a few times and he did drive—and very well.

Now John and Mary Foot left. It seemed that their departure was precipitated by the fact that Mrs. Alfaro, Mabel's housekeeper who had to do the cooking as well as the overseeing, against her will, and was not strong, threatened to leave and Mabel decided to close the guest rooms to reduce the table work to a minimum.

I suppose that the trip to the Apache Dance was abandoned.

On Monday morning Mabel asked me if I would like to go. Said there was still just time to reach the place on the day of the dance if we succeeded in getting through and finding the roads which she had never traveled before. It was wild country and would mean camping out at night, of course. I said that I should like to. Alfred was alarmed and distressed at the prospect of being left alone with his father (he had been with him all summer, to be sure, but no *so alone*) and pled that I take him with me. I said that he should ask Mabel if he could go too. It took mighty argument and persuasion to coerce him into making this request himself—I would not let him back down. If he wanted to badly enough he must overcome his timidity and fear of her refusal.

Tony represented that the Ford must be taken along with the camping outfit as there was not room enough for it in the Buick which he was to drive Mabel in.

"Would I drive the Ford with Alfred and the pack?"

"We should start at once—in twenty minutes."

I said that I would not think of getting out on such a trip where we would not run near a garage or any place of supplies in such country, and reported road conditions, without having the car overhauled and equipped, but Mabel exclaimed that it was in the best of conditions and that John had just made a record-breaking trip from Santa Fe with it in four hours.

I said, "I will try it," and Mabel added that "we will not say that we are going to reach the dance, but will enjoy the trip as far as we go."

Meanwhile I was getting into my khaki breeches and puttees for chauffeuring and camping and directing Alfred, who had just had experience on their Snake Dance trip, to bring whatever he needed.

My menstruation was just beginning, and having no opportunity to get any napkins as I had expected to do that morning before I knew of our going, I asked Mabel if she could lend me anything. She exclaimed, "Are you going to have *that* on the trip? It will give you a cramp if you sleep on the ground."

I said that would not trouble me if I kept warm. Mrs. Alfaro lent me a towel, and so very meagerly supplied—in hopes that we could come to water sometimes where I could wash and make the towel go as far as possible—unable to take one change of underwear because it was wet in the wash, I helped them pack the workbody of the Ford we started. No time to see whether we had any extra parts, beside one spare shoe without rim and a patched inner tube which Alfred found and put on board on his own initiative. Dasburg lent his army spade as he bade us goodbye and helped Mabel get food at the store.

The canteens were filled with a potato in one and corn cob in the other by way of corks— I took the gallon of oil I had bought and Tony and I both stopped for gas as we went through Taos and then we headed for the Rio Grande and Embudo, at the foot of the Canyon.

Mabel said that the idea was that "I should drive the Ford far enough in the rear to escape their dust and so that she would not hear our noise." (John had removed the muffler to facilitate climbing, therefore, we made plenty of noise. Mabel hates it—and so do I, but she claims that I don't mind it because I am inclined to be noisy and let doors slam. My nerves were in good condition so I did not let it trouble me, nor the thick adobe dust which we could not escape except in rare instances.)

Mabel has developed a fear of fast driving, she claims—at any rate she must have Tony drive so slowly on the straight, open going that I was often obliged to put the Ford into low speed or stop repeatedly to allow a space to be gained between.

She said that I could go ahead here where I knew the way as far as Española, but having had experience and knowing Mabel, how she would not stand being behind a moment, I quite cheerfully followed and swallowed the dust and noise. For it was wonderful, real New Mexican weather and, after all, I was going on a new trip with Alfred which I had hoped to do once while I was there, and until that morning had seen no prospect of doing. I say I was quite cheerful with emphasis. I was acclimated now and felt well and happy as we crossed the sage brush plains and then dove into the Canyon where we reached a spring at the bottom. It was about noon and we watered ourselves and our cars and at the Gerson Gusdorf (Taos General Store) sandwiches brought along with the addition of cress from the brook, I at least, with plenty of relish.

From there along the water's edge some 60 miles to Española, the fruitgrowing settlement, where the canyon spreads out wide and is entered by the Chama river at a right angle from the west, there is a bridge across the Rio Grande here which we crossed and headed up the Chama to Abiquiu. This was new and different country with sand dunes looking like great ant hills and some peculiar rocks like ruined watch towers, etc.

Abiquiu reached before sundown, was almost like some European mountain village high on a slope, looking across the gorge at a separated rock formation like the prow of a ship—very sightly and picturesque. All Mexican inhabitants.

Mabel had been here once before and knew the family who kept the post office, from whom she engaged rooms for the night, since, she told me, we might better start the first night under cover and not unload the pack.

Then she (or Tony) learned that we could get supper in another house, a very clean and good one. Mabel praised the Mexican woman for it, through Tony as interpreter into Spanish. Then, when Tony and I had got gas and oil at the general store and it was twilight Mabel suggests camping out after all and asks my opinion.

I said I agreed—but my opinion would be that since she had engaged the rooms and it would soon be dark, we should sleep inside tonight. She agreed.

By moonrise we were dispossessed in two Mexican rooms with cheese-cloth ceilings but apparently quite clean—Tony had a couch in the outer quadrangle—Alfred shared my bed.

Mabel warned of bedbugs, "unless I was immune to them like Mary Foote." I assured her that I was and could sleep through a million of them that night.

There was no sign of any in Alfred's and my room. The Mexicans through whose bedrooms we had to pass (being all on the ground floor, of course), while they were undressing, were now all asleep.

At 2 a.m., I was sleeping like a rock, when Mabel comes in and wakes me with, "Johnson, how can you sleep? I have not been asleep all night." "Is it bedbugs?" I asked, feeling sorry for her, because lying awake all night is one of the most miserable sufferings, I think. "Yes, they must drop down on one from the ceilng—it was unmistakeable—like fire all over one." She was going to take her sleeping bag and blankets and lie in the yard.

"Can I help you?" I said, lighting the lantern, which stood by my bed, for her. No, she would do it herself. I was asleep again soon. Before sunrise Alfred and I awoke with no bedbugs and began to talk, though not very loud.

"No fair talking in the morning," came in Mabel's voice—so we knew she had deposited herself right out of our window on the ground. We shut up like clams and soon all hands got up to cook breakfast in the Mexican kitchen full of flies.

Mabel and Tony made their coffee which I do not know how to do and which they did not want anyone to spoil, while Alfred went out to get milk. We found a halved watermelon inhabited by flies on the breakfast table from the night before and let it remain under the napkin, eating the large honeydew that we had got and cleaned ourselves. Then to the cars and down into the canyon of the Chama by the one track road along the winding wall into country that seemed very different and much wilder (perhaps largely because never seen before) than the surroundings of Taos.

Brick red earth appeared along a bank at the foot and then we got into the country of a painted canyon which none of us (except Tony in boyhood) had seen.

Our Rio Grande canyon is gloomy, dark, volcanic rock palisades with so many broken chunks of waste stone that one thinks of the cities which might be built of it, and one feels it a dead crack—but for the stream in its bottom.

Here was a brilliant wall (surrounding high plains all in light) banded red at the base, white in the centre and bright yellow above (the Tierra Amarilla). It skirted the smooth plateau irregularly like the bound of a festival arena and because it was so gay and the whole world so sunny there, it did not seem lonely, though there was no life to be seen miles without end, except an occasional long-tailed ground squirrel or little ones, like chipmunks, which look very ridiculous to an Easterner—since they have long squirrel-tails too, and hold them erect as they scamper. One of the large squirrels was run over by the Buick and all the acorns squashed out of his cheeks but he was not dead so I trained the Ford on him and still had to get out and kill him with my heel.

Dulce, the scene of the Apache dance, was, if I remember, supposed to be about seventy-five miles off by now. We had been told at Abiquiu that a bridge was broken through by a motor truck the preceding night.

We came to that bridge. It was large vigas (trunks of trees) with loose boards on top over a chasm in the rock perhaps 35 feet deep.

Tony and I got out to inspect it. Mabel did not want us to walk on it even, and it must be admitted that it was a treacherous looking thing. The trunks were large enough, but one was decidedly shaky, and a similar one was standing on end broken in the chasm.

If you drove with the wheels exactly on the centre of the trunks the probability would be that you got across all right—but if the weight of the Buick snapped the other viga there appeared to be no possible chance for car or driver. One could not take it other than slowly since the boards, many of which were short and breaking, had never had a nail in them—and if one kicked up! Mabel thought it was too great a risk for one Indian dance and I agreed with her—as far as crossing in the Buick was concerned. Tony did not want to turn back . . . The next village was only three miles away, and I would have liked to walk there at least, but Mabel did not feel like walking.

A couple of wagons coming from the other direction which we watched for many miles trailing down a distant hill, reached the bridge at last. Now these drivers had some Angora goats on board, one of which attracted Mabel and she talked of buying it! I reminded her "that she had got rid of all her Angora rabbits—and what would she do with it? And would she carry it home with her in the Buick, since the Ford was full?" (It was, or looked, nearly as large as the horses, tied, standing the prairie schooner, with its bows, but not its canvas up, white in the sun, with a fine head "like a Greek sculpture," as she said, appealing to me. I saw and admired, but did not weaken.)

We headed back toward Abiquiu and I know if I had any defined emotion it was one of mild relief, though, of course, it was disappointing to retreat at the last ditch, as it were. A mile or so back we stopped and cooked lunch. To be accurate, Tony made the fire, I opened the cans and Mabel made a good combination of them in the frying pan—and cocoa.

While in progress, as the party was divided, in two cars that were trying to keep apart, there was little time for conversation, but on halts like this we might talk. Mabel frequently brought up the labeling of peoples— characters by the date of their birth, which seemed to amuse her. She said I was a "water person" and she was a "fire person." I thought most of her analyses were correct, though its being determined by anything inherent in the 28th of July did not interest me any more than dream books and the Ouija board, and I asked her what was the effect on the subject if he were born under the Julian calendar, or the Jewish or the Chinese. This seemed to be a slightly new idea to her and she said that she had not asked the woman who taught her this game (as I called it) how that worked.

But I took up most of her points about myself and corroborated them to her, while she was telling me that I was a "one person—like Roosevelt and Wilson, always by necessity of their natures lonely and leaders—unable to cooperate."

"Yes," I replied to this subtle (?) flattery, "my father was born on the tenth of June and was that way; and my aunt, who strikingly resembled Wilson, was born on the 26th of March."

So we continued here and there. I went down to the stream to wash my share of the dishes and myself under the bank as well as I could, for I was very bloody, and though of course could not take time to undress, this may have made Mable think me dilatory.

We tried another way to Dulce, coming out on a high plateau right under the flat-topped mountain called Peternadel which we see from Taos 80 miles distant as the crow flies. We were rounding it, for it presented a narrow tower-like view. The plain was smooth and as easy traveling as Fifth Avenue without traffic, except that the ruts which constituted the road were rather deep for the Buick in places, it being too under-slung for some of this going.

But we skimmed along seeing only a bunch of wild horses and a Mexican cowboy picturesquely halting near the trail. . . .

I went gathering dead cactus and cedar for the fire and Tony started one. . . Made a comfortable bed prepared for rain, which Mabel thought was coming, saying that Tony said "they were wild clouds."

It did look threatening and there was a strong breeeze, which remained dry, however, all night. She asked me if I were not tired, saying that "she who had done nothing all day, was *dead*." Her last words were—"Remember, no talking in the morning!"

I was a little surprised that I was not tired, for that had been *some* driving. Dips with a mud hole at the bottom where the Buick had to nearly break backwards to turn its nose up for the almost vertical climb among stones, and the Ford followed like a little dog, with sometimes the advantage in point of size, but not daring to get into close quarters with the Buick at a pinch, so pausing at the top of a plunge, barking for the leader to go ahead, as it were.

No, my nerves were in fine shape, in spite of the fact that such a confined position and concentration all day was a bit hard on one in menstruation. I felt quite blissful under the open sky and Alfred who *was* a little tired slept in a minute. I soon followed him.

Mabel and Tony cooked and ate breakfast and called to me that it was getting cold, and "wouldn't I like some bacon?" "Yes," I said, "I'm hurrying," and I found the frying pan full of canned sweet potato and some hard chunks of fried-out pig, and I added (unfortunately)—"I should like a bit of bacon that was not all dried up."

I choked down a little, and went toward the Ford. Mabel called out, "Wasn't I going to do my share and wash the dishes?" I said, "Certainly," but my mind was beginning to swim. How was I going to get at the spark-plugs, as she was hurrying us off so? She said "it looked like rain," and she had decided to go right back as fast as possible. I was disappointed, of course, to miss the big tree country, and beside Jack Young had told us that if we could not get through to Dulce, he could put us on the trail to Peternadel by some pre-historic Indian ruins, none of which I have ever seen. But I only thought of these things and said nothing, because I realized that Mabel and Tony had had recent experience of roads in this country after cloudbursts—their opinion should decide, even if Mabel had not been head of the expedition. I certainly entertained some doubt of our being able to get back to Abiquiu by the trail we had come if it were wet—if my spark-plugs were not attended to, it would be more than a doubt and there was not a new plug in the car.

I turned to all the dishes bare-handed—this morning's, and those left from supper covered with grease and hardened egg and only a bit of clay

Grace Mott Johnson and
pony. *Deborah Park*.

Andrew with Alfred Dasburg. *Ann Dasburg*.

Grace holding Alfred. Andrew's mother at left. *Ann Dasburg.*

Andrew Dasburg, 1932.
*Courtesy Museum of New
Mexico, Neg. No. 59740.*

and unsuitable for scouring. So I did not make a perfect job of each. Mabel was urging me to hurry and got into the car to put them in the box herself. But she handed most of them back because they were not thoroughly cleaned. I said, "Those dishes are in an awful condition."

This was the first moment when I felt like making any *"remark."* The reason that it sprang to my lips was the fact that getting my hands full of grease and grime is no light matter for me. (At home we had many years of dishwashing but did it with a mop. For all the farm work I was obliged to wear gloves, even in summer, because I have a bad skin that cracks on the palms. I like to work bare-handed and it was eternal misery and nuisance to me, but if I did not wear them, even for a little job, they got so bad that they bled in the pail when I milked—and of course modeling would be impossible.)

I hoped to get to work in clay as soon as we returned from this trip and so the mean little job, though trivial in itself, was unfortunate for me. All this passed through my mind in a flash, of course, and in addition the fact that people can never understand about my hands no matter how much I explain.

Except for this one moment everything about the drive and camping was exhilarating to me—even the dishwashing, reminding of this work shared by the gang at home with much hilarity, was not disagreeable except for my hands.

Mabel said, "Why didn't you get up early and cooperate a little? Instead of criticizing?" I then realized that she was not in a good humor though she had volunteered that she had slept finely that night. Suddenly it seemed to me that I was being treated—not like a chauffeur and fellow-camper who was working hard (as I certainly was) but like a child or a servant who did not please.

I looked her right in the eye and said, "You know why I did not cooperate. I can't work as quickly as you can, but I'm doing my best."

This relieved my momentary resentment and I was not interested in getting at the Ford plugs and break-hands (which also began to feel loose). We went back to the Youngs for this, and I spent some time under the car and getting into the transmission—but not any more I thought than the average garage hand putting a Ford to rights while you wait. Jack Young and a crony warned against trying a certain "terrible hill" unless our brakes were in perfect working order, and Mabel declared that we were not going to try that hill.

But we all knew there were steep hills enough even if we did not go by way of this exceptional one.

Before I could touch the plugs she started ahead with Tony. There was a thunderstorm threatening before them.

Alfred (who had assisted me by handing me wrenches, etc.,) and I followed them on three cylinders—becoming two. But we skimmed along the high, smooth plain and were able to keep up with the Buick—or nearly—when my left forward tire went flat.

Alfred and I jumped out for this job while the Buick went on, but not out of sight. They stopped about a mile beyond and waited. Alfred and I changed tires and found that the valve was used up. While he was vulcanizing one of the inner tubes, none of which were good, I removed the radiator hose that was all screwed up out of shape when we started and now leaked badly—thinking that this might be as much the cause of our engine's missing as the spark plugs—and we could not afford to lose the water.

I had been rather sorry for Mabel sitting there in the car so long with nothing to do, and apparently not caring to get out and walk around for a change even. I did not envy her—and wondered if she had writing material with her or a book to read.

It was a bit hard to have to do garage work every moment while there, instead of being able to drink it in and dwell upon any of it and perhaps memorize some part, in this chance of a lifetime—I might never see it again—and this was the *first impression* that I was losing. But I took in much out of the corner of my eyes. . .

Inwardly, the possibility that Mabel would abandon the Ford for the time being gave me a sense of freedom and relief.

An empty stomach made one all the more limber to pump tires—I had eaten one Uneeda Biscuit since morning.

We drank the warm water from the canteen, since, arrived at the stream, we could get plenty of its brackish mud for the car.

A bunch of cattle came down on a peninsula of the bank opposite—a large Shorthorn bull among them.

The vertical, partly-colored cliff-face towering in full light as background made the group rich and dark by contrast, but every muscle was in clear relief, only half a stone's throw across.

Moving—drinking and turning to lie down, they varied the arrangement as on a stage.

God! What a scene to do in color, or bas-relief colored, perhaps!

People, by using swirling or extended lines and following some rule or idea of "design" try to do something "decorative."

While here it is! If they could do a thing like that—*as it is!*

Not something first required for a given space to fit into someone else's idea or sentiment, or weakened by that of the sculptor or painter himself, and lastly by his weakness in execution.

But this comes to the same old conclusion—We want a *great* artist or none. . . .

I felt very happy there, and since our delay was beyond our control, I enjoyed it and thought it in my favor.

We might be in for an adventure in case of storm or being unable to get the Ford up the canyon. Pumping tires is a little hard on the small of one's back during menstruation and in that rare air makes one bleed a good deal. When we had got all through, the Buick reappeared and I had to tell Mabel that I had lost the spare shoe. I knew she would psychoanalyze this. . . .

"Come right along and get to Abiquiu and have a mechanic that understands Fords fix the car," she said. We did—by the skin of our teeth.

Now we headed straight for Española. . . . Arrived at the garage. . . . At the Hotel Grenada we found Mabel had ordered supper, and I realized as I read the rates, though not high as compared to a hotel in the East, how much she had to pay for such a party. She looked quite fresh and like a lady in her silks.

She suggested to me that I had time for a bath before we sat down and Alfred and I went to our room and took one gratefully. It made up for the smothering heat hemmed in four close walls instead of the wind of the whole Wild West blowing over us the night before.

The amount of heat and adobe held in one union suit from three days on the road was such that I did not recognize the garment. I substituted an athletic camp shirt of Alfred's which we found in the bag. It fitted me down to the waist like a straight jacket. . . .

Dinner in my second-hand Army clothes and well scratched boots and face half flayed by the wind and sun made me feel far from a lady—but I had a soldier's appetite and the good food completed a strenuous day of fast with perfect satisfaction. . . .

Next morning we were on the home stretch, running fairly and having fair roads at first, where Alfred broke the monotony of his part as passenger-assistant by taking the wheel for some miles. . . .

Back in Taos

Next morning Dasburg, who was sleeping in his studio at Mrs. Young-Hunter's (the last house in the line) and eating some of his meals there, came over quite early and told me that Mabel had been interviewing him. (I was surprised because I had not seen her pass by and she seldom got up by that hour.) She had been telling him, he said, that "she had come home from the trip not on account of the weather, which she had given as an excuse, but because *I* had been very *unpleasant*."

I was thunderstruck—for I had not dreamed of such a thing.

The whole trip opened to my mind like a book in clear print in which I saw every page and line at once, and the keynote was that morning beyond Youngsville when I looked Mabel in the eye and said "*You know* why I did not get up early."

I said to Dasburg that "I was indebted to Mabel as a guest but since she had lied to me in this way and gone to someone else and talked me over I was done with her as a friend—and I would make arrangements to return East as soon as possible."

Dasburg was considerably excited and said that he had suffered too much from Mabel recently himself to take sides in the matter, but that he had stood up for me and told her that, with all my complexes, he believed I was honest.

"But," I said, "this matter was between me and Mabel and I did not need or want a champion or any quarrel or taking of sides. It was patent that this was just what Mabel was trying to foment and to bring about a *situation*, as she always does. All her best and oldest friends say this of her," I added—for it seemed to me that Dasburg was trying to be in a reasonable and fair state of mind and beginning to be open to see Mabel as she is. "I will write down the facts of this trip."

"But Mabel cares nothing for facts," says he. I agreed. "I'm writing them for *you*."

Then he went on about Mabel and her meddling in everybody's affairs and being interested in *Mysticism*—only as a means to gain power. And how she was just now interested in people's cooperating with her.

He said she had told him "to take *me* on a Camping Trip with *him* and prove how I did not cooperate."

My mouth must have opened at this. I said, "Can't you see that she wants to get us together and make us quarrel? She knows I did not come to New Mexico to go on camping trips with *you*. I told her last Spring I would not come at all if you were here—that she knew we never get along together as well as you do."

Here Dasburg got furious and strode away in the Russian thistle, calling out to me that "everything Mabel said of me was true—that I was a crazy woman!! Not fit to take care of Alfred, etc., etc."

I went in to write my facts, feeling pretty cool, but inwardly shaken and afraid that I might not remember and present things clearly. It all depends on a string of events seen in an opposite light by Mabel and Me—so I could not be concise.

Dasburg came around impatiently asking "if I were going to write all morning?"

"It may be," said I, "I can't do this fast."

But at length I handed him the paper—after he had been to town for mail and had time to cool down.

He came back from his studio after reading it and told me, "I think it is outrageous that Mabel should have brought you all the way out here to turn you out like that!"

"I must take Alfred back to school anyway, and since I cannot stay here under obligation to Mabel, after what has passed, I am going to try to get a return ticket as soon as possible."

He said that he wished that Alfred and I might stay over in San Geronimo, and he offered to give me $35.00 to cover our meals at the hotel if I would.

I accepted this, and thanked him—since our fares would finish my bank balance.

I said that "in the Spring when I wrote to Mabel, asking whether she knew of a studio in Taos which I could rent, I had expected to take care of myself, but not of myself and Alfred—supposing that you (Dasburg) and he were settled somewhere as originally planned. (Later, when I found that funds were low, Mabel's letter in reply saying that I could have John's house and should eat at hers, largely decided me to try the expensive trip.)

Yes, Mabel had promised Dasburg, he said, that he and Alfred "should have the Collier's place and camp at her ranch. But it was occupied all summer. The arrangements she makes for people are always most inconvenient." I replied, "it was so with Arthur Lee and all her other proteges. She has always been like this."

Dasburg did not think so, but he agreed that she was hard on people and told how she had given the horse that Mary Foote had bought (and liked better than anything she had) back to a Mexican who said that it had been stolen from him, without making him establish a claim, in Mary Foote's absence.

He said, "Mabel is the only person I can never feel sorry for because she has no compassion."

(I thought to myself, *"compassion,"* that is the word we must use now. it is good—but it is almost the same thing as "pity" which you so abhorred. I think it is used conjointly, as almost all synonyms in the Bible.)

"Mary Moore,"
one of Grace's
sculptures. *Sharon
Niederman.*

San Geronimo Day at Taos Pueblo. *Courtesy Museum of New Mexico, Neg. No. 4387.*

He went on, naming a certain Collector of Indian pottery who had been there, and had seen a very rare prehistoric specimen Mabel had. He was not rich enough to buy it of her, but offered one of his best pieces in exchange, and certainly appreciated it with all the passion of a lover. Mabel had not cared to part with it and it lay around and was used as an ash tray and broken.

This not only roused a poignant pity for the Collector, but a conviction in me that Mabel was really sadistic as well as ruthless. He thought her revengeful, too, though this I had doubted, because she lives too much in the moment, and is so childish.

But when he advised me to change my mail from her box because she had mislaid some of his, I could not help thinking that I might miss a letter from my Circus friend if I didn't—especially if she ever suspected how I rode away in the sagebrush with Sterne, from under her very nose, three years ago.

But I revolted against taking such a precaution about the mail. I said that "Mabel always wants to get people emotionally embroiled and that I had been surprised, first, that she had had me as a friend since I was neither in love nor divorced, nor anything exciting to her—and secondly, that this being so, she should go to the trouble to make a disagreeable situation over me."

But Mabel is not a sculptor or a painter primarily and has no conception of the necessity of getting settled in time to do some work in the place where you can use your materials, any more than she had any realization of what it is to plan what you can do on a certain amount of money and be limited to that. She feels that she gives one delightful freedom and opportunity, and she does—but when it comes to any practical arrangement you must look out for that yourself, and her sudden offers are too liable to change and too incompatible with other working conditions to make it worth while to bank on anything but your own resources and take her hospitality and excursions as something additional that you may or may not be able to enjoy.

That is the way to take her. She can be very good company. I have had the nicest horseback rides with her. She is stimulating when she feels interested. I maintain that she is an artist and has a taste and genius in her collections and arrangements of things that I've not seen in anyone else—her house is beautiful.

"Yes," he said, "she has the most beautiful house in New Mexico. She is a unique person."

Then he told me many things about Mabel and Nina Bull Witte getting together on the case of Mrs. Young-Hunter and how Mrs. Young-Hunter was hysterical when she heard that Eve and Jack Young-Hunter were likely to visit Mabel in Taos now. . . .

I had been chummy with Eve at the time and danced with her and Mr. Young-Hunter three nights running at San Geronimo in 1919—it being the corresponding season with this two years ago.

So things went on very quietly for a few days with no necessity for my going to Mabel's rooms and plenty of excuse for not going, if that were needed, in all the chores I had to do for Alfred's meals and mine and other things about the new house.

Dasburg presented me with some pastels which he had but did not use. I could not help thinking that it was another thing for me to pack. (He has left pastels and such like on my hands in Yonkers) but I thanked him—and tried them too.

Then Dasburg met a famous old bear-hunter (whose name was Lilly) while on a fishing trip with Ufer, who invited him to his camp—if he could find the trail—next Saturday.

Our baggage must be ready two days before we left on the 4th of October so that John Dunn (otherwise "Long John") who drives the mail, could get them to Taos Junction in time.

Having brought most of our winter clothing to Taos with me in anticipation of staying half the winter I had to mail this back in a laundry bag to begin with, and congratulated muyself that we were not yet wearing it, for though the nights were frosty, the days were ideal, and one rode with sleeves rolled up and open throated in the sun. Nevertheless, between camping duffle sent after, and a few Indian things acquired, such as a braided raw-hide lariat that was a great prize of mine, there was enough—and a problem how we could ride the last day and get into our city clothes in time to pack the others.

By doing everything possible in advance, I planned a little leisure for the three days of San Geronimo to spend them in the saddle, galloping from plaza to Pueblo and thence to the race track—lost somewhere in the sagebrush—and back to the plaza again, as the different events, coming off in true Mexican fashion hours behind time, or not coming off at all, should keep one flying around.

This would be the grand finale of my vacation.

I had been to the evening dances too, the other San Geronimo, but this time there was no Eve Schroer to fall back on, and I should be a wallflower—since I can't take a girl and lead (not being an experienced dancer) as I should like to do. Beside, none of the youths who danced with me two years ago and wanted to show me Colorado Springs, were likely to be around—and most of the old settlers were stiffs, in mind and legs.

Dasburg many times offered to help us pack—"later," he said. But I told him right now was the time to do it. Later would be too late to help at all, or save San Geronimo for us.

This, of course, he was too impatient to understand. So I buckled to and saved it for myself.

I was trying to hire a pony for the last week, since I had no horse of my own, having used Alfred's and Dasburg's when they were away, and taken care of them. Learned of a number but none were obtainable at once. Jo Lujan told me of a nice "Pinto" that an artist was painting up the canon and assured me that the family was coming down for San Geronimo and I could get him for a dollar a day.

I had got things running so that I could do some drawings in pastel during certain hours of the day, when, by hanging a large quilt over one window and stopping the chinks in the door, the light could be made usable in Alfred's and my house.

The second time I arranged for work in this way was Saturday morning and I was about to begin, when Dasburg comes in from Mrs. Young-Hunter's and says that he has just decided to try to trail Mr. Lilly; with Dick and the side-saddle and some provisions and his painting outfit, beside his sleeping bag and blankets, all on board—"Would I help him pack the horse?"

It sounded well-nigh impossible, as the sidesaddle has never a leather for anything and is particularly ill-adapted for attaching even a roll on the croup.

Here was easel, palette, gun and all. These things he was trying to balance across the animal's back, so making not only a most ticklish load, but one that would immediately block his progress in brush if the trail were narrow. . . .

So I lent him my nose-bag, circingle and some straps, as his were rotten, and helped him adjust this precarious and heavy assortment diligently, until he actually got out of sight, still ship-shape, in the direction of Canyone.

My morning's work was lost, but Dasburg was so eager, like a child, to try this adventure and had been trying to be so good-natured and actually thanked me for helping him!!—I could not begrudge him.

While waiting for my pony and the Fiesta I now felt almost free, and certainly perfectly cool, and wrote Mabel a note in which I simply said

that I was astonished to hear that it was my "unpleasantness" instead of
the weather which had brought us back from the motor trip, and that
since she had talked my conduct over with others, whom it did not concern,
instead of speaking first to me, I was leaving immediately after San
Geronimo. . .

So the incident closed: and Mabel sometimes looked in at our door, or
we took her mail to her as before.

One evening by the cedar log fire she talked to me about Dasburg and
his lameness, saying that she thought him somewhat exhibitionistic of it.
I had not thought of this, but in the course of the conversation his trial
of the osteopathis or other treatment was spoken of and I expressed myself
strongly—against anyone's making him believe that his leg could be
"cured," since he was ready to take up with such a hope, and I could feel
that the disappointment and above all the fear of doing himself a permanent
injury instead by manipulations might well have been part cause for his
serious illness last winter.

Then Mabel asked "if I were not worried about his staying away in the
Mountains so long—it was more than a week." No, "I had not worried
nor thought of him."

Meanwhile I had secured the Pinto Pony.

It proved to be a little stallion, so oddly marked in red and white that
it looked like the king's fool, the party-color extending even to the eyes.
But it was a delightful animal to ride. He certainly could run—and wanted
to. It was like riding a bird.

San Geronimo

San Geronimo began to arrive. The racetrack in the sagebrush a mile
out of town in the direction of Ranchos had been washed out by the
unusual rains and Tony was having a short, straight course smoothed
down—more or less—on land north of Mabel's house and overlooked
from her sleeping porch. For he wanted to run his black stallion and more
recently acquired chestnut mare. In fact he, or Mabel, as his backer, seemed
to be the principal promoter of the race this year. He asked me to exercise
his horses and take care of them preparatory to the race—but after my
experience with the Ford I declined to take the responsibility.

Jose (typical skin-and-bones Penitenti, Mabel's gardener) liked his horse
better than anything next to his yearly increasing family. They were very
poor, but they *could ride*. Jose's long bowed shanks seemed bent exactly

to the sides of the horse, and he raced bareback; others used the impossible stock saddle on the track, while it at last appeared that Tony (or Mabel) had imported a racing saddle, or something near one, from the East. . . .

The booths of five-cent dusty knick-knacks to be won for ten-cent chances were put up around the Plaza. Grapes and melons and pinones were bought and eaten all day long. Then the Apaches came to town. Handsome lads, some of them, and making the most of their looks, in paint, with their beaver-skin-wrapped braids, broad-brimmed hats, slim loins under the wide silver-studded belts and leather chaps and spurs like real vaquerors. In fact, these Indians are the only *men* (that I have seen) who perpetuate the style of the southwest. Their riding is their pride, and a posse of these youths gallop through Taos and onto the Pueblo with a flourish. The Apache families come frequently in wagons, and pitch tents in the Pueblo fields near the creek while they visit, trade and look on at the events of the Fiesta.

Some of the Apache and Navajo girls were beautiful, with round, bare heads and faces—high and broad cheekbones and small, delicately chiseled noses and even lips that, to my mind, make the American "pretty girl" white type look cheap, mongrel and vulgar.

The young Indians of both sexes have a delightful, shy smile and they can laugh and giggle too. But their whole physique has a rhythm and a grace of unhurried movement that gives them poise and dignity no matter how incongruous their array. As when you see the smooth black hair, the rich face enhanced by an unerringly decorative spot or line of red paint, gorgeous Indian dress, still in perfect harmony, but instead of beautiful beaded or white moccasins a pair of high-heeled, high-laced, pointed shoes from the store.

Interest was divided between the baseball game and the race. We on horseback took in some of each. Tony's black stallion won easily, because the other horse was ridden off the course on purpose.

Mabel had offered a prize of $15.00 but no one could make out the schemes of the Mexicans or how the betting went.

The great Day is the one at the Pueblo.

Mabel did not go. She sent Tony with the Buick and said that Nina Bull Witte and Alfred and I might go as passengers. Mrs. Witte accepted and Alfred preferred to look on at ease from the car.

Pinto flew up to the Pueblo with me on the wings of the sunrise wind, through the harvested Indian grain-fields, very familiar to him, and I was among the first arrivals—really enjoying the ride better alone. (After a lifetime of doing things alone and enjoying nature and laying up one's memory pictures and sensations, even the company of a congenial son is likely to be a detriment.)

It was delightful in the frosty dew. When I reached the first houses, or suburbs of the Pueblo, on the roofs of which I could look down from the saddle, I saw gathered plums reddening there in the sun.

(The day before, the open space or Pueblo "Plaza" where the creek runs through and the races and dances are held, looked like the Valley of a Thousand Smokes, for all the Indian women had their adobe ovens burning for baking the holiday bread and cakes. I had ridden home eating a loaf of the bread which I had to toss from my bridle hand to the other and it burned my teeth at that.)

The huge pole, with the sheep's carcass and pumpkins hung at top, had been erected, as every year, to be "shinned" for today.

I enjoy the day of preparation when this is done and the booth is made at the end of the foot-race-track with gold-leaved aspen sprays from the mountains, as much, or more, than the big crowd at the Mass and the Race and Dance of the Day itself—September 30th.

This morning the sun took a long time to shed much warmth. I rode up behind the Pueblo to the Glorieta (the wonderful cottonwood grove) and back again. There were a few Indians, their sheets drawn close over their faces, walking seriously to or from the Kivas where they were preparing for the race.

I rode about the Pueblo. There were signs this year which ordered all automobiles to keep out and I was glad, but presently I saw Mabel's Buick driven by Tony in his best blanket right inside the walls.

"So you're breaking the law," I said, "didn't you see the signs?"

There were some other tourists parking where they shouldn't now, and some masters of ceremonies were going toward them. "I hope they put them out and you too," I said. "Nothing spoils the whole scene like a mixture of these black cars." Mrs. Witte in her half-dreaming state of "Cosmic Consciousness" through which she claimed to be passing to arrive at "Individual Consciousness" had not thought of that. Tony did drive on beyond the city wall and park inconspicuously along the racetrack.

I tied Pinto under the large racks such as Esquimoux have for keeping fish from the dogs, there used for drying things, preparing buckskins, etc., here. I shinned up a post and took my position with sundry Indian and Mexican lads, whose ponies were also below, where I could look directly down on the race and up the length of the track.

The runners in their paint and feathers were coming up from one kiva and sounded like coyotes. They formed in procession and were met by the troupe from the kiva of the other Pueblo across the bridge. The two processions joined in the preliminary dance, a sort of lock-set with hands on shoulders in two sideward-moving columns to the drum beat—all singing.

Then they form in two horseshoes at the two ends of the track and run the relay race. Two pairs, of one from each Pueblo, starting, the lead being picked up by the other end by the pair running back.

The goals are marked by a willow and spruce bough for the respective Pueblos.

They are laid on the ground, and the runner touches or jumps them as he gives his place to the next man.

An old man stands behind the "horseshoe" and touches each as he starts with an Eagle feather to give him speed.

When all have run they form in the double dance-line again and the drum beats and the women throw cakes and fruit among them from the walls.

. . . The sun struck in under the black cloud which was pouring a curtain of rain against the background of the Pueblo Mountains, and a complete rainbow formed, showing the whole gathering within its span.

Such a group and such a setting with the live air and light on them from the west was too wonderful to be real—It held so long that one felt it was worth coming all the way from the Atlantic coast to see—as if it had been planned as the last unimaginably beautiful picture of the season.

I cannot imagine anything more striking that this scene on the sagebrush, framed in the mountain rainbow as I saw it, fresh, frosty-gray with the shower.

The only thing that hurt was to see the smallest pony there, an iron-gray colt with a touch Mexican boy in the saddle, dealt repeated blows over the right eye for nothing at all, but to show off his rider's prowess and manliness.

Galloping the length of Mabel's long house, Pinto leaped ahead of the posse—but so lightly did he come down even when held in at the turn that it was like the bouyant, dancing motion of a bird in flight—a swift small bird.

I turned in at our house where Alfred and I ate the nubbins of sweet corn from the stalks left standing before the door. (After eating corn raw you never want it boiled.)

We stumbled over my nosebag, bereft of its straps, in our doorway that evening. I said to Alfred, "See, your father is back." When he appeared in person from his studio, he was looking very hearty and ruddy. Even

Dick, his horse, which he had ridden down from the range of mountain all day, did not seem done up and was then eating an extra large feed of oats.

Dansburg told his adventures that evening sitting in our house to Alfred and me and Mabel who came in and lay down on my matrress on the ground.

It was a good story and well told. He described the long trail which he followed by the occasional print of the old hunter's hob-nailed shoes then lost it for miles and never saw the "quakin asp" which his eyes were peeled to find, that was left to denote the fork in the way—but somehow he arrived within a stone's throw of Mr. Lilly's camp far back of Wheeler's Peak without knowing it!

Not finding Mr. Lilly he returned and the horse was gone, the greater part of the rope left with the tree. At a distance he discovered him lying on his side with the rope broken off short around his neck and every article of his working outfit smashed and scattered, especially the tubes of paint, also the "grub" and the sidesaddle horns.

Rescuing the sleeping pouch he got the horse on his feet and tied, without saddle, for the night and turned in himself. Was nearly asleep when the sounds of many wild horses careening around and visiting Dick gave him to understand the cause of his breaking away and the loss of his outfit.

Next morning Mr. Lilly found him and took him to his camp. Took long walks through the day, observing unnoticeable signs of the movement of game.

The big bear that he was after had a 60 mile range.

He was at his best with that audience in the old adobe house that evening, and all our faces were aglow. Afterwards, he asked me if there was anything he could do to help us get off since the trunks must be ready next day—and Alfred and I were leaving early Tuesday morning. He was leaving then also for Santa Fe. So I said that he would probably have no time to help us with his own packing, but if there was any, I should be glad to have him help Alfred pack his trunk.

But, I said emphatically, that I was not asking him to do anything. We expected to be able to manage for ourselves.

I realized that he must be tired after his trip and he admitted that he was somewhat, though he was so much keyed up that he did not seem so.

Next morning, Sunday, Alfred and I were up early clearing our house into our trunks. Alfred's was half-packed, including his motor boat, which had to be laid in right, and I sent him over to Mabel's to clear out his photographic darkroom.

This took him a couple of hours and he was absent when the following things transpired.

I was working over my trunk and other parts of the room when Dasburg came in. He said that, since he was going to Santa Fe with Dick, and his buggy, he wanted to take an old carved Mexican chest that he had collected on the wagon. He sat on the cot and began to ask me if Jose's wife came to clean the house, etc. I told him, and continued packing and said that this was our last day to get things off, and since there was a lot to think of and fit in and remember at each moment, I could not talk then. He took out a map I was packing and began to peruse it. . .

After sundry remarks and questions from him as he sat looking on I made some broad hints to the effect that I had to keep my mind on everything just then and that visitors were in the way. He pointedly remained in the way and speaking of various things. Then, (remembering that he considered "hinting" odious,) I requested him flatly to leave while I finished my job.

He responded by sitting hard where he was and directed at me the most hateful expression of which he is capable—which is by far the most hateful expression that I have seen on any human countenance.

I had felt perfectly calm until that moment and even regarded him with exceptional good will for it seemed to me that he had begun to be friendly and treat me on good terms, almost of comradeship, before he went on his trip and I was determined to meet him more than half way and, above all, let him wind up his stay here and get off to Santa Fe successfully as my stay was winding up successfully, and all hands would have a pleasant parting in forty-eight hours.

But that look was the same that it had been ten years ago—only much worse—a look that above all others I would not take from anybody, the expression and attitude of a German boor enraged at his wife—a concentration of venomous ferocity and contempt. No, he would not dare look like that at a man. His jaw would be smashed before he had time to rise if he tried it. No doubt I met it with an equal expression for it never failed to call forth on the instant the intensest hate of which I am capable. He remained. I showed him the door and said, "My God, can't I ask you to leave my house while I'm working? I'm not asking you to do anything but go!"

He rose with clenched fist and teeth. My contempt wished him to see himself. I said, "Why don't you hit me, you know you want to?" He plunged out and went to his studio.

Well, I thought, that is not the pleasant farewell all round that I was having in mind, but I guess there is no danger of seeing him again. I felt confident that that was final. Drew a free breath and finished everything in the house.

When I go across to the outbuilding where Alfred's trunk and the large packing box were, I meet Dasburg dragging the trunk on end by one handle, the tray being out on the floor. "Let me pass," he says.

"Why are you taking this trunk away? It was nearly packed and you have upset everything. It must be ready for New York today."

"It is not going to New York," he replies between clenched teeth, "nor Alfred either. He is going to Santa Fe with me to stay."

"He is going to New York with me, I believe," I said. "That trunk stays here." "Does it?" he sneered, "What right have you to say so?" "Is that your trunk, did you buy it?" I asked. "You can't stop me," he said. "I'll call the sheriff then," I said.

My hand was on the handle of the trunk. He made a pass at me and said, "Let go or you'll be killed!" "And perhaps you will," I said, leaning quickly across the rubbish and taking up Alfred's rifle which stood against the wall.

I stepped back to the further end of the room with it. Dasburg left the trunk and went to his studio precipitately.

There was nothing for it but to pack it over again as fast as possible. Alfred came now and wanted to know what had been done to it. I said "his father was very mad because I had asked him to leave our house when he came around this morning and hindered my work, and he had upset it, that was all."

We got things to rights again and locked up, and went to town for dinner.

As we were locking our door, Dasburg passed and asked me if I had any fruit for him. Inwardly amazed, I said, "I believed there was some inside," and began to unlock the door; then he yanked away saying he would not have any.

On the afternoon, as I was packing the box, he comes over and says that he "can't stand this. It is making him sick. Let us not fight."

I said, "I did not want to fight"—and continued my work. He goes on that "Mabel had come over to his studio and found him weeping and he had told her what had happened, that is (he said) that I had been so very unpleasant to him this morning."

She had been surprised and could not understand it—unless it was my jealously of his trip to the Mountains.

Shrewd analysis of hers, I thought: That might have been true once. But if she knew the power of a look, and anything about her own demand of "cooperation" she would be aware that envy of his trip while I was having San Geronimo on "Pinto" was far from necessary to supply the animus of any "unpleasantness" of mine that morning. And she had seen him in tears, too, and timed her visit just right—to prove that he was exhibitionistic of his weakness. "Mabel, you win!" I exclaimed to myself.

ELEANOR WILLIAMS
Rebel in the West

Born in 1906 into a well-to-do Pittsburgh family with both Rockefeller and Frick connections, Eleanor McClintock Williams might
well have spent her life comfortably as a proper Eastern lady. Instead,
drawn by the West, she became a champion trick rider, performed
on the rodeo circuit and in the Ringling Brothers Barnum and Bailey
Circus, and struggled to build and hold onto her Quemado, New
Mexico, ranch during the Depression and the war years. After going
through two stormy marriages, she wed rancher Frank Williams in
1940. While raising five children, she also found time to run for the
New Mexico legislature, publish her poetry, and, at age 45, pick up
her paintbrush and portray the people and places of her beloved
New Mexico.

Eleanor first fell in love with the West as a teenager while on a
summer vacation at the Montana ranch of Nan Hart, the woman
she called "my dear western Ma" and with whom she carried on a
lifelong correspondence. Eleanor described that point in her life
when her heart turned west, writing: "I will never forget the bursting
feeling of contentment that I had on my first morning at the Dot S
Dot, when I woke up down in the 'green room' and smelled the
heavy sweetness of the new Montana air, and heard the turkeys
chirping peacefully outside my window. . . ."

Two distinct interests conflicted within Eleanor—her love of art
and her love of riding. While studying art at Carnegie Tech, she
spent summers at Yellowstone National Park working as a "pillow

puncher" and escaping to the stables every spare moment. She studied
animal husbandry briefly at Penn State, then, returning to art, enrolled at the Art Students League in New York City. The following
summer she worked as a wrangler on a ranch near Jackson Hole,
Wyoming.

Returning to the Washington Square apartment she shared with
the daughter of a Bar Harbor family friend, she continued her studies
at the League, one of the nation's premier art institutions.

Later in 1928 she attended a rodeo in Madison Square Garden,
where backstage she met rodeo cowboy Walter Heacock. Two weeks
later, Eleanor and Walter eloped. Although the wedding announcement reported that "the bride and groom are taking an extended
trip to South America," the truth was that Eleanor had joined her
new husband on a Wild West show bound for Chile.

After a number of shows the manager ran off with the gate money,
leaving them stranded. Walter and Eleanor headed back to California
on a Japanese cargo ship. While Walter searched for a job, Eleanor
wrote Wild West stories under a still-unknown pseudonym. When
she married Walter, she vowed never to ask her family for financial
help.

Walter and Eleanor worked the rodeo circuit in the early 1930s.
When offered 300 acres on Apache Creek near Quemado for $2 an
acre, they bought the land. This, the Rising Sun Ranch in the Apache
National Forest, would be Eleanor's home for the rest of her life.
Between riding in rodeos dressed in scarlet costume, Eleanor returned
to the ranch to work with the men hand-digging the well and cutting
logs for the barn, corrals and house. She also made a series of pencil
sketches of her fellow rodeo performers.

Then, in 1934, after six years, her marriage broke up, a personal
tragedy Eleanor attributed to Walter's ". . . unfortunate blend of
charm and inconsistency . . ." Packing her horse, Sonny Boy, into
a trailer, Eleanor drove to her parents' home in Pittsburgh, where
her daughter, Nanny, was living. In Febraury 1935, a telegram arrived from Tim McCoy's Wild West Show, offering her a job as
trick rider and aerialist.

That season she toured the country with the Ringling Brothers
big top. When the circus came to Pittsburgh, Eleanor was chauffeured
to her performances by her cousin, Helen Frick, wife of steel magnate
Henry Clay Frick. Helen was so horrified by Eleanor's tightrope act
that she offered to recompense her whatever wages she'd lose by

stopping. Eleanor refused, but later a broken thumb forced her off the high wire.

While performing that season, Eleanor met and married circus cowboy Earl Cline. She separated from Earl in 1938, putting herself in the position of raising her two children and running the ranch alone. Using every resource, including driving the school bus and tending the cattle and horses herself, she managed to keep going. "I feel comparatively secure and peaceful when I'm here alone, even though I haven't much money," she wrote.

Then, when she was at her lowest point, fate intervened, and Eleanor fell in love with and married Frank Williams, a neighboring rancher who was, she felt, "the first man to supercede my love of the west itself." Frank was the embodiment of the western virtues Eleanor admired—a self-made, honest, determined man who'd supported his family from age sixteen on and didn't even have a high school diploma. He was "not a 1941 model—but like the men who once typified the west, full of old-time courtliness and kindness," she wrote.

Frank and Eleanor had three children. To make ends meet, he hired out as a foreman on another ranch while Eleanor managed the Rising Sun.

Not until 1951, at age 45, when she began to get out from under constant worry about mortgages, drought, severe winters, the cost of hay and surgery to correct old injuries, did Eleanor begin her oil paintings depicting her family, neighbors and the landscapes she saw every day.

Throughout the 1960s and 70s, Eleanor continued actively running the Rising Sun. Frank died suddenly of a heart attack in 1974, and Eleanor died of peneumonia on June 21, 1979.

During the twenty years she set her art aside, Eleanor was occupied with the practical, daily concerns of marriage, children and—predominant in her thinking—the ranch. When her children were older and she was somewhat more financially secure, she was able to once again turn her energies to painting. As the eldest daughter of an artist father, Eleanor follows the pattern of many women artists, having the possibility of a career, the materials and access to training at hand.

But the pull Eleanor felt for the West outweighed any commitment she may have had toward building a career as an artist. In following that pull, she cut herself off from the training, influences, and connections necessary to build a career. While living in Quemado, she associated neither with the neighboring Hurd-Wyeth group nor with the Santa Fe and Taos painters. For her, painting was a purely personal expression.

Beginning in 1935 and spanning almost two decades, Eleanor's letters to Nan Hart reveal the vulnerability of a woman who lived outwardly as a brave rancher and daredevil rodeo queen. Offering a rich response to a deeply trusted confidante, these moving, colloquial, insightful letters touch on many issues facing women today—marriage, divorce, separation, child-rearing, economic and emotional self-sufficiency, the battle between self-doubt and self-trust, and the juggling of commitments to professional and creative growth and personal responsibilities.

In the presence of a loving, non-judgmental friendship that endured well beyond her earlier marriages, Eleanor could gather perseverance through the exchange of clarity and honesty. With Auntie Nan she feels free to recognize and express her thoughts without censorship and so come to know and trust herself more deeply.

Eleanor refused to allow social convention or other people's expectations to overshadow her personal drives. Standing in the generation between homesteading women and contemporary feminists, her character mixes the grit and guts of the pioneers with contemporary women's striving to express their talents and build authentic, complete relationships.

MAY 27, 1935
PHILADELPHIA, PA

AUNTIE NAN DEAREST,

How sweet of you to write your neglectful western daughter who has been much to blame for not writing to you, but who has nevertheless thought of you many many times. It has been on the tip of my fingers for a long time to write you—the first few weeks on the outfit were spent in getting acclimated and adjusted, and letters were quite impossible—but just as I was getting used to everything one of the blamed fingers got broken, which again made letters impossible, since it was on my right hand—and a thumb at that. It is still in a splint, but I am learning to manipulate it a little better now.

I had a time after I saw you that day in Pittsburgh. The Allegheny mountains were a glare of ice, and it was colder than Greenland's glaciers—

and we broke down near Ligonier and had to sit in a frigid country garage while the car was being worked on. We ran into heavy storm clouds and frequent flurries of snow, as I made up my mind to keep on going till I got out of that neck of the woods—figuring all the while that it would be easier to stay congealed than to stop for the night and thaw out and then have to freeze again. By ten o'clock that night I got to Frederick, Maryland—where I wired Mother, and by five o'clock next morning we were in Richmond, Virginia. I kept right on going till I got to Augusta, Georgia, and there I had more trouble with the car and had to lie over for seven hours getting it fixed. After that, the trip was warm and uneventful.

It was quite hectic in Florida, getting settled, and used to the long hot hours of training that we had to put in every day. We were there till the fourth of April, when we started our long trek northward by train. We were all on one train—horses, giraffes, lions, acrobats—even the man on the flying trapeze—and honestly I thought that trip would never end. We were traveling at a third class freight rate, and fully half of the time en route was spent sitting on railroad sidings waiting for "regular" trains to whizz by. We had no chair cars of any description, and the Ringling pullman bunks are all built in to stay put—they don't turn into seats by day. We had to either sit all hunched up in our berths or else go out and sit on the train platforms. Results were, that when we got to New York after four days on the way, we were all pretty well tuckered out. The weather in N.Y. was plenty nasty for two weeks after we got there, and on top of everything else they kept us worn down practicing in the early mornings, so that with our resistance lowered we all contracted beautiful colds. It was tough sledding those first few weeks, but now things have eased up a bit; so as long as I got through those first hard days I know I can stick it out for the rest of the season—especially since I broke my thumb! I can do very little, so I lead quite a lazy life. I can ride my trick horse and ride high jumpers, but my hard riding and trapeze work is out.

. . . Ringling's does not overlook a single detail. We have grooms for our horses, so that we don't have to worry about looking after them. . . . In fact, all we have to do is to go out and do our work during the show. That is all that is expected of us, and so it is really an easier life for me than I have been used to for years. Of course, during the show we really have to scramble, changing costumes, etc., but when the show is over we are free to rest or do anything we want to. We are expected to live very respectable lives—otherwise we could not hit the riffle. That is one noticeable difference between circus and rodeo life. Rodeo hands are many of them pretty loose livers, and there is no one to lay down the law to them, because if they go to pieces from parties and drinking, they are the only losers. But on a circus it is a different matter. We are kept tabs on like boarding school girls, almost. If a circus girl starts going around with a man from the "front door"—she loses her job, if caught.

Your offer of a job on the Dot S Dot is terribly tempting. After all, that seems like my country out there—and like home. The most fascinating job in the world would never have the lure for me that that place has, and that life. I love it, and if I was away from it the rest of my life I would never stop missing it, and all of you. But right now I am afraid it would be mighty impractical of me to pick up and leave here. I am drawing fairly good pay, with no living expenses attached; and my horse is here, while my car and trailer are in storage in Florida. Leaving the show would mean probably a lot of grief and expense in getting the horse parked temporarily in some out of the way Oshkosh, and a trip to Florida. . . . So it looks as though I had better stay in the buggy for this season, anyway. But you don't know how much I appreciate your wanting me there—or how much I would love to be there. Believe it nor not, it is a real temptation to just pull up stakes and fly out. If I was a lady of leisure instead of a slave to the necessities of living I most certainly would do that very thing, and no two ways about it.

It is time for the two o'clock show now, so I must stop and put on my scarlet and sweltering costume for the grand spectacle. A heartful of love to my dear western ma and pa always, from ELEANOR

9/20/35

DEAREST AUNTIE NAN

I've thought of you a thousand times this summer, and pictured you out there on the ranch; but it's been so darn hard to write letters. My time is so completely cut up into little pieces that when I finish one thing, I have to almost start right away to get ready for the next. And the only time that I really get to write is here in the dressing room, with everyone talking at once—the biggest hug-bub you ever heard. This letter, as a result, may not make sense; but it's a try anyway, and something that I just don't want to put off any longer.

How are you anyway, and have you had a good summer? My, I do hope so. This summer has been quite an experience for me, and in a lot of ways I've liked it very much; but would hate to think of having to do it the rest of my life. . . .

About a month or so ago I got a letter from Walt, written on Dot S
Dot stationery. I guess I am just sentimental enough so that the letter
gave me an awful start. It seemed like a voice from the past, coming from
that country where we had lived together, and where little Nan was born.
It hit pretty deep; especially as he wrote as though nothing had ever
happened. And only two or three days before that—almost at the time
that he wrote that letter, I guess—I had decided to legally put an end to
things and had started action for a divorce. I certainly was loathe to come
around to doing that—it just went against my whole nature and everything
that I ever believed in—Walt wrote me such pathetic letters last winter
that I relented and intended to give him another chance—I thought that
perhaps the separation had taught him the lesson that nothing else would;
and that he would really try to make good at least one of his many promises.
But, as always, when he thought that things were going his way again,
he went right back to his old ways—chiseling and not telling the truth,
and being most unfair. One letter from him would work on my emotions—
He wanted me to leave the circus and go and make rodeos with him;—I
had sent him one hundred dollars not three weeks before that to help him
make two back payments on the truck, and did not have enough saved to
get out there with horse and trailer, even if I had wanted to—

And of course I felt that it would be a most foolish move on my part,
even if I could have afforded it. As it was, I wrote and told him it was
financially impossible—Instead of trying to understand all that, he wrote
back quite a cruel letter, saying that if I did not think enough of him to
make rodeos with him, that we might as well "call it quits," and that I
would hear from his lawyer in a few days. The lawyer part was seemingly
all bluff, because I never heard from him. But that letter was the turning
point for me.

I never answered it, and after a month or so I started action for a divorce.
He never wrote again either, until the letter that I got from Melville. Then
it was too late, because I have made up my mind now, and there will be
no turning back. But just the same, the letter from Melville struck an old
chord, and it took me several days to gather myself together again and
get my thoughts straightened out.

Walt's unfortunate blend of charm and inconsistency, of nice qualities
and overshadowing faults, is the greatest tragedy that has ever directly
touched my life; and my inability to help him or change him in any way
is a disappointment that I will never never get over. I will feel baffled
about it to my dying day, I know that.

I still worry about him, as I would over a little boy, and I do hope that

Eleanor Williams.
Helen Baldwin.

Eleanor and Sonny Boy. *Helen
Baldwin.*

Eleanor and Walter
Heacock. *Helen Baldwin.*

Eleanor and Sonny Boy. *Helen
Baldwin.*

he will succeed in taking care of himself, or that someone else will take
care of him. I hate to think of his going down—down—down after years
of fighting to keep him from backsliding.

. . . Dearest love to you always, and to dear Uncle Harry & Bob—I'm
sorry this has been such a stupid missive, but it's the best I can do today.

Always devotedly,

EL

HOTEL CHARLOTTE
CHARLOTTE, N.C.
NOV. 4, 1935

DEAREST AUNTIE NAN—

I came down and got a hotel room today, partly to get a good warm
bath, and partly so I could answer your letter where I would have a little
comparative peace and quiet. And what a dear sweet letter it was! As I
read it, a lot of the warmth of that atmosphere and of your loyalty and
generosity and love seemed to go into me and make me feel fairly glowing
with it.

I wish that I could unhesitatingly say that I could come, but I still don't
know. You see, my ranch is all in my name; and as Walt never put out
any of the actual cash that went into it, it ought to be. But nevertheless,
there is a law in N.M. whereby land is considered as "community property,"
regardless of whether it is recorded in the name of husband or wife. Walt
claims that he can get half of it by this law, even though he knows that
it is rightfully mine, down in his heart. If he deserved half, I could be only
too glad to share it with him; but he doesn't. It is just one more bit of
chiseling that he hopes to put through; and I feel this time that as a matter
of pride and practicality and everything else, that I must not let him get
away with it.

I am going out there and see the best lawyer I can find, and find out
just how hard or easy it going to be. Also how much of Walt's attitude
is bluff, and how much of a fight he really means to put up. If things are
too awfully lengthy and disagreeable I may agree to do what he wants me
to do; sell my share to him. I know by doing this that I could ultimately
get it anyway, because he never *never* has been able to pay for things, and
he always is the first one to make a perfectly hopeless deal. He cheerfully
plunges into the deepest of waters without a cent to his name, or an idea
of where any more is coming from; so that I could easily fix up a mortgage

and close right down on him. Only thing is, it would take much longer, of course. Also, it too would be a disagreeable proceeding, and as long as I have to go through so much disagreeableness, I might as well go through it now as later.

But about your lovely invitation. If things are bad when I get out there, I may take a mortgage on the place (my share), and in that case, I could come north as soon as I get it drawn up. And if I can win the property, I might lease or rent the ranch to someone, and then come to Montana. . .

The circus comes to a close one week from tomorrow, November twelfth, in Miami, Florida. From there I have to go back to Sarasota to pick up my car and trailer, and I intend to trade my old '31 Chevy in on another car, as it has 62,000 miles on it and is getting very dilapidated. I would really be afraid to trust it on another long trip. The Chev. agency in Sarasota offered me $150 for it on a trade, which is more than I ever expected, so I think I'd better cash it in. Dearest love to you all, and to you, my dear Auntie Nan, heartfelt appreciation for your unfailing devotion. It is certainly mutual.

Always your old hay-hand & source of general annoyance.

EL

FEBRUARY 15, 1936

MY DEAREST AUNTIE NAN—

. . . I guess when I wrote you last, that the circus season was almost over. If it was from Georgia, that was fun just a week before closing time, and cold as Greeland's icy mountains. We had to build charcoal fires in the dressing room to keep from freezing, and our necessary daily bucket baths were accompanied by shreiks and goose pimples. Even Jacksonville, Florida—next to the last spot we played—was plenty cold. We closed at Miami, and from there I went back to winter quarters and picked up Sonny Boy and the car and trailer. Besides my baggage, I had two additional head of livestock—gifts, both of them—an old Airedale dog;—Gaspipe, for five years a circus mascot. . . . Now Gaspipe lies by the fireplace evenings, and chases bunnies daily. He chases them so ambitiously that none can be found for shooting purposes within half a mile! My other gift was a three months old chow puppy—a little darling. I traded my old '31 Chevy in on a new '35 Chev. sedan in Florida. So we made a good start; but I was held up for three days at a small and very second rate tourist camp a few hundred yards from the famed Sewanee River. If you look it up on the map you'll find that it rises I know-not-where;—but the part I'm interested in runs into the Gulf of Mexico about one hundred miles south from Talahassee. The country around there is thickly wooded swampland—high spots of oak, and low-spots of big bottomed cypress. All of it dense and dark with hanging moss and peopled sparsely by poor whites who live in unbelievably shabby frame shacks and are largely illiterate and ignorant. At this tourist camp I lighted my first night from Sarasota, tied Sonny boy to a tree in front of my cabin, and went to sleep. Sonny Boy, who had always been a model camp horse, decided to commit flagrant crime, broke his halter rope and ran away into the land of the unknown. Next morning I trailed him seven miles up the highway, lost his track, and spent the rest of the day frantically driving over terrible back roads in the impenetrable swamp country, stopping at little house after little house to inquire if he had been seen. No success! The second day brought no better luck, and I drove literally hundreds of miles over terrible roads. By this time, gnarled Florida "crackers" were drifting into "Jo's Camp," where I was staying, with varying tales of a "potted hoss," as they described him. One had seen him at midnight, the night he broke loose, and that report I knew to be a prevarication, as I had been up and looked at him at 3 AM when I heard him stamping, and he was still fast tied. On the afternoon of that second day, I posted a ten dollar reward for him at the village store, four miles from the camp; and next morning, Jo said, there were darkies and whites searching the swamps in three counties.

About noon, on the third day, a man drove up in an automobile to say that he had Sonny Boy safely penned in his chicken yard. I dashed up there in the car—twenty miles away, it was—and almost wept on his spotted neck, I was so glad to see him.

From then on, my journey was unhampered by any more mishaps. Two days after I got home I filed suit for divorce in Albuquerque. I found Walt at the ranch when I got here. First he wanted me to give him money for what he claimed was his half. He always seemed to think that I had an unfailing source of ready coin—where he got the idea, I'm at a loss to know. When he found out that I had no cash to part with—or *would* not, according to him—then he took whatever settlement I would give him. My lawyer assured me that I would not have to give him an acre, since it was all in my name and listed as my separate estate. Also, I could prove non-support; and even if I did not have all the evidence that I did, I could get the ranch for alimony. But rather than have a lot of wrangling and perhaps a court fight, I gave Walt about one hundred and thirty acres of land, and some of the personal property. That gave him a right to hold his forest permit, and gave him the feeling, at least, that he had won his part of the battle. . . .

MAY 10, 1936
RISING SUN RANCH
QUEMADO, NEW MEXICO

. DEAREST AUNTIE NAN:

The trouble with you, you write such swell letters, that I always wait for a time to answer then when I think I have enough time on my hands to do them, and you, justice. And those moments just never seem to come. My letter to you, now, has been something that I have on my mind to write for *months*, literally, and I have put it off from day to day, saying, "Tomorrow I won't be so busy." But you know how deceiving anticipated moments of leisure on a ranch can be, I guess. . . .

We drove to Minneapolis a week or two after I got it. The roads weren't bad at all, so we did not take a train. But instead of going to Mayos, as I had intended, I decided to put it off until I got through the building up part here on the ranch. I have had so much organic trouble, which troubles me almost worse than the back, and is all a result of the same accident, that I did not know how much Mayos would find they had to do to me, and if so, how useless I would be afterwards, and for how long. So I decided to wait until after I could play my most useful part here, helping and cooking for those working. Then, perhaps, I can give a sigh of relief and a look after the rest. I have an inexpressible dread of operations anyway, and a tendency to wait, hoping that things will improve themselves. . . .

Since we got home, the days have been very very busy. We get started about six in the morning, and keep going pretty steadily until dark at night. And then we are both so tired that we spend our evenings very unillustriously indeed by going to bed. It makes me so mad to think that fatigue can make you forego the advantages of the only leisure time that you have to read or have fun or write letters or talk, and that when you busy yourself with hard physical tasks during the day, your body won't allow your mind to have its fling at night, but demands sleep, like a dope addict. Earl and I haven't even been to any of the town dances or school plays! We have had from two to four extra men working here all the time, and of course that means cooking three squares a day. I have been cooking for from three or four to eight for quite some time now. Of course I used to do the same thing when the Heacock menage was here, but in those days it was just plain discouraging labor for nothing, while now things march forward in grand style, and I don't notice it as work at all, because it is a happy feeling to be doing one's share of work toward a good end, and a goal that one can really see and not just dimly hope for.

Last week we branded most of our cattle and threw them out on the forest. What are cattle selling for up there now? We have been able to pick up pretty good grade Hereford stuff—not registered or anything like that, but still a pretty good grade—for twenty two and a half a head, two year olds. We have gotten some cows older than that for twenty five. We bought two three year old cows about a month ago for twenty five apiece, got them from a man who needed exactly fifty dollars to pay a grocery bill; and now both cows have calves, which alone ought to be worth twenty dollars or so by fall. Cattle are lots higher than they were around here though, and we can't find cows just anywhere at these prices. We were just lucky in getting a few bargains. I find myself wishing that I had even half of Uncle Harry's "cow sense" about now. There's an awful lot that I don't know about cows, but we're never too old to learn, are we? No one in this country ever saw a bunch of cattle like yours and Uncle Harry's anyway. Most of it is Mexican Chiwawa stuff—ring-eyed and goat-horned.

Our big log house is really shaping out, and we think that inside of a month or six weeks we will be ready to move in. The roof is on, and we have sent after a 50 Unit Heatilator for our living room fireplace. When all is finished, I figure that we can accommodate from six to eight people, to help make things pay, but it is awfully late in the year now to try to do any canvassing for dudes. If you have any overflows that you don't know what to do with, give them a steer this way, as we would sorely like to see a little money coming in after the steady outflow of the last few months. We will be definitely able to accommodate a few by the first of July anyway. We have a few good horses and saddles, and will be able to take care of a few very well—that is, if we aren't too late. I didn't dare to write anyone before I knew positively how things were coming out.

. . . Well, no more of the nomadic existence, I hope, and a thousand thanks to you, Auntie Nan, for looking after those belongings of mine for so long, and so well.

Walt and his frau have left this country and returned several times. . . . Walt lost his car, the big Buick. A merchant downtown had made two payments on it for Walt, and he left here afoot. I heard reports that he and this girl that he married are already at odds and ready to split, but I hope that that is not too true. Walt seems a very different person than he used to be. I can't even realize sometimes that he *is* the same one. So hard and so greedy, and brazen about things. I kind of wish now that I had not been so lenient about the divorce settlement, because he quite obviously doesn't appreciate it. He is supposed to have sold the land to his brother in law, but I rather suspect that it is just a shift in title to avoid attachments for debts. He has none of his sweetness left, and what charm remains seems to be very much put on in order to gain his own ends. It is most terrible to see the fast development of his self-destructive nature. What *will* become of him, Auntie Nan? Even his eyes seem to have become smaller and meaner looking, and his mouth has a cast of cruelty to it now that I never noticed before. He hardly seems good-looking anymore, and I always had thought that he would have his looks, no matter how deceiving they were.

I must stop now and go to bed, as being up at ten o'clock tonight is a rare accomplishment for me, and one that is beginning to show its stamp on this letter. As I look up the page I see y's where E's ought to be, and everything else. Earl is reading Detective stories in bed, and I think I had better stop him before he gets powder-burnt.

We had a new colt yesterday, whose Pa was Walt's pretty Silver horse, the palamino stallion. The colt is out of a bay mare, and is a real buckskin. I am breaking another dun filly in my spare time. She is three years old. A little young to break, but there are no horse breakers around here now but me and so I have to take advantage in every way that I can. I have ridden her three times and she is coming nicely. It's such fun to be doing things around the ranch without looking forward to having to leave in the near future and make rodeos or circuses. We expect two hundred baby chicks (three weekers) to arrive next week. Then the work *will* begin, won't it!?

Much love to each and every one of you, dearest Auntie Nan, and I hope that things will be starting off with a bang for you in the very near future.

Always your devoted,

El

Rising Sun Ranch
Quemado, New Mexico
August 16, 1936

Dearest Auntie Nan:

I got your letter yesterday, and feel more than badly that I haven't gotten a letter off to you long before this, so that you had to take the time during your busy season to write and find out what had become of me. . . .

August 20

Four more days have sped by, during which I've had a surplus of things to keep me busy and interrupted so that I could not finish this letter. When the Bible says that "a thousand years are as but a day in His sight" I'm sure that that applies to the God of the wide open spaces too, else how can a month seem like just a few days, when it comes to accomplishment?

All these weeks that you have not heard from me I have been terribly busy, and not too well besides. The combination has made the worst kind of procrastinator out of me, when it comes to letters or any of the little extra things I'd like so much to be doing.

We have been very busy on the new home, but have had so many delays that we still aren't moved in, and thank goodness I had no dude prospects for this season that had to be cancelled. . . .

Our plumbing fixtures got held up along the road somewhere, and we did not get them for over two months after we ordered them, which was the main hold-up. Then we had trouble with our workers, and had to fire the whole bunch, and getting someone new in this country, what with the CCC and the WPA and other loafing institutions to harbor (what used to be) the main part of the working class, is anything but easy. We finally got lined out again, but I have not been able to keep my end of things up the way I should, and have finally had to get a girl to help me. One day of hard work would put me in bed the next, and poor Earl could not be expected to have to labor in the kitchen and work outside too. The trouble is all caused indirectly by that miserable accident. My back does not bother me so terribly much, because I have not been on a horse in months and hardly ever even set foot in an automobile, but the other organs that got knocked out of place at the same time have been behaving badly. I have started to have another baby, which I really very much want, but whether I'll be able to get through with it is an open question. Only days in bed have kept me from losing it half a dozen times already, and in some way the embryo seems to be very much out of place. I haven't been able to navigate the sixty miles to a fairly good doctor yet, so I don't know just what we will find. As far as I know, it will happen in January, and we are hoping that it will go through without a hitch because this is the first time in years that I have had the leisure to have one, and goodness knows when I would again. Earl is crazy to have a child, and I think it would help him to feel freer of the stigma of a previous husband. As long as we are here on the ranch there are constant reminders of Walt to get under his skin. Next summer will doubtless be busy in one way or another and if I have the baby in January I will be able to be in good trim again when I need to be.

I feel the need of having one too, since little Nan and all her baby life have been more or less lost to me. I wrote Mother the other day that I was ready and able now to take her again, and I am deathly afraid to get the answer to that letter because I am almost certain that Mother and Daddy won't want to give her up. Of course I don't know, but they have had her for so long that she is like their own, and they have a strong argument in *favor* of keeping her when it comes to good schools. Their taking her when it was so impossible for me to have her with me and being so perfectly lovely about giving her a wonderful home during all these years has put me in a position where I cannot very well pull a "Gloria Vanderbilt" and get her for myself. I could not be ungrateful now. I can only hope that they don't anticipate keeping her indefinitely as much as I am afraid that they will.

I have not told Mother about the new expected arrival yet, partly because I did not want her to worry so early in the game, as she invariably does, and partly because things have been so uncertain that I did not want to break such important news to her one day and perhaps lose it the next.

We are in a pretty serious condition in this country with the drouth. Today it is raining pitchforks, a slow steady rain that three weeks ago would have done worlds of good, but since yesterday was our first good rain this summer and the poor grass is burned to a crisp, we are afraid that our moisture now is too late to do much good. This native grass can do surprising things in the way of quick growing, but it will hardly have time to ripen and mature now before the frost hits it. We usually get a frost in September that puts an end to fast growing.

Must stop and start lunch. The boys are finishing up the big Heatilator living room fireplace today, and we are very anxious to see how it will work. Then they are going to work on another little fireplace in a small room adjoining the big one. We have our bedrooms completely finished and furnished, and really about the only main chore left to do now is to put in the water system. There is a party of surveyors working north of Quemado, one of whom is a first rate authority on plumbing, and he comes up here every Sunday, his day off, and helps us with our plumbing fixtures. We have about half of them in, but we have to get our overhead supply tank still. Our cess pool is all dug. Everything we do seems to have its hitches and go slower than we figured it would, but it is gradually working out, and at least we can see lots of light now.

Please forgive me for not writing before, but you know what it is to be snowed under and "cripping" around trying to do your work, so I know you will go easy on me. I think of you and Uncle Harry so much and try often to picture you all and think what you might be doing in that land that always lies nearest to my heart in so many ways.

Always with so much love to you all and most devotedly,
EL

RISING SUN RANCH
QUEMADO, NEW MEXICO
MAY 28, 1938

DEAREST AUNTIE NAN:
    . . . This winter has been the most worrisome of any that I have ever known. It has been a nightmare of financial worry. With mounting bills and several debts, I finally got desperate this spring and took a job on a big wild west show that opened in Chicago in April, riding bucking horses. Earl got connected with it too, as one of the assistant cashiers. It was really a big thing, supposed to replace and surpass the old 101 Show, and the backers put $450,000 into it—one of them was a Dupont from Wilmington. They had riders from the Argentine, from Italy, from old Mexico, from Australia, from India, from England and from our own country. There were two hundred American Indians alone. All wore native costumes and used native saddles and regalia. The show was headed by Col. Tim McCoy, who made a minor name in moving pictures and whom I worked under on the Ringling Show. It was a really beautiful show, with colorful acts and wonderful up-to-date equipment. We traveled on trains after we left Chicago and went on the road—the show had thirty brand new stock, flat and pullman cars.
    At Washington, D.C. a horse pulled away from the pickup man and reared back with me, hitting my face with his head and knocking me unconscious. One of my teeth was driven through my upper lip by the impact, but fortunately did not knock out or even loosen the tooth, and my cheek-bone was cracked. That accident, added to the fact that word that very day had reached us that things at the ranch were being terribly mismanaged, made us decide that the wisest thing to do would be to leave

the show and come home. My original intention had been to leave anyway, in June, although Earl thought that perhaps he might stay on the rest of the season. That was the first day of the Washington engagement, and I drew out what money I had coming to me that night, as did Earl, and we left the next day. And what a break for us that we did! That was on Monday, and Wednesday, creditors closed down on the luckless show and it went into the hands of receivers, and everyone got five dollars apiece. It was tragic, really, for it was a beautiful show, but for one thing they had too enormous a payroll, and overhead, and they struck a very bad season to launch a new show.

We came home to find an added eighty five dollar grocery and feed bill that had been run up entirely without our authority and knowledge during our absence, and all kinds of skullduggery in full swing at the ranch. We had left an elderly and apparently very dependable couple here on the ranch—I think I bragged to you in a letter some time ago about being fortunate in having them here. She was looking after the children and he was running the cattle and affairs, and our old boy that we had when you were here, Lloyd, was also here. We found that they had, among other things, butchered one of our yearling steers, and sold part of the meat in town—can you picture it? And Lloyd was supplying an impoverished and neighboring brother and his family with groceries from our cellar and with some of the feed purchased in our absence. It was all very disillusioning and very disgusting. We had a very complete and thunderous shakeup, and are now doing our own work temporarily, as it is very difficult here to pick up anyone new at short notice. I expect to do the planting next week myself, as soon as I can rent a planter from a neighbor, and put in a field of cane that we are going to try to irrigate with a small centrifugal pump.

That plus a lady dude who arrives the eighth of June is presenting quite a problem, but we will work it out somehow.

Nanny and the baby are the very pictures of health. Nanny is developing wonderfully and is really cut out for a ranch. I don't know, of course, whether that is a fact that is really to her benefit or not, but being in love with the west as I am myself, it gives me a grand feeling to think that Nanny's tastes run along the same lines. She is a great help, and has certain chores that are relegated to her and which she does most efficiently. The baby is a regular platinum blond, which makes me feel like an old hen with a duckling child. Both children are living monuments to this climate and the air and sunshine that they get from one day's end to another.

Now I must stop, and as I say goodbye to all you dear and much beloved people for another while, I will say too that I hope this summer will be a good one for you, and bristling with dudes.

Much love to you all, always from your ever devoted,
EL

JANUARY 16, 1940
RISING SUN RANCH
QUEMADO, NEW MEXICO

DEAREST AUNTIE NAN—

It was a real boon to get your letter—and how you do read between the lines of things! No matter what I tell you, you seem to already know it.

Yes, Mother did want me to come back there but I don't know yet whether I will go—and if I do it can't be for quite a while. Really, my whole being rebels terribly against "bedding down" anywhere in the east. I don't see how I can ever do it, but of course, as you say, the children have to be thought of first. However, I am not sure that I can ever offer them much back there—and I do feel that no matter how small the financial returns are from whatever I undertake, that I should do the providing, and not allow either of my children to become "wards", so to speak—of other people. It is true that they might have access to more material things by such an arrangement, but in the long run it would be morally devitalizing to all of us—so I feel that we should stick together, even if the fare is only cornbread & beans.

. . . I don't know whether I told you or not, but Earl is in California trying to get a job, and I am holding things down here and running the school bus with my car for $40 a month. That isn't great wealth, but it keeps us going; and then I am also looking after about twenty head of horses and twenty five head of cattle—the remnant of what we sold fall before last & from which (pardon the change in ink, but I am writing this down in Quemado!) I had hoped to build another herd to run on our forest permit when grass conditions improve—when & if! We have had bad luck with other people looking after our stock, & I feel that I can take care of them better myself. I do love to work with stock, & it is a much more economical arrangement. . . .

I have not made any definite break with Earl because he wanted me to give him another chance, & he has promised to try to stop drinking & get a job—and I thought that it would be criminal to discourage him, if encouragement on my part could in any way help him to help himself. Whether it will or not remains to be seen. So far, he hasn't any job, and if he comes rolling back to the ranch without one, then will be the time to worry. Not so much because of his failure to get a job, but because of what I know will inevitably follow—constant griping and running up bills that I may not be able to pay; and probably having to sell out to alleviate the situation. I feel comparatively secure & peaceful when I'm here alone, even though I haven't much money; but I don't really require much to get by & be happy, while with Earl it's a constant heartache not to have all he wants to go here & go there etc.—

You see things so clearly & so logically that I wish I could see you and talk to you. No one has the same clarity & force of thought that you have—or at least, no one that I ever knew. And it is a wonderful feeling to me, believe me, to feel that you & Uncle Harry are really more like my father & mother—you know I have always called you my *western* mother! Certainly the bond of affection with me is just as strong as if you were.

Please do write me again, & if you come anywhere near here, *please* stop for a visit!

With a great deal of love to you all—Always your devoted
EL

JUNE 15, 1940
RISING SUN RANCH
QUEMADO, NEW MEXICO

DEAREST AUNTIE NAN—

I certainly do owe you a letter—or rather, I owe you some *news*!

The longer I live, the more I believe that we have precious little to do with what happens to us. We are given the power to struggle and endure; but the underlying structure of our lives is built in spite of us—by what hand and for what reason we do not know. Sometimes we cannot see for years and years what motive there is in what befalls us; but thank God—at last the skies have cleared for me—and I feel as though my ship had been steered out of the rough waters and into the calm that I have long been wanting. I've been fighting all along to try to keep afloat—but a hand stronger than mine has been at the helm & done the steering—it's a cinch that *I* didn't know until now where I was heading for.

When I wrote you last, things were just about as bad as they could be. I hated to admit it; but I had pretty well lost all real hope. I think I explained at the time how things were—I realized what a second rate affair my marriage with Earl was—Really & truly—it was never much else—but that's not to my credit. As I look back, my marrying him in the first place was a reaction against loneliness—and a tepid notion that we could make each other happy without being deeply in love. I was tired of struggling—of being without Nanny—& Earl offered a certain amount of security. I didn't want to live alone the rest of my life—& he seemed hell bent to live on a ranch & to marry me—and my decision to marry him was a form of defeat. What I got was, I guess—what I deserved. Earl was not satisfied with ranch life—he drank heavily—& we neither of us were in any way suited. But the worst of the deal was to me, that instead of his realizing our incompatibility, he came to rely on me and need me—even though we did not get along at all. Weak by nature, he would decide one day to get up & get out—would tell me that he was "through with me & the ranch & everything" and then the next day everything would be all off. Waves of remorse would be followed by waves of anger. It was an awful existence & I sank lower than I ever had with Walt—because this time I felt largely to blame—and as though I would have to "stay in the buggy" and help Earl as long as I could. I knew I'd never love him—& I knew he would shuttle back and forth all of our lives between wanting me to help him and blaming me for every bit of hard luck he had ever had.

At last he went to California, as you know. He was supposedly getting a job out there—& I was going to give up the ranch & go out there & join him. In the meantime I was here alone, driving the school bus, looking after the cattle, and doing what had to be done. After the hardest winter months were over, he came sailing back—without the job—and having apparently had a very pleasant time out there. It was then that my heathenish tendencies broke loose. I decided then & there to make the break & have freedom at any price. I took the children & moved into a little shack across the road & told Earl that if it was the ranch he wanted, he was welcome to it all—lock, stock & barrel. He said at first that he would certainly stay there, & run it himself; but after a week of batching—he came across & agreed to let me get a divorce, if I would put the ranch up for sale and give him 40% of the sale price. This I gladly agreed to do—and so it stands. I am to stay here until it is sold—which probably won't by until it rains. He gets the baby two months out of every year—& I have her the rest of the time.

But you haven't heard the real news yet—and when I tell you—please take it seriously, because to me it is still unbelievable and is the most wonderful thing that ever happened to me. A young cowman from Magdalena leased the ranch next to this one and moved in here with his cattle—and fate decreed that he should fall in love with me & I with him. It seems strange that I can say now that I never was *really* in love before. This is the end of the trail. Frank is a native of New Mexico—his father before him was an Indian fighter, and scout to the old covered wagon trains—as well as a cowman. He has never known anything but ranch life and has been foreman of some of the biggest cow outfits around this country. He went partly through high school—has a love of knowledge— even a poetic turn of mind; but when his father died he had to leave school and take a man's job to support his mother & younger brother—when he was just sixteen years old.

He has had a hard life, but through it all he has held on to his natural sweetness of character. He is resolute & determined, yet not hardboiled or bitter in any way. He has had seriousness of purpose enough to build up his own bunch of cattle from a start of absolutely nothing & at a great sacrifice to his own pleasure and material comfort—and yet he is still full of fun & has a swell sense of humor. He is extremely unselfish—and thoughtful of other people—sincere and honest and kindly.

We have been married a little less than two months—but those two months have done more to change my life than all the rest of my life put together. Where before there seemed not to be much rhyme or reason for existence—now there is a real meaning—& joy in looking ahead into the future—where for the past twelve years I've been afraid to look ahead a week.

Whether we ever have wealth doesn't seem to cut much ice. I was much more materially ambitious before I was in love. Now I don't care—except that I hope we can live decently & enjoy a certain amount of independence. We will always be in the west somewhere, I suppose. But as long as I am with Frank I don't much care where I am. He is the first man to ever surpass my love of the west itself. If he went to China, the west would lose its lure for me pronto. But it's a pretty safe bet that we'll always be in some part of the west, because it is native to us both.

I am calling both Nanny & Ethel by his name. As long as he loved me enough to take them both with me, and to be so kind & good to us all, I think that we should all be one family—whether it is ever done legally or not.

I am sure, Auntie Nan, that you will understand & be glad of all this—and you can tell as well as I can that this time I'm on the right trial. I've never been so sure—never been so happy. And I can't say that I regret the past, either, because if I had not had each & every sorrow that I have—& all the hard times & disappointments—I would never have met Frank. What

I'd like to know is—whose was the hand that was guiding me through these rough waters—? And who could see—when I couldn't—the peace that lay ahead? Things like that certainly prove that there *is* something, don't they?

Devotedly,
ELEANOR

NOVEMBER 13, 1940

DEAREST AUNTIE NAN:

It's been a long time between drinks! How are you anyway? And what kind of a summer did you have? I hope the very best.

This has been a wonderful year for me—not financially—but certainly rich in the things that really count. It seems incredible that after so many years of disappointment there should be this wealth of happiness that can come only of true love and real companionship—It makes the past absolutely unregrettable, and the more so to me because I think that if I had met Frank at the very beginning, before all the rest had happened, that I might have taken our happiness too much for granted—might have thought that such happy combinations were a run-of-the-mill, everyday occurrence. Now I know, both from observation and personal experience, that they are not—that they are comparatively rare—and it makes me appreciate doubly what I have now, and treasure each day—the past, and what is now—and what God may give us in the future. Even material losses and setbacks, that I had always thought would be devastatingly discouraging, would seem relatively unimportant to me now. Frank and I have been married for several months now—and I know beyond a doubt that no one else ever did really matter—or ever will. He is not at all a spectacular sort of person. He is quiet and unassuming—and on certain types of people who expect personalities that impress and flash with positive, aggressive qualitites he might make no impression at all.

But if they took enough trouble to look—or if they were discerning enough to see—they would find a rare inner sweetness, a character abundant in integrity and gentlemanliness—the true kind—a sensitive and responsive spirit—and yet a man with a will of his own and humor—and human-ness. I know that the more I knew Walt & Earl—the less I respected them—and the more lacking I found them; but for Frank I have a boundless respect and admiration that grows each day. . .

We had very few dudes this summer, really, only enough to be a nuisance! Mother registered us with the Foster Agency, but they did not prove to be as high-powered as I thought they would be. . . . Three people were the only result—two for a one week's stay, and one for a two weeks' stay. Not very lucrative. We had three more besides that—one for a month, the fourth year in a row that she has been here.

To offset this, I got a few rodeos to ride in—all in this state and Arizona—and we got a good price—8 and a half cents—for our yearling steers; what few we had. They weighted out well, thanks to the fact that we finally got some real rain this summer. The country is knee-deep in our beautiful native curly-topped black gramma grass. It's a sight that is grand to us, drouthed out as we have been for the past few years! Our cattle are all in grand shape for the winter—& here's hoping it won't be too severe.

. . . Now I must go as we are driving the school bus again this year, and it seems as though the hours just fly between the morning and afternoon bus time. Before I know it, it is time for me to go to town and I've hardly accomplished a thing. Much love to you.

EL

MARCH 24, 1941
RISING SUN RANCH
QUEMADO, NEW MEXICO

DEAREST AUNTIE NAN:

. . . Peewee is having her afternoon nap, Nanny is at school, and Frank is working on our contrary old well which has a sanded-up cylinder for the second time in a week.

Outside it is snowing right down. We've had a screwball kind of winter. Last summer our eight-year drouth broke with a vengeance. The skies opened and the grass grew and everything was fine. If it had only known when to stop! It rained all through September and all through October—and when our two real storm & cold months came along—January & February—it never did get cold. We have hardly had a night below freezing all winter. But oh, the moisture! Rain, most of it—and wet heavy snows that melt almost as fast as they fall, and keep everything a sea of mud. It's been light on the stock, but hell on the roads. We still drive the school bus, and we have fought mud until there is just practically nothing left of the poor old sedan. If it wasn't for Nanny's education, I would tell the school board that as far as I was concerned, school was out! But it's the only way we have to get *her* there, so we can't be too independent. . .

I was optimistic and sent away for fifty baby chicks—twenty five many-starred Leghorn pullets for layers, and twenty five rhode island red cocherels for fryers. They hatched Feb. 10th in a Colorado hatchery & arrived here next day. Frank had built me a little brooder house, and I have coddled them like babies, and had good luck with them in spite of the weather. We still have forty six out of fifty, and they are six weeks old today. . . . Last year the coyotes got two of my twenty hens when they stole their nests—and about two thirds of the babies that did hatch met freakish fates—washtub drownings on a large scale and smotheration at the hands of Peewee etc. . . .

The twentieth of next month, Frank and I will have been married a year. It has seemed *such* a short year. I guess because it has been so very happy. There never was anyone quite so nice as he is, I'm sure of that—surer every day. I sometimes think that we won't ever get out of the rut of financial worries. Frank isn't scheming enough for this day and age. He is too trusting—too simple—too unwilling to think that anyone else has anything but honest intentions. Yet I have seen so many chiselers—so many dashing handsome and aggressive heroes that are contemptible at heart—that I would rather do without the money and have Frank just as he is, with his spirit of rare sweetness and his direct forthright nature—not a 1941 model—but like the men that once typified the west, full of old-time courtliness & kindness. "His word is his bond"—Where do you find that last anymore, even out here?

. . . Must stop now. With a heartful of love to all three of you—Uncle Harry, Bob and your dear self.

Devotedly,
EL

ARRIVED!
At Rising Sun Ranch
Quemado, N.M.
A New Hand
Frank Matthew Williams Jr.
Weighed in at 7½ pounds
May 15, 1941
On the Receiving End—Frank and Eleanor Williams

JANUARY 12, 1942
RISING SUN RANCH
QUEMADO, NEW MEXICO

DEAREST AUNTIE NAN:

. . . The last two months have been quite a strain on Frank and me. We have embarked on a venture that I will tell you about. . . . Peewee was thoroughly delighted with her green silk handkerchief and wears it proudly around her shoulders in true cowgal style. She is a little dyed-in-the-wool westerner, if there ever was one. She wears Lee pants, sweaters, is a thorough tomboy; tells everyone that she is a cowgirl, and thinks, talks and breathes horses!

. . . You are not on the national forest there, are you? Well we are, you know. Our land is bounded on both sides, longitudinally, by the Apache National Forest. We are only allowed to run 50 head of cattle on it, according to our permanent forest permit. We have over one hundred cattle, and have been able to run them on our allottment by virtue of a "temporary permit"—due to the fact that the other man who shares our allottment has moved away and has had a non-use permit for three or four years. A permittee cannot go on indefinitely under such an arrangement, however. He has got to either restock, or sell out (patented land *must* go with the transfer of a forest permit.)—or else lose his permit. The latter is uncertain, because the forest is more lenient with non-users than it really should be. If he restocks, we are automatically cut down with our bunch to the allowed 50 head—which is no living. So our only choice—or chance for the future—is to try to buy him out. That gives us almost two sections more of patented land, and an added permit on the forest for another 100 head of cattle. We will have the allottment all to ourselves, and can let our bunch increase to about 200, which they will do quietly speedily now. And that will be more like it! In order to swing the deal, we have had to arrange for a $3500 loan from a bank—which means mortgaging of course. The appraiser has been out and sniffed around and counted all the corral bars, and all that is holding us up now is the record-breaking slowness of the bank's lawyer, who is dawdling around with a couple of abstracts that he could have had ready weeks ago. We are sitting on pins and needles in fear of war conditions changing the bank's mind about making us the loan. But that evidently does not worry the lawyer!

In view of all this, and the fact that we will have to keep our noses right *on* the grindstone for about three years in order to pay out of the hole. Frank has taken a job as foreman of another ranch, leaving me to look after this outfit—cows, babies and all. He is so persevering, and digs in so patiently "from the bottom up"—He has always come by everything the hard way, and this is no exception. So that I am overjoyed to think that I can help him at this end. It's a chore though. I should be riding every day that I possibly can—but I can only really cover the territory on Saturdays and Sundays, when Nanny can be here to keep the house warm and look after the baby. On weekdays I can only go for brief hourly spins during Matt's nap periods, to pastures that are near where we have some of the weaker cows and leaner calves. This job takes in everything—even chopping wood. Frank only gets home about once a week and sometimes not that. And when he *does* come home, I don't want empty woodboxes staring him in the face—or other chores that he did when he was here. I would rather have the time to visit—and sometimes he helps me ride if it's on Sunday. It's awful without him, though—and I miss him constantly. Especially when down in my heart is the gnawing realization that perhaps sometime this year or next, the army may call him along with other husbands and fathers. In view of that fact, it seems as though each day that he is away now is a day lost from both our lives, and he feels so too—but what else can we do? We have been trying to swing this deal for a long time—long before war was declared. . . We feel that we must plan for a future and believe in it, even though security is an unknown quantity just now. If everyone became paralyzed and afraid to act or to play at all, the Japs and Germans could whip us all in two weeks time. Well, quien sabe?

So that is why I haven't written you sooner. It's five thirty every morning—light the fires, cook breakfast, bathe little Matt & fix his bottles—and then a day of variated jobs. Maybe a washing—maybe bringing in a thin cow—maybe a session with the woodpile! And although Nanny and Peewee and Matt are all slumbering by eight o'clock, I am too sodden then to take advantage of leisure time. My eyes fall shut in spite of me, and I might as well "pull off the road and take a doze"—as night-driving motorists say. . . .

A heartful of love to you all—always and always—from
ELEANOR

FEBRUARY 8, 1942
QUEMADO, NEW MEXICO

DEAREST AUNTIE NAN:

I hope this isn't answering your letter discouragingly soon; but I just had to write and tell you that our loan went through and we have our place. We are so happy about it. The prospects of "paying out" are scary alright; but we would have been so very sunk if something had gone haywire and we *hadn't* gotten it. At least now we have something really worthwhile to work and sacrifice for, and we both feel more than hopeful, and glad that we got our fling at it. $3500 isn't so much of a debt, comparatively speaking, but it's plenty big enough for us, and with our present setup, I would not want to take on a cent more.

. . . These are surely busy days now. Frank's mother is here to be with Matt when I have to get out and ride, etc.—and the *etc.* part is quite as strenuous as tending the cattle. Last week I wrecked a two room house that was on some of the land that we recently acquired and which we thought should come down. I did not think I could do it, but Frank said about all there was to wrecking a house was to notice carefully just how it was put together, and to take it down in the order that it had been put up, in reverse. So I took a wrecking bar and a claw hammer and went to work on it. After I got the windows out without breaking any of them I felt encouraged. The roof came next, and I believe was the hardest part for me, because the nails were all huge and very rusty, and I tore up some of the lumber getting them out, and I found that the bending over was harder than doing the parts where you can move around more. The most tedious part was a half a day spent in unclinching nails in the walls. Whoever nailed up those walls put them there for eternity, because practically every nail was clinched. But when that was done and certain essential framework and brace parts removed it was rather fun—I just gave all the wall boards a gentle push and over they went, with soul-satisfying squawks from the nails at the bottom as they pulled out. After that was all done, I had to build a crossing so that we could get the pickup over a deep ditch to haul the house lumber down to the ranch. That called for one whole day with a pick and shovel, three loads of rocks and one of poles; but I felt more than compensated for my sore muscles when I could report to Frank that it was a finished job.

In all of this, we have had just one nasty break—or at least we feel that way about it now, though we may not—and probably will not—later. I find that I am going to have another baby who will make his or her arrival sometime in July—only fourteen months or so younger than little Matt. It's the first time I ever had a real "slip"—one that wasn't planned or wanted, and you can readily see why we would not want one just now. Because you see I was still nursing Matt when it happened. I was furious at first and heartily wanted something to go wrong. But nothing did and I don't feel that way about it now, and neither does Frank. I would not want it on my conscience to interfere artifically—not with Frank's child certainly. There must be some good reason why we are supposed to have this one, evn though I can't see it just now. Right now, I am still well able to keep up and do all the work and all the riding that I would any other time; but of course as time goes on it's going to slow me up whether I like it or not, and I don't know how it's going to work out with Frank's job—which he needs to hold for a year, at least.

   . . . With dearest love to you, each and everyone, from your always devoted

ELEANOR

JULY 25, 1942
RISING SUN RANCH
QUEMADO, NEW MEXICO

DEAREST AUNTIE NAN:
   . . . The baby and I have been home since about the seventh of July. Helen is doing very well, and so am I. I felt so rotten before she came that I feel more than atoned now, because I never felt stronger or better after any baby than I do now. I had a few flare ups with my heart even after the baby came, but that condition seems to be getting so much better now that I feel sure that it will all clear up and go away. . . .

We are in the throes of another drouth here. There is still time for the grass to grow if it would only rain, but it will have to do something soon, and we cannot help but feel uneasy with the first of August almost here and not a sign of rain—no grass—and the poor old cows going downhill fast and calves dogieing. If it doesn't rain soon we will either have to sell everything or else lease some grass somewhere, and grass is hard to find. I feel that we would be making a big mistake if we sold out. Of course, prices are good now, but if you sell out now, with the world in the shape that it's in, you don't know just how or when you can ever get back into the cow business again. It would be different in normal times, but things are in an awful muddle now if you ask me. Frank has worked so hard and has sacrificed so much to build up this little bunch that it would be a kind of a near tragedy to see him have to sell them. Surely we can work something out so that he won't have to.

   . . . I don't think we will have a single guest this summer. . . . When even just one person is here we don't feel at ease as a household the way we do when we're alone; and with the selective service silhouetted against the horizon, I would rather we would have this summer to ourselves, because there's no telling what the next few months might bring.

And now goodbye for the present. We all send our love, and especially your ever devoted

EL

APRIL 18, 1944
QUEMADO, NM

DEAREST AUNTIE NAN:

I'm wondering if you are still in Tucson? It must be getting warm down there, although if it's like the weather around here, we are having an unusually late cold spring. Even down on the river, as we call the land that lies along the Rio Grande, where it is three thousand feet lower than we are, and usually where the trees leap out two to three months ahead of ours, it has been very wintry. The trees down there are just now venturing to bud, which is pretty unusual.

I had the best intentions in the world of writing you from Socorro, as soon as I arrived there to wait for the bambino, but I never got there! For once, my habit of allowing too narrow a margin for such Acts of God failed to work. I didn't get by with it, and the baby was born here on the ranch. The doctor set the date as April 19th—I figured about the 12th. We planned to leave here the 5th, and Frank was going on to Belen to see about a section of land that we are selling. We had sent for the tax receipts on the land, which hadn't come, and as I felt pretty well and hated to leave the family, I decided to wait for Friday's mail to see if the receipts wouldn't come in. Early Friday morning it was too late and I knew I'd have to have the baby here, so Frank went rushing down to Quemado to get the old country medico who brings lots of the backwood babies around here. We had no assurance that he would be in Quemado—his two sons have ranches 40 miles north of Quemado and he spends about half his time out there. But as fortune would have it, he was there, and Frank was back here with him in less than an hour.

I thought it would be a fairly quick birth, but something was wrong. The baby's head was too big, or he was turned wrong, or something. Anyway, he wouldn't come. Finally, after what seemed like an eternity, the doctor used instruments and brought the baby. He warned us that the baby might be dead, but we were terribly lucky. He wasn't, and now we have another nice little son, James Oliver. He weighed eight pounds which was Nanny's weight when she was born. It has taken me longer to snap out of it this time, but the baby is eleven days old today and I am trying to get around a little. I'm a little dubious about the condition of my insides, but I guess the best bet would be to wait a while until I gain a little more strength and then go to some doctor and get checked over.

After the baby came, it seemed awfully nice to be home instead of in a hospital. Hospitals give me the willies, and I always miss the family. Mrs. Lane has taken good care of me and Jim, and Frank calls himself the "night nurse." And he's a good one, too. Frank had to help the doctor when the baby was born, so I think we both had quite an experience. . . .

Do write soon to your devoted

El

MARGE ARMIJO
Our Times Were Special

Growing up in Albuquerque before World War II, Marge Armijo enjoyed a childhood secure in the traditions of church and extended family, celebrating the interwoven cycles of nature and community. Her family lived together, each branch on its two-acre parcel of land, inherited from the "ancestors," who no doubt received it originally as land granted from the Spanish throne. Like many of the comfortable, self-sufficient, agricultural Hispanic villages clustered along the Rio Grande north and south of central Albuquerque, Marge's Los Tomases hadn't changed much in generations. Although her parents worked outside the home, within the larger economy, the family seemed untouched by the Depression, for they carried on as always, sustaining themselves with their gardens, orchards, and animals with no lack of abundance. Today we look at such a childhood with nostalgia, seeking to touch this simple, independent, harmonious New Mexico way of life at least in our imaginations through a film such as *The Milagro Beanfield War*.

Although raised within strong, unquestioned traditions of her tribe, Marge emerged as an individual, an individual who continued to live within the tradition. She chose to live as a single woman, and she became one of the first two female general contractors in California, as well as a businesswoman heading her own company.

Her oral history evokes the charm and goodwill of a fairy tale with a happy ending. It is simply told, a series of personal recollections, one memory triggering another, and full of the golden sunshine which can still be seen on a summer afternoon's stroll along the ditchbanks of Albuquerque's North Valley.

*M*y name is really Margarita Graciella Armijo and I was born on April 16, 1936. My mother says that was the happiest day of her life. My dad was Epimenio John or Juan Armijo. My mother was Pauline Salazar, but her mother was an Armijo. She was born in Villanueva, up in northern New Mexico. My dad was born in Albuquerque. He went to San Felipe School, and so did my nieces and I. I was brought up in northwest Albuquerque. My baptism certificate says I was born a half mile north of St. Anthony's Orphanage. That's about how they described it. And at that time it was called Los Tomases, and it was its own little barrio. They had their own little chapel over off Menaul, east of 12th. They used to have fiestas—I remember, I was four years old, my grandfather took me to the fiestas in Los Tomases. They had a man playing a bass fiddle, a guitaron, and I remember my grandfather carrying me and dancing with me. Los Tomases is no longer in existence, unfortunately. Anyway, my ancestors had sold a lot of property there to the government for the Indian School.

I felt really loved in my life; I felt so lucky. My grandfather Jorge, George Armijo, absolutely adored me. He had a fantastic sense of humor, but he was very much the patron. He ruled the roost. He had a truck and used to grow all kinds of vegetables. He had a truck garden, and he'd go along 12th St. where all those big homes were and he'd sell vegetables, and that's how they lived. They had goats, they had horses, they had all kinds of animals.

My grandmother would make cheeses. Her name was Aurelia Garcia and she was born on Central, and that's how come I think I'm related to everybody in Old Town. So people from Duranes, Old Town, they're all my relatives.

People from Albuquerque used to go out, apparently out to the country. They were in the country, but they'd go out even further. And they used to go to this place called El Coyote, and I think it was over in the Manzanos. It was a mineral springs, and it was a big Sunday thing to go out and picnic there. So I described this scene to my mother, and I told her there was a little baby in a basket, and I told her the people that were there, and she was just shocked. She said I must have been two years old. So I have to say that's my earliest recollection.

We were very family-oriented. My mother and dad worked outside the home, but they worked in a way that we didn't have baby sitters. They managed their time so they could be with us, one or the other. And my dad really helped with us! He took care of us almost as much as my mother. My dad worked in Parks and Recreation for the City of Albuquerque, and my mother worked for TWA for 30 years; it was then Transcontinental and Western. She said she was the original stew for the Wright Brothers. She had a fantastic sense of humor. She brought us up to really care for each other as brothers and sisters. She brought us up to worry about our neighbor, and to worry about earning our space. God put us on this earth for a reason, and we were to relate to each other as human beings and help each other any way we could. She did a lot of volunteer work; she was very involved with the community. She found time! My dad, of course, helped. He felt he wanted to support all her activities.

They were completely opposite. She was a complete extrovert and he was a complete introvert. My mother was a very strong role model and very important in my life. My dad was, also; he was a dear, dear person. I remember having a library card really young, and I became interested in books and in music. My mother said I would hang onto the radio and dance, and my diaper would fall off! It could have been because my mother was older when I was born. I had a sister who was 16, who moved away to Seattle when I was two, so I ended up being the oldest. And then my mother had another group of children; I had two younger brothers.

My grandfather adored me. They had all grandsons till I was born. And I have to say, my reign was short. It was 29 days, and then I had a girl cousin. But I was still first. And I was always first in his eyes. My grandfather always used to bring me little presents; my grandmother used to bring me little wrapped-up things in her arpon. She was a beautiful woman, fair, with beautiful green eyes. And she wore little hats on Sundays. I used to go to church with them, because I liked going to the Mass at San Felipe—my parents would go to St. Anthony's, to the orphanage. My grandparents would to to the same pew every Sunday. And my grandfather used to put (you know I was his favorite grandchild) his truck had wooden spokes, and he used to put a board across for me to sit on. And I had a hat, it was one of these big Breton sailor hats with sashes, and my grandfather and grandmother used to be up front, you know, putt-putt, off to church, and my hat would fly off and my grandfather would stop and pick it up and put it back on my head, and then he'd go a little further, and the same thing would happen. It seemed like it was forever to go to church; it's really not that far now. Any my grandmother—she was very patient— would finally take the hat and put it on her lap.

I went to San Felipe School because that was the school that all the family had always gone to—my aunts and uncles, my mother and father. I spoke Spanish at home and English in school. I remember making my first communion—and my girlfriends—matter of fact, we still see each other. And I was very much involved with San Felipe. We all grew up together, the same group, all the way up to ninth grade. And some of us are distantly related. I remember belonging to the Ignacitas. It was a Jesuit order at San Felipe at that point. We were like Girl Scouts. We used to wear veils and have prayer services. In the month of May we went to church every day carrying little flowers, like baby's breath. We'd take our little bouquets from our yards and say prayers. The month of May is Mary's month, and we were very much involved with Mary. I remember my mother saying, "The Blessed Mother wouldn't like it, if you did that." And I remember growing up with this. It would make us really stop and really look at things. And October was another month we did this. It's also Mary's month, the month of the Rosary. And for the May crowning, we'd carry our little flowers and somebody would get chosen to crown the Blessed Mother, and put a crown of flowers on her head and we had this beautiful ceremony.

And at that time we had Matachines. Matachines were—they were spirits, I felt. They dressed differently and they used to dance and come in ahead of us. We had processions—our big processions were during Lent. We'd march not only around the plaza, but we would go beyond that, all around Old Town and down Central. One of the things we did on Holy Thursday—my grandmother Armijo would take us all, she'd get the cousins, the primos, and say, "Cousins that are that close, they are like brothers and sisters, they do not fight, they do not argue." And this is how we were brought up, like we were all brothers and sisters. My grandfather would gather us around and tell us cuentos. This was our story time. Stories of things that happened, legends, sometimes religious things—a combination.

Summers were fantastic, we did so many things. I remember on the 24th of June, my grandmother used to take us down to the ditch. The property was huge, and they had this apple tree that had special little apples, they were called "manzanitas de San Juan," you know, for San Juan's day, his feast day. So we would all go down to the ditch, the one that used to feed off into the others. Right now it would be north of Menaul and west of 12th St., in that area. There was a dairy around there. She'd take us all like little ducks, she'd go up to the ditch, and she'd say, "Today is the day of San Juan, and this is the first day you can swim." And she would put water on our moiera, the crown, just a little bit, and that way she'd make everything well, so we would not have problems with drowning, and then we'd swim. Being as my mother worked for the airlines, we used to travel summers. We used to go to New York and Washington, D.C.

Marge Armijo and her brother. *Marge Armijo*.

Marge Armijo and her brother. *Marge Armijo*.

We did have some neighbors who weren't relatives, the Blairs, and Ruth was their daughter. She was like a relative. We all lived together up and down the street, because all that property, remember, belonged to the ancestors. So we all had parcels of land, maybe two acres. During the day we had chores. We fed the animals. We had pigs and goats and geese and chickens. Of course, we had chicken every Sunday. And we had huge gardens and a big orchard. We used to pick fruit. They kept us busy.

My favorite animals were always the pigs. My mother would say prayers with me at night, and she'd see all these lumps underneath the blanket and she'd lift up and here she'd have to gather up all the piglets and take them out. But I was still very much a little girl, wore frilly dresses. . . . I used to have a pet pig, Gus-Gus, and I used to take him out on a walk, with a stick. But Dixie, my Dalmatian, was so loyal, she followed me everywhere I went. You always knew that wherever Dixie was, that's where I was.

My grandfather used to finish his work about 3 or 4 o'clock and my grandmother used to fix a big meal for him. He used to count his money, and I used to help him. I was the only one he would allow in the kitchen.

I lived with my maternal grandmother, Josefita Salazar for a while. She lived in Martineztown, on Edith, across from Mt. Calvary Cemetery. I lived there for the school year I was in second grade. That was all I could take, being away from my mom and dad and my brothers. So my mother came by every day and my dad came by twice a day to visit me. My grandmother was alone, and I was the one chosen to stay with her. They had velorios—wakes—where they would carry statues of saints to different houses, mostly in the spring. It was more urban than I was used to.

My grandmother canned her own things, and she did a lot of praying. She made me kneel down and pray long prayers. I mean, for a child in second grade, it was really hard on me. She gave me little pinches when I didn't settle down. All I had at my grandmother's was a dog named Lobo and a cat. And I remember the cat because in the winter—my grandmother had a woodstove—and I was sitting next to it in a little rocking chair with the cat, and the cat, all of a sudden, just swung up, flew off, and landed on the stove with all fours! Yeoow! And just hit the ceiling. And my grandmother came in, and boy, did I get a spanking. And I didn't do a thing!

During the war something funny happened. It was my mother's day to water, and she had the three of us. And it was an open field beyond us where the horses and cows grazed and there was a plane coming over on a maneuver, and a bomb came out! My mother threw herself on us. It killed several horses.

My mother and dad told my sister, who was about 18 or so, forget it, you're not dating. They just didn't let her go out with any of the people from the Air Force, from the Base. She didn't take it well. Katherine was really rebellious.

My mother said she saw a big change in me when I was 16. Up till then I was a dear, dear, very obedient child. I went to a girls school; I did what was expected of me, then the minute I turned 16, my mother said, I all but got horns and a pitchfork, a tail with a little point. I became completely my own person. But it was really because of my mother! It was because of her influence that I became so independent. She gave me lots of strength.

I was named Margarita, but I was really named after Peggy Howden, my mother's best friend, whose father was Bishop Howden of the Episcopalian Church. So I grew up very ecumenical, really.

I took piano and folklorico dancing in Old Town. At that time, there was a post office on the side of the church. There was a grocery store where the basket shop is now. There was a chile parlor on the other side. There weren't so many shops. You socialized mostly at church, after church. Where the fairgrounds are now, that was really out of town!

In California I went to UCLA, majored in education, minored in history. I went to school for an education major, but in California I didn't like the system, so I became a supervisor for the telephone company. And then I met a neighbor, we became very good friends, business partners. And I beame one of two women who were licensed general contractors at the time in California. We had a large business, with 200 employees, but the unions in California are very . . . it's very hard for an employer. And after a while we saw that our employees were making more money than we were. So then I became an analyst for a development corporation and I traveled around—we had work in Arizona, Chicago, Texas, California.

All of a sudden, my parents passed away, and I said, I'm tired of all this, it's time for me to . . . so out of the clear blue, in 1971-72, I moved back here. I wanted to get back to my roots. I had enough money set aside for rent, and I did volunteer work for San Felipe, and I worked with the youth and the elderly in Duranes. I still do some of that. Then I taught school for quite a while. And I became involved in cultural affairs, and I'm doing that now, for the City of Albuquerque, it's community cultural affairs and I do that through the KiMo Theater and the South Broadway Cultural Center.

I loved being a single woman. I was very, very strong. I didn't get married . . . Efren Griego and I were together for twelve years. He was the most fantastic man I have ever met in my life. We met through church. I was in my 30s, and he was about six years older. The most interesting man I have ever known. He was from northern New Mexico, from Dixon. And they are a breed . . . they are very real. They look at life in a very real way. They appreciate things, even in nature. Efren and I just hit it off. He was my dear, dear friend. He went through a lot of physical challenges, and he rose above them. He had polio when he was a child, and one leg had atrophied. He'd had arthritis in his spine. He wore a brace. He had a disease called syringomelia, you get cysts on your spinal column. He became paraplegic, and he could not accept being dependent. And he was completely dependent on me in his later years. Had I married him, he would have lost his disability, his social security. I'm still very close to his family. As I say, I was really very, very lucky in my life because I was loved by my grandfather, by my father, all his affection was for me, and by Efren.

I remember asking Efren once, Efren, do you love me? And he said, better than that, I like you. And his made for a fantastic relationship. I think one has to come before the other. I think you have to be friends.

We used to go out for a long drive on Sunday, and he loved picnics, so we went all the time, even in the winter! Efren loved to fish, and I would take my schoolwork and correct my papers, or read, because I never did like to fish. Matter of fact, I used to feel sorry for the fish. I used to say, you've got to throw that fish back in! So we'd drive out to Corrales or maybe up to Dixon, where he was from. . .

I did a lot of the same things other children did growing up, but I still think our times were special.

CREDITS

Agnes Miner: The Colorado Historical Society

Flora Spiegelberg: Special Collections Department, Zimmerman Library, University of New Mexico

Yavapai Woman: Arizona State Museum, University of Arizona, Tucson

Mary Annetta Coleman Pomeroy: The Mary Annetta Coleman Pomeroy Papers, MS660, Arizona Historical Society, Tucson

Mary L. Stright: Menaul Historical Library of the Southwest, Albuquerque

Marietta Palmer Wetherill: Special Collections Department, Zimmerman Library, University of New Mexico
Oral History by Lou Blachly, The Pioneers Foundation

E.J. Elliott: Biography Files, Arizona Historical Society, Tucson

Isabella Greenway: John and Isabella Greenway Papers, MS311, Arizona Historical Society, Tucson

Katherine Davis: New Mexico State Records Center and Archives

Frances Beebe: Golden Library, Eastern New Mexico Univeristy, Portales

Beatrice Nogare: Huerfano County Ethno-History Project, Pueblo Library District

Mary Cabot Wheelwright: The Wheelwright Museum of the American Indian, Archive MS1-1-128

Grace Mott Johnson Dasburg: New Mexico State Records Center and Archives

Earlier versions of introductions to Flora Spiegelberg, Marietta Wetherill, and Eleanor Williams chapters appeared in *New Mexico Magazine*